The Global Politics of Sport

Sport [...] advanced cases of 'globalisation', arguably because [...] and political obstacles to the development of trade a [...] er in sport than there are in other fields. Thus there has bee [...] e nature of the politics of sport since the end of the Cold War; t[...] ust be rewritten to acknowledge a twenty-first-century world in whi[...] rnational sporting organisations and transnational corporations have become far more important than states.

The Global Politics of Sport presents a range of essays examining the emerging global political issues in twenty-first-century sport including:

- The role and power of organisations such as FIFA and IOC
- The influence of US exceptionalism
- The construction of global sports heroes
- Tensions developing within traditionally 'alternative' sports in a global commercial culture.

The Global Politics of Sport presents new and fresh exploration of different conceptions of sport as a purely commercial activity and as an activity as embodying 'higher' social and ethical values. It is a sequel to *The Politics of Sport* and *The Global Politics of Sport*, which were previously the leading works in the field.

Lincoln Allison was the founding Director of the Warwick Centre for Study of Sport in Society. He is currently Visiting Professor in the politics of sport at the University of Brighton and will be Emeritus Reader in politics at the University of Warwick.

Sport in the Global Society
General Editor: J.A. Mangan

The interest in sports studies around the world is growing and will continue to do so. This unique series combines aspects of the expanding study of *sport in the global society*, providing comprehensiveness and comparison under one editorial umbrella. It is particularly timely, with studies in the cultural, economic, ethnographic, geographical, political, social, anthropological, sociological and aesthetic elements of sport proliferating in institutions of higher education.

Eric Hobsbawm once called sport one of the most significant practices of the late nineteenth century. Its significance was even more marked in the late twentieth century and will continue to grow in importance into the new millennium as the world develops into a 'global village' sharing the English language, technology and sport.

Other Titles in the Series

The Global Politics
of Sport

The role of global institutions in sport

**Edited by
Lincoln Allison**

 Routledge
Taylor & Francis Group

LONDON AND NEW YORK

First published 2005 by Routledge
2 Park Square, Milton Park,
Abingdon, Oxon OX14 4RN

Simultaneously published in the USA and Canada
by Taylor & Francis Inc
270 Madison Ave, New York, NY 10016

Routledge is an imprint of the Taylor & Francis Group

© 2005 Edited by Lincoln Allison

Typeset in Goudy by Keyword Publishing Services

Printed and bound in Great Britain by St Edmundsbury Press,
Bury St Edmunds, Suffolk

British Library Cataloging in Publication Data
A catalogue record for this book is available from the British Library

Library of Congress Cataloging in Publication Data
A catalog record has been requested for this book

ISBN 0-415-34601-0 (hbk)
ISBN 0-415-34602-9 (pbk)

Contributors

Lincoln Allison is (Emeritus) Reader in Politics at the University of Warwick and Visiting Professor in the Politics in Sport at the University of Brighton. From 1993 to 2002 he was Director of the Warwick Centre for the Study of Sport in Society. He has been editor of a number of books on sport and is author of *Amateurism in Sport*. His other published academic work is mainly in the fields of political theory and the politics of the environment. He remains an active cricketer and tennis player.

Alan Bairner is Reader in the Sociology of Sport at the University of Loughborough, having previously been Professor in Sports Studies at the University of Ulster. He has written extensively on Irish sport (often in collaboration with John Sugden) and is most recently the author of *Sport, Nationalism and Globalization*. He remains a supporter of Dunfermline Athletic Football Club.

Ken Foster is now semi-retired and living in the North York Moors National Park. He was a full-time member of the School of Law at the University of Warwick until 2002, where he continues to teach a course on sport and the law. He has published extensively on sports law and his recent publications include, 'Is There a Global Sports Law?' in *Entertainment Law* (2003). He continues to support Middlesbrough Football Club and now has more time to follow his horse-racing interests.

Paul Gilchrist is a research assistant at the University of Brighton where he is working towards a doctorate on the ideas of heroes and heroines in sport. He previously completed a BA in Politics and an MA in Sport, Politics and Society at the University of Warwick where he was captain of the university darts team.

Terry Monnington is Director of Physical Education at the University of Warwick. Most of his career has been as a teacher of physical education and he has published widely in the fields of British and African sport. He previously played Rugby Union for Moseley, whom he captained, and for the North Midlands. He coaches rugby and volleyball.

John Sugden is Professor of the Sociology of Sport at the University of Brighton. He is the author of *Boxing and Society* and has also written extensively on Irish sport (often in collaboration with Alan Bairner). With Alan Tomlinson he co-authored *FIFA and the Contest for World Football* and co-edited *Power Games*. He has coached the Northern Ireland Universities and Brighton University football teams and continues to play the game even in his mature years.

Alan Tomlinson is Professor of Leisure Studies at the University of Brighton. From 2000 to 2003 he was editor of the *International Review for the Sociology of Sport*. Apart from his collaborations with John Sugden (see above) his books include *Consumption, Identity and Style* and *The Game's Up*. He continues to play tennis and to support Burnley Football Club.

Belinda Wheaton is Senior Research Fellow in Leisure Studies at the University of Brighton. She is principally interested in the politics of popular culture, especially of 'lifestyle' sports. She is the editor of *Understanding Lifestyle Sport* and has contributed to a wide variety of journals and magazines in the field. She is herself a surfer, windsurfer and snowboarder.

Preface

This volume is a successor to *The Politics of Sport* (1986) and *The Changing Politics of Sport* (1993). The pace of change requires an entirely new body of work and the range of the subject prohibits a singly authored volume.

I would like to thank the University of Warwick and particularly the Department of Politics and International Studies for the support they have offered in the production of this volume and especially for financial assistance in bringing the contributors together to discuss the issues and themes raised by the book. I would also like to thank my son Michael for his help with the editorial task and my wife Ann for her support, particularly in bringing the contributors together.

Lincoln Allison
Leamington Spa

Series editor's foreword

According to Richard Vinen, '... all social history and sociology and social anthropology is political in that all history is about power',[1] while according to Robert W. Stern, '... change is the condition of everything that lives (and) the condition of social continuity'.[2] *The Global Politics of Sport* bears witness to the prescience of both remarks.

'While everyone else was changing, so were we. We were changing too'![3] *The Global Politics of Sport* is the third volume of a trilogy on the politics of sport and reflects the editor's latest change of approach in response to changes in the relationship between sport and politics. Mutant moments characterise all change. Of course, continuity in this relationship continues as the present furore over Mugabe, morality, politics and cricket demonstrates. Change and continuity in history go hand in hand.

In the changes that characterise modern sport, globalisation is a 'leading player'. Consequently it receives due prominence in *The Global Politics of Sport* and the term is adapted to circumstance rather than circumstance adapted to it. The quality of analysis is thus enhanced.

The 'Great Universal Churches' of the IOC and FIFA, as *The Global Politics of Sport* makes very clear, now exert a powerful doctrinal, liturgical and 'theocratic' influence – with their propensity for architectonic control – over countless millions. FIFA has indeed created a borderless international community. The English Premier League illustrates this perhaps too well. In one weekend of April 2004 'foreign legionnaires' outnumbered 'native footsoldiers' heavily. Only 65 of the 220 who started in the games were qualified to play for England. The top 5 teams had a mere 14 English players![4]

Arguably *The Global Politics of Sport* leaves the best till last in the question it poses: is global sport moving into an era of a post-Westphalian or even a neo-Medieval system of international politics far more autonomous of state systems than in the twentieth century? This question stimulates others. Does this shift, if true, have future dramatic consequences for the use and abuse of power? What have the IOC and the European Union in common, in addition to canonical texts, centralisation, corruption and unaccountability? In fact, are such organisations linked, not divorced (as *The Global Politics of Sports* suggests) in their use of power? Do Blatter and Chirac share the dystopic 'papal qualities of haughtiness, self-righteousness and pretension'?[5] Do the politicians of power-bloc politics and sports politics systematically construct distancing mechanisms from accountability? Is it time therefore for 'un certain tour d'esprit' involving atomistic resistance in the global politics of sport?

Academic analysts of sport can only watch and wonder.

It is all a long way from the ideals if not the practice of Corinthianism, 'fair play' and amateurism.[6]

The great attraction of *The Global Politics of Sport* is that its questions raise questions.

J.A. Mangan
Series Editor
Sport in the Global Society

1 Sport and globalisation

The issues

Lincoln Allison

What follows is a second sequel to *The Politics of Sport* in 1986 and *The Changing Politics of Sport* in 1993.[1] The 'Politics of Sport' in its 1986 sense can now be seen as the 'Old Politics of Sport', its assumption being of a 'Westphalian' system in which states were the dominant actors in international politics. To discuss the politics of sport required describing the policies of communist and African states in using sport to achieve greater recognition and legitimacy, the use of sport in contests over the relationship between nationality and statehood and the consequences of state policies – primarily apartheid in South Africa – which challenged assumptions about the 'autonomy' of sport and its irrelevance to politics. If there is a single word with which to label the era, it is 'boycott', in reference to the numerous and escalating attempts by states to withdraw their competitors from international sporting contests in pursuit of broader diplomatic goals.

One paradox of the weakening of the primacy of the state is that in many cases in Western states government is considerably more involved in the domestic politics of sport now than it was twenty years ago. Certainly in the United Kingdom (as Terry Monnington and I argue later) government is involved in programmes to achieve sporting success and acquire major championships to a degree that was almost inconceivable in the 1980s. It is difficult to conceive of the events of 1980, when Mrs Thatcher's government attempted to boycott the Moscow Olympics but the vast majority of British sports federations ignored the boycott, taking part. In Africa, we shall argue, there was a heyday of successful intervention lasting from the 1960s to the 1980s during which governments were able to achieve goals of international prestige and internal unity through sport. This capacity has now diminished considerably, partly because of general economic failure, but also because the competitors themselves have been spirited away beyond the control of domestic politicians in the direction of American campuses and European football clubs, though in some countries, such as South Africa and Ethiopia, there is still clearly a 'sports dividend'.

The broad truth is that within the international system states are much less important than they were. In sport, they generally (and to a remarkable degree) compete with each other within agendas set by transnational corporations and global non-governmental organisations. Imagine – if it is not already the case – that you are concerned about some aspect of the future of sport. It might be the shape and survival of test match cricket or the development of surfing or the survival of small town football clubs or the use of drugs in track and field athletics: all of these are matters which concern the contributors to this volume. Almost entirely, at the time of writing, your concerns would not lead you to monitor the activities of governments, but they would lead you to want to know more about what was going on at Newscorp, at the Federation Internationale de Football Association, at the International Olympic Committee and at the World Anti-Doping Agency, among others. This stands in sharp contrast to the situation in environmental politics or human rights where states remain much more important and international organisations much less powerful.

The pace of change has been remarkable. A good proportion of the policies and contests which defined the politics of sport in 1986 had disappeared by the time *The Changing Politics of Sport* was published in 1993, replaced by a situation of much greater fluidity with a much less 'Westphalian' shape. There was talk of a 'new world order', but it seems more realistic to describe it as the collapse of an existing order without the emergence of anything very clear to replace it. Everywhere – inside and outside the academic world – the concept of 'globalisation' was invoked. I will not here define 'globalisation'; different, though broadly similar definitions will be invoked by individual contributors in this volume. But there are two points which must be stressed about the importance and unavoidability of the concept.

First, the use of the concept of globalisation is 'self-fulfilling'– to use Robert Merton's term – which, in a sense, means self-realising. People assume and perceive a 'global' reality where once they assumed a 'Westphalian' state system, though it is important to note that 'globalisation', like 'charisma', 'elite' and others and unlike 'Westphalian' is a term now well-imbedded in a variety of ordinary languages. Demonstrators on the streets now conceive what they oppose in terms of globalisation where previously they might have conceived it in terms of free trade or imperialism or thought of it at all only in terms of a lower level of generality and abstraction. Second, we would expect a priori that globalisation in sport would be relatively well developed and the evidence suggests that it is. The aspirations of sport, from the start and as represented in the constitutions of such bodies as FIFA and the IOC, are parallel to those of a 'great universal church'. But the hostility to sport within national and globally regional cultures is markedly less than to the proselytising of a real church and the opposition both to the general idea of modern sport and to specific sports has declined markedly in the past century. It is much less subject to cultural defensiveness than are institutions concerned with language and the arts. 'Borderlessness' is easier in sport, particularly since the collapse of communism. In the labour market 'professional' footballers can cross borders with none of the limitations – not even language – that limit their contemporaries in the older professions. There exists a global system of cores and peripheries in which, for example, leading Irish, African and Scandinavian footballers rarely play in their countries of origin. In the capital market, the governor of Siberia can become the owner of Chelsea Football Club. In the image market it becomes possible to choose between three different live cricket matches on television while living in the United States, a society which has an historic disdain for cricket, while the England footballer David Beckham acquires fans in East Asia on a different scale from the followings for players in previous generations. In the political dimension it is normal to conceive of globalisation in terms of the development of 'systems of governance' and the emergence of effective 'regimes'. Here again the broad judgement must be that the major sporting bodies operate at a level of coherent global power unknown to aspirants in fields such as the environment and human rights. Compare, for example, the way in which the People's Republic of China treats representatives of the International Olympic Committee with its treatment of international non-governmental organisations in the other fields mentioned! For whatever reasons – and those reasons will be discussed in this volume – it is clear that states find it much easier to 'pool' sovereignty in the regulation of sport than they do in other fields.

Generically, three types of issue arise out of the globalisation of sport, though it would be only proper to acknowledge that they could be classified in alternative ways. First, there are issues of regime development. Parallel to the theory that in the development of states a gangster-like central power is a necessary stage before the rule of law, is the idea that a raw global power is bound to develop before mature regulation is possible. The issue is whether global power can be turned into a mature regime capable, for example, of dealing successfully with problems like doping and of aspiring to spread the benefits of the regime to a global public. The context is one in which the personnel and practice of international organisations often look more Robber Baron than Civil Service. The chapters by John Sugden and Alan Tomlinson on FIFA and by the latter on the Olympics are concerned with these generic issues. As a sports lawyer, Ken Foster offers an important perspective on these issues by contrasting American perspectives on the regulation of sport with those in Europe. American law (predictably?) conceives professional sport as a primarily commercial activity, though it has to accept some odd implications of that assumption. European approaches to the regulation of sport, after a brief flirtation in the mid-1990s with the idea that the regulation of such matters as the regulation of the labour market in football should be the same as in other commercial activities, has reverted to the more typical European idea that sport, including football, should be handled primarily as a 'social' or 'cultural' activity, albeit one with a commercial dimension. To some degree these alternative models are competing for hegemony at the global level. In general, the prognostications for the development of global sporting regimes in this book offer a mixed picture, though not without a good deal of pessimism.

A second sort of issue concerns the relationship between emerging global institutions and existing institutions, including states, but also including nationalist parties and movements and national sports' associations. The chapter by Terry Monnington and myself falls under this heading, as does Alan Bairner's analysis of the relationship between globalisation and nationalism. To some degree – to borrow a favourite academic analogy – the story here is of a dog that doesn't bark: there are surprisingly few conflicts between the institutions of sporting globalisation and other movements and authorities. But this is a situation which may change.

Finally, to borrow a German term with no precise English equivalent, there are the issues of '*Kulturkampf*', cultural political struggles arising out of the tendencies to create a global culture, the contests over them and the opposition to them. Belinda Wheaton's analysis of 'lifestyle' sports like surfing is an account of sub-cultures which are often in opposition to the idea of globalisation and to the defining ideas of modern sport, but which are also themselves global and subject to global commercial pressures. There is a political contest for the 'soul' of surfing and also for many other sports which offer a 'lifestyle' and a specialised relationship with natural phenomena. Paul Gilchrist's essay, by contrast, investigates the idea of the hero, till now mainly conceived in a national and even nationalist context. My own chapter on the 'curious' position of American sport in the global context presents what is in some ways and from some angles the inversion of the idea of 'coca-colonisation' and Eurodisney as the 'cultural Chernobyl', in which we find American cultural conservatives berating the challenge of 'soccer'. Though at a deeper level, I argue, in fairly close resemblance to Ken Foster's account of a challenge from an American model of regulation, American ways are setting a radical agenda for global sport.

These issues will be at the heart of the politics of sport for the foreseeable future and perhaps for the twenty-first century. They make it a fascinating subject.

2   Sport, prestige and international relations

Lincoln Allison and Terry Monnington

In an essay written in the mid-1980s, Trevor Taylor concluded that, '... international relations scholars show little sign of seriously considering the place of sport in global human affairs' and prescribed that '... international relations should take more account of sport ...'.[1] We might have expected some change in the period since then, not least because the academic study of sport has established itself in such fields as politics and law and has made further advances in sociology and social history. The 'myth of autonomy', which suggested that sport should and did have little effect on other human activities, has been largely undermined; indeed we would argue that in some cases there has been an overreaction against it. Modern sport is increasingly and perhaps essentially international and has had an international dimension almost from the outset. It has developed highly autonomous international organisations, most notably the International Olympic Committee and FIFA, the international (association) football federation. Sport is unusually free from constraints on the development of global markets in images and labour. Sport is an important part of the images of nations and states and of the process of socialisation of young people into global society: Lothar Matthaus, Michael Schumacher and Bernhard Langer have been more importantly formative of young people's images of Germany in the last generation than have Fichte, Hegel and Bismarck.

Yet the sporting dimension of international relations still often plays almost no part in education in the subject. We might expect to find no mention of sport in a collection called *Classics of International Relations*[2] but it does seem strange to find it entirely absent from recent monographs, textbooks like Michael Nicholson's *International Relations*[3] and William Nester's *International Relations*.[4] An honourable exception might be Joshua Goldstein's *International Relations*, which manages two references to international sporting organisation in over six hundred pages.[5] It is not as if sporting relations are part of some new study of 'globalisation', of international organisations separate from the state and a global 'civil society' which fits oddly with the traditional study of relations between states. They are, but it is also the case that states have used sport in a variety of ways in their foreign relations. As a preliminary categorisation we can note that states have used sport in two principal ways: to sell themselves and enhance their image and to penalise international behaviour of which they disapprove. Even at this preliminary stage it must be remarked that each of these categories divides further into two. The 'image enhancement' effect can be a question of success or merely of acceptance. A Soviet academic account of Soviet sports policy insisted that 'each new victory is a victory for the Soviet form of society and the socialist sports system. It provides irrefutable proof of the superiority of socialist culture over the decaying culture of the capitalist states'.[6] In this case the success of the policy was entirely dependent on success on the field of play; we shall be suggesting some doubts about the efficiency of this form of policy and even whether it was what it purported to be as a policy. But many states have looked to sport merely to symbolise their acceptance in the international community. In the strict diplomatic sense this has been an issue most notably in divided countries such as Korea, China, Germany and Ireland. It must be remembered that in 1969 only thirteen states recognised East Germany and in the Olympics of 2000 Taiwanese athletes paraded under the banner of 'Chinese Republic – Taipei', an appellation which might be thought to suggest that Taiwan was ultimately a 'special region' of China, like Hong Kong. But even some established nations whose existence is not in doubt look to sport to express their status. It has been widely argued that China's enthusiasm for the Olympics is principally motivated by a desire to secure and demonstrate its acceptance as a mature state in the international system.[7] This desire must be seen in the context of China's fragile self-image as an ancient culture whose proper status is not fully acknowledged by the established (Western) powers.[8]

The politics of international sport has been more overtly coercive where states have instituted sporting boycotts as sanctions against the behaviour of other states of which they disapprove. The largest of these have been the US-led boycott of the Moscow Olympics in 1980, the Communist reciprocation four years later and the series of boycotts primarily by African and Commonwealth countries of the South African regime in the quarter century before it collapsed. Of these, the South African boycott was easily the most important and is generally attributed with a direct effect in bringing down the *apartheid* regime.[9] It included a number of secondary boycotts of countries which had allowed sporting contacts with South Africa, of which the most prominent was New Zealand. But there have been other, lesser boycotts and until it was overthrown in 2001–02 a variety of global sporting organisations were boycotting the taliban regime in Afghanistan.

It has often been remarked that sporting boycotts appealed to governments as strategic low-cost alternatives to other political methods. Trade sanctions against South Africa by Britain, for example, would have imposed high costs on some British workers and capitalists, whereas sporting contacts with South Africa proved largely substitutable. This remark applies also to the secondary and weaker sense in which governments seek to apply sanctions through sport, by their influence on the allocation of games. For example, a British parliamentary committee in 2000 recommended that the British government oppose the allocation of the Olympic Games in Beijing in 2008.[10] The rationale was that the Chinese economy was becoming too important for a serious trade embargo and that the 'New' Labour government's stated aspiration to pursue a 'moral' foreign policy would have to be pursued by other means in the case of a state which had become (especially in relation to its policy in Tibet) one of the major violators of Western human rights doctrines.

In short, sport seems to claim some attention even according to a traditional definition of international relations. That it should be so thoroughly ignored does seem to require further explanation and the most obvious hypothesis is that it does not have to fit into the established paradigms and debates of the discipline. These have been couched to a considerable degree as a contest between 'realists' and 'idealists' with (of course) a number of interpretations and revisions of each approach. A 'classic' version of realism, as put by Hans Morgentahu in 1960 has it that:

> International Politics, like all politics, is a struggle for power. Whatever the ultimate aims of international politics, power is always the immediate aim . . . When we speak of power, we mean man's control over the minds and actions of other men.[11]

Correspondingly, idealism suggests that there is at least a dimension of international relations which consists of genuine attempts to create or maintain an international order based on shared values. The degree to which idealism or realism is the assumption of a foreign policy can be a political issue in itself. In the late 1870s and early 1880s the clear difference between Benjamin Disraeli as Conservative leader and his Liberal opponent W.E. Gladstone on foreign policy was that Disraeli thought that British policy should be based unequivocally on British interests whereas Gladstone thought it should be based on the aspiration to a universal, Christian morality of international affairs. Turkey appeared as a natural ally of the United Kingdom from a Disraelian perspective, but as a morally errant despotism in Gladstone's eyes. There are shades of this dispute in the differences of emphasis (at least) between Democrats and Republicans since the end of the Cold War.

In order to demonstrate how the realist-idealist dichotomy might unduly marginalise sport, it is useful to consider an example. There was a vigorous contest, resolved in 1993, as to which city should hold the 'millennial' Olympic Games in the year 2000. The endgame involved Sydney and Beijing with Sydney being awarded the games despite the clear commitment of the President of the International Olympic Committee, Juan Samaranch, to the Chinese cause. The whole issue presented an interesting reversal of fortunes for the Olympic movement insofar as the games held less than a decade earlier, in 1984, which were ultimately held in Los Angeles, had at one time been threatened by cancellation because of the unwillingness of any suitable city to hold them. The decision was influenced by both China's suppression of democracy, especially the brutal response to a student demonstration in Tiananmen Square in 1989, and its reputation as a haven for sports coaches who used drugs. The result of the decision was particularly offensive to the Chinese: here, after all, was a country which is small in population and peripheral in world politics being awarded its second games (the first being Melbourne in 1956) before the world's most populous country had even hosted the games once.

What did Australia get out of hosting the games? Sydney 2000 was considered a great success: the atmosphere and organisation were adjudged by the great majority of those who could make the comparison to be clearly superior to those in Atlanta in 1996. This image was enhanced by the success of the Paralympics in Sydney shortly afterwards and the comparison between the genuine enthusiasm for this event in Australia with the tokenism and lack of interest in Atlanta again went Australia's way. A sense of what Australians thought they had gained from Sydney 2000 can be judged form the comments of Peter Fitzsimmons, Australian sportswriter and former rugby international, on the aftermath of the games.

> And did I mention already that Sydney has never seen the like, never done it better, never been so exuberant and I mean never? Never mind that the Olympic flame has been doused – the city remains agog with how well everything went, the reception it seems to have received from an international audience and the simply staggering brilliance with which we pulled the whole thing off!... don't think this is just me raving on. One of the most influential sports writers in the world, Rick Reilly of Sports Illustrated, devoted an entire column last week to mounting the argument that Sydney should keep the games for perpetuity; that it 'was the most beautiful city in the world' and made 'Paris look like Lubbock, Texas'. He also raved about the hospitality, how efficiently everything worked, the sheer Aussie panache and everything else Down-Under delicious he could think of.[12]

Even allowing for a certain (self-confessed) over-writing, we must surely concede that the games allowed the 'happy country' to be seen as it wanted to be seen by the rest of the world and that the vast majority of Australians would share some of Peter Fitzsimmons' pleasure and enhanced self-esteem as a result of them. The success would also prove beneficial in terms of tourism and investment (though the figures remain highly contested) and at least marginally in terms of the status and opportunities for individual Australians. Getting the Olympics and holding them successfully was good for Australian individuals, Australian society and the Australian nation and the benefits in these terms clearly outweighed the damage done by Australia's immediately previous appearance on the world stage as a society with something of an identity problem, deeply divided on the fundamental question of monarchy or republic.

At the same time it would be absurd to assess these benefits primarily in terms of the enhanced power to the Australian state in its important relations with Indonesia and the United States, just as it would be risible to think that China's achievement of third place in the medals table at the games in any way strengthened the hand of the Chinese state in its negotiations with the World Trade Organisation. We must surely allow that there can be benefits in status or prestige which are distinct from power. If the distinction is allowed it would also follow that in the absence of 'great games' like imperialism and the Cold War, the importance of prestige would increase at the expense of power. A less state-oriented international society might contain many states and regions whose interest lay primarily in their brand image rather than in any sense of 'power' or 'control' they might seek to exercise over the rest of the world. A Welsh person, whose country lies within the United Kingdom and the European Union (as well as being part of the state-like England and Wales) can coherently and patriotically welcome enhanced Welsh prestige as a result of the success in the rugby field or in the Commonwealth Games while being entirely opposed even to the existence of Wales as a player on the international stage.

There are at least two ways in which a defence can be mounted for the sort of 'realism' put forward by Morgenthau. He allows

> First, not every action that a nation performs with respect to another nation is of a political nature. Second, not all nations are at all times to the same extent involved in international politics...[13]

In this light, realism is not so much false as arbitrary, misleading and increasingly trivial, suggesting an analogy with the traditional ethical thesis that all human beings are selfish. It is apparent that 'politics' in this sense is narrower than it might usefully be and that non-politics is becoming more and more important. The other possible salvation is to insist that any benefits can be construed as 'power' (since the latter includes the general category of 'influence-over minds'):[14] if people like or respect Australia, then that country has power over them. In this case the theory is simply tautologous and uninteresting, incapable, *inter alia*, of allowing for shifts in the nature of international politics.

Let us assume, therefore, that prestige can exist separately from power and that states and other agents can seek it on behalf of nations and civil societies. Sport is a natural source of prestige. A number of questions follow: what kind of prestige can be achieved? Which means are most effective? How does international prestige relate to the other, domestic, objectives which sports policy may have? It is to these questions that we now turn.

An 'age of goodwill' and an 'age of prestige'

Before 1939, governments regarded the role of sport in international relations, if they regarded it at all, as being primarily a source of goodwill. To different degrees they accepted the orthodox accounts of sport's own spokesman, such as Pierre de Coubertin, that sporting encounters naturally engendered friendship and goodwill between nations. Peter Beck's account of relations between the Foreign Office and the Football Association suggests that the former saw potential in the latter as low-level, populist ambassadors for the country.[15] A notorious image remains of the footballer-as-ambassador: it is of the England team raising their arms in Nazi salute in Berlin in 1938 before the game against Germany. At the same time, it was obvious that sport did not always engender goodwill as the Colonial Office and even the Cabinet found when they had to pick up some of the pieces of the 'Bodyline' controversy in 1933, a major problem in Anglo-Australian relations which arose out of tactics on the cricket field.

It may be that the Foreign Office saw sport as only a minor and low cost opportunity to foster an atmosphere conducive to diplomacy. But there were those who put much more faith in sport. Phillip Noel-Baker, for example, saw sport as the principal means of developing international understanding and furthering the cause of peace. In a long life he was twice an Olympic silver medallist, a member of the British Olympic Committee and the International Olympic committee, a Labour M.P. and a campaigner, *inter alia*, for the League of Nations and the Campaign for Nuclear Disarmament.[16] He brushed aside the bitter Anglo-American rivalries which had been part of his own Olympic experience as creations of the press, insisting that the atmosphere '... at the Olympic Games has now become one of friendship between the teams, one of personal acquaintance among the runners. Everyone who was in Antwerp will readily accept that view: and everyone who has seen the Games from the beginning will know that every year it becomes increasingly true'.[17] It was the kind of naïve optimism about sport and peace, which Noel-Baker represented, which was George Orwell's target in his essay *The Sporting Spirit*. Orwell's comments are widely quoted (especially the description of international sport as 'war minus the shooting') and frequently misunderstood, but they do include the bald assertions that 'sport is an unfailing cause of ill-will'[18] and that 'international sporting contests invariably lead to orgies of hatred.'[19] They are the natural response of the natural polemicist to the kind of pious optimism expressed by the likes of Noel-Baker and espoused from time to time by the Foreign Office.

But for all the intensity of rivalries in international sport before 1939 there is very little evidence of governments seeking prestige by winning sporting contests. The world's first minister of sport was Jean Borotra, appointed by Marshall Petain under the Vichy government in 1940. The appointment undoubtedly arose out of a concern with French decadence and (lack of) virility, but it was in a context in which international competition was scarcely possible.[20] It is only with the Soviet Union's change of heart about international sport at the end of the Second World War that we have a significant example of a government devoting resources to achieving prestige through victory in competition. Of course, such a policy would have been extremely difficult to conceive in the context of major sporting nations before 1939. Sport was considered to be an 'autonomous' activity, part of a civil society independent of both the market and the state. In order to have a sports policy the British government, say, would have had to either break a fundamental rule of statecraft by putting on

the political agenda something which it could not control and to have introduced a new form of state intervention which the (elite) sporting norms of the
time would have declared distasteful.

To a greater or lesser extent most governments have imitated the Soviet
Union in trying to increase national sporting success. Paradoxically, the
British government imitated it more thoroughly in the 1990s, after the demise
of the Soviet Union itself, than it did before. During this period the Major
government shifted sports policy towards 'excellence' and allocated some of the
vast sums made available by the introduction of a National Lottery in 1994 to
the financial support of elite competitors in non-commercial sports.[21] But in the
thirty years after 1945 most governments developed programmes of support of
sporting achievement complete with ministers, funding and appropriate agencies. One could argue that this might well have happened even if there had
been no USSR to serve as model, exemplar and competitor. Compared with
previous and subsequent periods this was a time of *etatisme* when people looked
to states to solve almost every kind of problem. The rapidly growing technologies of air travel and television created, respectively, many more opportunities
for international competition and a much higher profile for such competition.
In many cases popular and press pressure would have been on government to
create programmes for sporting success. In the British case those pressures arose
in the period 1948–53, during which the English cricket team were soundly
beaten by Australia (in 1948) and the football team was beaten by the USA in
their first venture into the World Cup in 1950 and lost their unbeaten home
record to Hungary 3–6 in 1953.

It is important to note that though there was a shift in government attitude
towards sport from a belief in its value for establishing international goodwill to
a concern for prestige through success, the rhetoric and the practices of goodwill
continued. The expression 'ping-pong diplomacy', after all, refers to the Nixon
government's overtures to the People's Republic of China in the early 1970s and
involved the choice of the sport at which the USA was least likely to win. The
Foreign Office continued to look to the FA to provide teams to visit targeted
countries, though as the pressures of international competition increased this
was less and less likely to be a full England team and more likely to be an 'FA XI'
or an individual club side: at the time of writing the Foreign Office is negotiating with at least one Premiership side to play in a country with whom relations
have been fraught. The Soviet Union itself, away from the competitive glare of
the Olympics, sent teams and coaches abroad, particularly to Africa, in a spirit
of goodwill, sometimes even with instructions to lose. The rhetoric of goodwill,
perhaps even an abstract faith in goodwill, survived Orwell's scepticism intact.
Jaoa Havelange, President of FIFA from 1974 to 1998, who presided over an era
of rapidly increasing competitiveness and commercialism in world football, was
nevertheless able to assert, on the occasion of the organisation's ninetieth
birthday in 1994, 'whenever people can find an outlet for communication
and – especially – play, you will always find peace and harmony'.[22] Even so,
it is clear that from 1945, despite the survival of these practices and this kind of

faith, the new and predominant drive of governments' interest in sport was a concern for prestige which could only be attained through success.

A political analysis of Soviet sports policy is bound to suggest considerable doubt about whether the official justification for it was the real drive behind it. It was overtly an expression of a Marxist philosophy about the development of mind and body (a kind of Russian version of the nineteenth-century English public school idea of *mens sana in corpore sano*). The drive to win international competitions (and the Soviet Union headed the medals table in all but one of the Olympic Games in which it competed) was thus a kind of 'hearts and minds' campaign to convince people outside its boundaries of the virtues of the Soviet 'way of life'. The other dimension of the policy was that it functioned (like the space programme) as a mighty demonstration of the power and success of the 'Soviet Motherland' within its own borders, especially in the fourteen non-Russian constituent republics which Russians called the 'near-abroad'.

This emphasis fits much better with what it is now orthodox to believe about the Soviet Union. The party leadership did not, for example, harbour aspirations to world domination but were primarily concerned with maintaining full control over their own territory and existing sphere of influence. The idea of a popular sporting way of life involving exercise and athletics decayed rapidly as the Union stagnated leaving the country with a population which was less healthy and less active in sport than in almost any Western country while the elite programme remained successful to the end.

There is a danger of a fallacy of a collective will in generalising about the reasons or motives behind a policy. A wide range of actors and institutions were involved in the policy over a period of nearly half a century. Many of them may have believed the official ideology, and it can only be a broad, intuitive judgement that the reality was about national identification rather than about Marxist-Leninist philosophy. However, we can make slightly firmer statements about the success and the failures of the policy. It clearly did not enhance Soviet international prestige in anything like a proportion to the statistical Olympic success. On the other hand, Georgians have told us that though they regret it now, the sight of three Soviet athletes, complete with flag and anthem, standing triumphantly on the Olympic podium did make them feel more proud to be associated with the 'Soviet Motherland'.[23] It is very important to note, in this context, that though the Soviet Union allowed a variety of international cultural representation to take place at the level of the individual republics (such as the world tours of the Georgian State Dance Troupe), and even had four members of the United Nations, it was insisted that international sporting representation was at the 'Motherland' level.

The hypothesis about Soviet history is that, despite its overt rationale, sports policy is to be understood primarily as something designed for internal consumption. An extension of this hypothesis would be to suggest that all modern governments see the benefits of sports policy primarily in domestic terms. It is not at all convincing to suggest that the successes of New Zealand Rugby Union teams or Brazilian football teams in any way strengthen the hands of the respective states in international relations. But it does seem convincingly demonstrated that those successes enhance the general image of those societies abroad and contribute to a sense of national self-esteem, a 'feelgood factor' at home. Governments' interest is surely in fostering that self-esteem and being seen to be associated with or to contribute to that success. It is therefore to be understood primarily in terms of its domestic pay-off, though in many Western countries it has been a response to pressures from the electorate whereas in the Soviet Union it was an elite initiative. We now propose to explore these themes by examining the development of policy in Britain and in Africa.

From public school to public interest: the evolution of British concern for prestige

The long established traditions in British sport of pluralism and voluntarism created a barrier to state intervention in sport, which in the second half of the twentieth century came to be seen as a justification of the need for intervention. The numerous governing bodies of sport in Britain jealously guarded their autonomy and maintained the assumption that the state should not venture out on to the playing fields of sport. For much of the nineteenth and twentieth centuries successive British governments were also largely indifferent to the needs of sport and to its potential social and political value. Action in this sector was only deemed appropriate when crises relating to public health or public order warranted legislative action. In these contexts sport and leisure were to benefit occasionally as a consequence of their presumed instrumental value. The provision of open space in public parks, the eventual location for sports pitches, was justified on the basis of the need for public access to fresh air in towns which had become grossly overcrowded and polluted by industrial effluent.

Such attitudes to state involvement in sport were to guide government action well into the twentieth century. Demands for government support for sport were voiced, on occasion, to facilitate an improvement in the physical fitness of the working classes in preparation for work or war. In the late nineteenth century, defeat in sport of our supposedly national teams engendered only limited serious national concern. Even the defeat of the England cricket team by the Australians in 1882 that prompted the famous obituary notice in the *Sporting Times* only had significance for the dedicated cricketing community. However, with the restoration of the Olympic Games, the concern of the nation was aroused and more particularly our status in the world community was thought to be compromised if our athletes proved to be unsuccessful. The comments of the author F.A.M. Webster, following the failures at the Stockholm Games in 1912, were considered to reflect the view of many British people. He referred to '. . . a feeling of shame that we should fall so low as to be beaten by the even lesser European nations, who for generations past have been our pupils in all sporting pastimes'.[24] A further comment of Webster's apropos the 1912 games, reinforced his views on the damage to Britain's prestige that defeat on the international sporting stage could now bring: 'For remember we are a nation holding vaster possessions overseas than any other country ever has held, and once let us lose dominion and we sink to the level of the least European peoples'.[25]

Webster was one of a number of individuals who expressed concern and frustration about British sporting performances, but for the most part, the attitude of the government and politicians was characterised by indifference. There were, inevitably, however, a few individual politicians who supported the view that sporting success could deliver credibility and prestige to a nation. In 1927, 1929 and 1931 the Air Ministry successfully supported the entry of British seaplanes in the Schneider Trophy Air Race. These successes produced an 'immediate fillip to British prestige and a long-term benefit to aircraft design and even victory in the Battle of Britain'.[26]

National concern over sporting failure was further expressed following the failure of the British team at the Helsinki Games in 1952 when our gold medal tally was one. The failure and the other high profile defeats in the period leading up to 1952 in international sport prompted a group of physical educationalists at the University of Birmingham to publish their report entitled *Britain in the World of Sport*. The argument was that British sporting failure could only be reversed through some form of state intervention and financial support. Such a move was heresy to the traditionalists in British sport, but support for the principle of intervention grew steadily. Even the highly influential Wolfenden Report, commissioned by the Central Council of Physical Recreation and published in 1960, which in many respects provided the 'blueprint' for future British sports' development, was dismissive of certain forms of direct government involvement in sport.[27] The Report even questioned the real value of success in international sport and we can note the irony that a body which is acknowledged to have played an important historical role in the development of British government interest in the prestige value of sport should have expressed such clear scepticism about such value:

> To talk, as some do, as if sport could be properly used as a major instrument of international diplomacy, or as if a nation's authority and influence in world affairs at large are to be measured by its successes and failures in the Olympic Games, seem to us to reveal a serious lack of a sense of proportion.[28]

Despite the concern of many of the Wolfenden Committee, they were well aware that certain governments abroad were already more than willing to exploit international sporting success:

> There are many more nations taking part (in sport); increased and improved means of communication enable a much wider public to be emotionally involved in the result; in countries with a highly integrated political structure, sport and its prestige values can be consciously

exploited. We may deplore this feature of international competition; we cannot ignore it.[29]

Nevertheless, the re-elected Conservative government in 1959 did make some concessions to international sport during its term of office, including offering a modest grant of £20,000 towards the 1964 Olympics appeal fund. But Mr Denis Howell, later Minister for Sport in the 1964 Labour government, berated the government for underrating '... the importance attached to international prestige gained at the Olympic meetings'.[30] Of particular note was his suggestion that this prestige was important to the British public; he overtly acknowledged the value of international sporting success for domestic consumption. The 1964 Olympics was a success for British athletes and there followed a vigorous press campaign to force government to offer essential support. Mr Christopher Brasher of the *Observer* commented about the athletes that '... the money can only come from the government, and a cheer went up from most of the team when the news came through that Labour had won the Election'. [31]

When the Labour government entered office in '64 there was initial disappointment with the level of public funding in support of sport, including a real fall in public expenditure on sports facilities. But, through the efforts of the new Minister for Sport, Denis Howell, there was an increase in financial support for international sport, which generated much favourable comment towards the government. It was inevitable that the Soviet Union's use of sport as propaganda was seen to be paying substantial political dividends both at home and abroad. Politicians around the world could not fail to be impressed. The victory of the English football team at Wembley stadium in 1966 provided further evidence to the government of the value of international sporting success and was seen to '... provide one euphoric moment when austerity measures announced on the twentieth of July could be forgotten in a haze of national pride'.[32]

In 1968 Goodhart and Chattaway offered a prophetic comment when they suggested that

> Under the stimulus of popular concern, governments are certain to spend more heavily upon the development of successful sports teams, and to intervene in these affairs more regularly. In Western democracies, governments may have been slower to look at sport in this light, but attitudes are changing with the growing belief that a country's prestige is involved on the sports field.[33]

State intervention in sport, once legitimised in the 1960s, was rationalised primarily to reinforce state hegemony in a period where the working class, especially the young working class, were deemed to be a threat to social order; policy favoured access to more sport and range of leisure opportunities. Public funding of new sports facilities was primarily through the locally determined actions of local governments. The advisory Sports Council, established in 1965 and chaired by Denis Howell, provided advice and encouragement for sports development for masses. Elite sport was not as yet prioritised by this body or government as no real political agenda for sport was identified nor was their recognition of the value of potential of sport in the generation of national prestige. The situation was to change, however, from 1975 when the incoming Labour government decided to accord elite sport equal priority with the solving of social problems through sport. 'Success in international competition has an important part to play in national morale'.[34] To this end, government financial aid for elite sport rose significantly, supported by a 'Centres of Excellence' policy, which was overtly designed to foster national morale and prestige. By the 1980s, the government was increasingly usurping the *de jure* independent role of the Executive Sports Council, created by Royal Charter in 1971, as it increasingly prescribed an agenda for British sport. On occasions Margaret Thatcher marginalised the Minister for Sport, as issues relating to sport were perceived to be too serious to be handled by a junior minister. Likewise, the advice of the Sports Council was also regularly ignored or not sought by the Prime Minister. She was motivated, not by any love of sport, quite the contrary, but by the perception that international status and prestige were at stake, particularly in the issues raised by the Moscow Olympics.[35]

Thus, despite Thatcher's indifference to sport, it was indisputably on the political agenda, guided by a corporate plan identified by the government's own Sports Council; it was often considered too important to be left to the sports administrators alone. *Sport for All* was to be the responsibility of the local authorities, while alleviating social unrest in the inner cities and the promotion of elite sport were to be the main focus of attention of central government, with policy initiatives implemented through the Sports Council. However, as these latter issues were perceived by government to be increasingly important, the supposedly independent Sports Council was required to mirror the values of sport that the government articulated. The Council was also required to initiate programmes in support of these values. More and more the Sports Council was becoming '. . . the Government's executive arm for developing and promoting sport'.[36]

The election of John Major as leader of the Conservative party in 1990 heralded an increased profile of sport on the government's agenda. Publication of the government's sports policy document, *Sport: Raising the Game*, focused much of its attention on the creation of an infrastructure to support elite sport. The expressed view of Major, that reflected an importance that he attached to sport, which was widely accepted as sincere, saw sport as

> . . . a binding force between generations and across borders. But, by a miraculous paradox, it is at the same time one of the defining character-istics of nationhood and of local pride.[37]

His support for construction of a state-funded institute of sport confirmed the significance he attached to international sporting success. The establishment of the Department of National Heritage, with a minister of cabinet rank, and sport being identified as a key area of responsibility in this Department, further raised the profile of sport. Creation of the National Lottery in 1994–5 and its clear predilection to support elite performers and the construction of national facilities reinforced the status afforded top-level sport in the priorities of the government.

Conservative party publicists were constantly eager to exploit Major's professed commitment to sport by encouraging identification with the efforts of senior sports administrators to attract prestigious sporting events to this country. Most notable was his close identification with the bid to host the 2000 Olympic Games in Manchester. In July 1996, John Major wrote an article in the *Daily Telegraph* commenting on the three weeks of Euro '96. His conclusion was that '... football brought the country together in a way only sport can. The performance of the side lifted the spirits of the nation'.[38] The actions of the Sports Council and those of the remaining home nations continued to support government strategy ever more closely. The eventual division of the Sports Council in 1995 into the English Sports Council (now referred to as Sport England) and the UK Sports Council (now UK Sport) reflected the need for a separate organisation, the latter to direct elite sport, the element so crucial to government in the creation of national prestige through sport.[39] A change in government in 1997 has not derailed movement towards ever-greater government involvement and control of British sport. Tony Blair does not share Major's passion for sport, but there is no evidence of a downgrading of sport's importance on the political agenda of government.

During the latter half of the twentieth century, British sport has experienced a significant, but not total, metamorphosis. Much of this experience has been led by government as increasingly, as the Birmingham University report prophesised, 'he who pays the piper calls the tune'. Government investment in support of sport in Britain has not come without strings. Political agendas for sport in Britain, set by governments, have emerged and evolved, not always in a coherent and carefully considered manner. The politicisation process has been gradual but relentless and the consequences dramatic. British sports' administration, with its multitude of governing bodies, remains superficially intact. But for the majority, state-funding support has brought a significant degree of dependency to a corporate plan led by Sport England but ultimately prescribed by government. Even the relatively affluent and seemingly independent government bodies have been subjected to increased government influence and direction.

The machinery of government that has emerged to support British sport has brought many benefits. But the superficially hidden political agendas that are increasingly directing sport to facilitate social policy implementation and to generate prestige can be challenge. Indications are that very substantial additional funding is likely to be made available to sport through a number of major government departments and ministries in pursuance of educational, public health and crime prevention agendas. Under such circumstances, many of the traditional values and requirements of sport could be lost.

Sport as a last resort:
the rise and fall of the African dividend from sport

Sport was widely accepted as one of the few locations for super power competition during the Cold War years, even if the rhetoric was directed more for consumption of the media than believed by political leaders and their policy advisors. Many Third World leaders, however, embraced sporting success even more earnestly, not least because they had far less opportunity or power to effect political change. Sub-Saharan Africa provides many examples of national leaders exploiting sport and international sports stars for political gain. The weak and precarious nature of many political regimes in this part of the world following independence meant internal stability and future economic prospects were almost invariably at crisis point. Post-independence euphoria soon passed and existing linguistic, ethnic and tribal divisions that had been evident for generations were to cause much tension and concern. The fight for independence had often suppressed these divisions, but in most cases they now re-emerged.

Economic exploitation of the African possessions by the colonial powers had left the countries with only limited industrial capacity through which to develop new economies. Self-interest among tribal groups seriously hampered all aspects of development. Economic prosperity and political stability required unity and common goals, but they were rarely in evidence. The reality was invariably political insecurity and economic stagnation that owed much to the colonial inheritance. The world recession of the 1970s and early 1980s compounded already serious situations. African economies took a serious downturn as demand for exports declined and costs of imports escalated. Natural disasters, including severe drought and famine, crippled already faltering economies. Social unrest and disaffection were fuelled by a failure to improve the economic fortunes of the African peasantry. Unemployment was endemic, while real wages failed to keep pace with inflation and what prosperity was accruing to many independent nations was being enjoyed by an increasingly isolated elite. Essential foreign aid was only exacerbating the economic problems, as the African nations had now to service massive foreign debts. Revolution and military coups were regular consequences of public frustration. Successive governments across Sub-Saharan Africa flirted with every conceivable political ideology.[40] The progress made by Asian economies from the 1970s and by many of the economies of South America from the 1980s has generally eluded African countries.[41] In desperation, many African leaders have turned to sport for a lifeline to provide some credibility for their failing regimes.

To secure authority over sport and the necessary power to permit its use as a political tool, many African governments established Western systems of sport and physical education, but often with stricter government control and direction. By the mid-1960s the majority of African nations had established government sport offices, either as separate ministries of sport, or as sections of existing ministries. Direct control was invariably vested in a sports council or commission with extensive powers, including organising and financing sport on a national level. In particular, the objective was often to dictate sports' policy, an essential objective when considering the use of sporting boycotts in the international arena. The political role of African sport, in particular its potential in legitimising both individual regimes and nation-states, as well as its perceived value as a cohesive influence on domestic politics, is not solely the prerogative of athletics, although during the early years of independence this particular sport caught the attention of the world media.

The breakthrough for African athletes came at the Olympic Games in Rome in 1960 when Abebe Bikila of Ethiopia won the Marathon, followed home by a Moroccan. There followed throughout the 1960s and 1970s a succession of pre-eminent African athletes who became household names across the world, following their victories at major athletic meetings, including the Olympic and Commonwealth Games. Kenya proved to be the most prolific producer of middle and long distance track stars, with Kip Keino perhaps the most famous.[42] Their arrival on the athletics scene was to herald an East African domination of distance running that has been challenged, but rarely surpassed. A definitive explanation for their success is probably impossible, but certainly the athletes had the incentive of fame and material benefits were lavished on them. Keino, in particular, was lauded by politicians, including the head of state, Jomo Kenyatta, and regaled with the most prestigious honours. President Kenyatta was sufficiently astute to appreciate that this popular sporting hero could become a focal point for the diverse peoples of Kenya, generating a feeling of nationhood among a society that had long suffered from often intense tribal and consequential political divisions. Keino's victories, along with those of other Kenyan athletes, could also be construed as victories for an emerging and perhaps internationally significant new member of the world community. Prestige that could be exploited domestically and internationally could come cheaply, but with apparently significant rewards. The sporting infrastructure that supported these athletic victories was truly basic. A visit by the author to Kenya in the mid-1990s confirmed this reality. St Patrick's Boys' School and the nearby Singore Girls' School in the Rift Valley, near the small town of Iten, have produced many of the country's and the world's finest athletes. But the facilities for sport available at the school are poor; the girls' school relies on a cow pasture to prepare its athletes to compete on the world stage. The boys' school has a worn-out grass volleyball court and a dangerously slippery tarmacadam tennis court. The athletes train on the nearby track in Iten.

The list of African political leaders who have endeavoured to follow the lead of Kenyatta, from the 1960s through to the 1990s, in identifying with and exploiting sporting success for political gain has proved extensive. The heads of state in Ghana, Libya, Zambia, Cameroon and Morocco are among many whose political ambitions were in part vested in identification with prestigious sporting contests, successful teams and sports' heroes.

Football, however, is the most popular participant and spectator sport in Africa, regularly attracting crowds of over one hundred thousand. The mass euphoria the game generates was confirmed in April 1993 as a consequence of the death of thirty of Zambia's national squad and associated officials in an air crash near the Gabonese capital as the party were travelling to Senegal for a World Cup qualifying match. One hundred and fifty thousand mourners joined the funeral cortege at the six-hour burial ceremony, outside the National Independence Stadium in Lusaka.

This sport has, in consequence, been credited with similar political functions to those of athletes. Kwame Nkruma, the first President of Ghana, had a vision of a new Africa that had thrown off the shackles of colonialism and the associated exploitation and subjugation. He saw the continent's future as a united states of Africa in which sport had a role in enhancing the dignity and pride of its peoples and a vital role in moulding and mobilising the youth of a nation. President Mobutu of Zaire also recognised early on the potential of sporting success for the benefit of political leaders in their search for personal and national prestige. The success of Zaire's national football team in 1974 in qualifying for the finals of the World Cup represented a first for Black African football. Mobutu endorsed a trend, to be mirrored subsequently by many African leaders, of rewarding successful sportsmen with lavish gifts and national honours. The status afforded the footballers in 1974 was considered to be vindication of his Africanisation policy and systematic removal of symbols of Belgian colonisation and suppression of African traditions.

The success on the world stage of African football has been limited and few commentators of the game would be willing to suggest that there is much chance of an African nation winning the World Cup in the future. Nevertheless, moderate African success in this tournament has been an excuse for national celebrations and the appearance of national leaders to emerge from the shadows to bathe in reflected glory.

Despite the reservations felt, but rarely expressed, African sport clearly had some considerable success during the early post independence years. The success was extensively used by political leaders to further their own political ambitions as well as the wider objectives of developing national integration or nationhood, national identity and international recognition. Success in international sport is highly visible and is perceived to offer quick returns for relatively minimal financial investment if, as was the case, elite sport is the priority.

Unfortunately, however, the potential role of sport in fostering prestige for African political leaders and providing other political benefits has not always been long lasting. The concentration on developing an elite nucleus of athletes in an often very narrow range of events has brought success and gained a high profile for both the athletes and their country of origin. But international recognition in this form is invariably a temporary testimony to the strength of a nation. The success of the great Kenyan athletes of the late 1960s and early 1970s certainly brought their nation a high profile that was fully exploited by her political leaders. Yet subsequent international boycotts through the 1970s and early 1980s along with the luring away to the USA of many of the outstanding Kenyan athletes on university scholarships certainly contributed to the loss of Kenyan status both in sport as well as in the broader realms of international diplomacy.[43] There is now a discernable trend for African leaders to be more careful about associating with specific sporting contests to further their political ambitions.

There are several possible explanations for this development. The important context is that Africa over the last two decades of the twentieth century was the disastrous exception in global economic history with an estimated negative growth of around 15 per cent, while many Asian economies were doubling and trebling in size. Inevitably sports investment suffered. But it is also true that the continued violence associated with domestic as well as international sport has often discredited the name of sport and those associated with it. Success in sport, by its very nature, cannot be guaranteed even with the support of science, both legal and illegal. For politicians to identify too closely with sport can have regrettable and sometimes serious consequences. For politicians it can result in embarrassment, bring identification with failure, evidence of a lack of leadership skills and, at worst, gross incompetence. A visit to Zimbabwe in 1995 for the Sixth All Africa Games confirmed the inherent danger of politicians identifying too closely with sports stars and sporting spectacles.

The occasion was the opening ceremony of the Games in the new National Stadium of Harare, a stadium funded by the Chinese in recognition of their support for the country's Marxist leader, President Mugabe. The games had been established as a pan-African event and was regarded by many as one more means by which modern Africa could express its modern ancestry and celebrate the individuality of its multifarious cultural traditions, but also its unity. The history of the All Africa Games has been beset with problems, most notably as a consequence of mismanagement and political exploitation. But in 1995 it was planned to be different.

President Mugabe was eager to impress his guests with the capacity of the Zimbabwean people to organise a showpiece Games. His guests included many African and international leaders and senior representatives of the International Olympic Committee and other supra-national governing bodies of sport. Unfortunately, there were not many other spectators in the stadium. The time of the opening ceremony had been changed without notice and public transport to the stadium had been commandeered for the athletes. The mass of the population of Harare could not reach the stadium, even if they could have afforded the entrance charge. The start was delayed by half an hour as the torch was caught up in the traffic of Harare. When it did arrive, it had to be constantly re-lit on its lap of honour. Disaster followed disaster, culminating in the failure of the public address system, thus precluding our listening to the swearing of the Games' oath, the welcome of the President and the playing of the National Anthem.

For President Mugabe an opportunity to enhance his personal reputation as one of Africa's senior politicians was lost through the incompetence of the Games' administrators. The opening ceremony was a political embarrassment, a lost opportunity to paper over some of the cracks that were already in evidence in the country's economy and political system. The strength of the South

African team and their outstanding successes at the Games further undermined the value to Mugabe of the Games as a political stage.

Yet despite these risks, during the second half of the twentieth century, politicians were often eager to identify with sport. But towards the end of the twentieth century sport was changing its nature and becoming much more overtly commercial and globalised. Political attitudes towards sport were also changing as politicians became more astute and less willing to risk reputations and status on activity that they were increasingly unable to control because of the uncertainty of the outcomes of sporting contests.

As globalisation proceeds, organisations like the International Olympics Committee, FIFA and IAAF are able to wield power and influence superior to many Third World countries and they have the budgets to match. They are major players in the creation of a global sporting culture, with their own identifiable political economies. They are in reality emerging and increasingly significant players in the global economy alongside governments, multi-national corporations and other interest groups that have similarly become active across the globe, endeavouring to spread their influence and flex their economic muscle.[44]

In the context of sport, as the controlling bodies become more powerful, presidents of these organisations, along with the management agents of the athletes, have increasingly taken elite sport out of control of the politicians, governments and even the competitors themselves. The ability of governments to control these international sporting bodies and competitors diminishes as they vie with one another to attract sporting spectacles to their country. The political and economic power and influence of many African and other third world nations are usually significantly inferior to those of the large international sporting bodies. The success of the major sporting extravagances such as the Olympic Games is regarded by many as attributable to the IOC and its president rather than the host city, more a celebration of the supra-national governing body of sport than a nation-state and its political leaders. The hosting of such events is becoming increasingly a mere dream of most countries rather than a realisable ambition. The cost is well beyond the means of most national budgets. For those nations that continue to dream of hosting a major national international sporting tournament, the inevitable need to turn to external funding agencies to support a project will once more, for many, re-kindle images of neo-colonialism and economic dependency.

The athletes themselves were once the ambassadors of their nations, but they too are often commodities in the sporting global economies. Many are extremely wealthy, international personalities, even away from the context of sport. But they are, nonetheless, subjected to market forces that require them to respond to the needs of the market place. This invariably means competing in events around the world and for many, particularly in athletics, it means basing themselves in Europe. Many African athletes and footballers are no longer based in their home countries where they should be available as role models for future generations of sports men and women. They are certainly less available to their political leaders to be used to further political objectives or personal goals. Interference by senior politicians and presidents of African nations in team selection, particularly the national football team, has been in the past, a common occurrence. The Cameroonian football team experienced such interference at the World Cup in 1990 and 1994. By the year 2000 such interference only brought embarrassment and ridicule. In February 2000, following the apparent failure of the team from the Ivory Coast, the President incarcerated the team in a military camp near the capital. He seized their mobile phones and lambasted them for their poor performance. Somewhat frightened, the majority of the team was desperate to be released, have their phones returned and be able to return home to their clubs far away in Europe. Their priorities lay elsewhere. In the context of Africa, particularly in Sub-Saharan Africa, the success of elite sports men and women and national teams has thus become a potentially less valuable and valued tool in the political armoury of leaders of many of the countries of the region.

The great promise of the early years of independence has for many African countries evaporated as natural disasters, economic mismanagement, corruption and poor leadership have crippled their economies and political systems. The world media has regularly chronicled the demise of many of these nations. The United Nations and the World Bank have produced vast quantities of statistics to confirm the faltering nature of their economies and the plight of the people. The message included in a report of the IOC in 1986 has now even more poignancy than ever. It was, essentially, 'Do we have the right to offer sport for all when we do not have bread for all and work for all? Do we have the right to play and dance and to take seriously the measuring of our physical strength and the exercise of our physical skills so long as penury and illiteracy exist?'

From a political perspective, investment in sport and physical education at the elite level or for the masses is also not likely to engender much support when the social and economic infrastructure of society is being subjected to the level of pressure which is now evident across the continent. Sport can only bring temporary respite and transient pleasure for a beleaguered society. Sporting success and the associated prestige for all concerned, including the political 'hangers on' cannot hide the consequences of a collapsing, corrupt economy. The 1970s slogan that *'there can be no normal sport in an abnormal society'* has become increasingly relevant to Sub-Saharan Africa because of its failure to develop. Sport is simply not a priority for people fighting to survive. Education and employment inevitably and rightly rank higher. From a political perspective, sporting victory is increasingly less valuable in a failing society. In extremis, sporting victory can mock the condition of the majority. Thus, politicians are less eager to step out into the sporting arena, and if they dare, they present an increasingly less credible image. In short, though there was a period following independence when African politicians could develop and identify with sporting success in the interest of national unity and morale and in furtherance of their own careers, the potential for doing so has declined. Power has moved from states to international organisations and the African athletes and footballers themselves have moved from Africa to Europe and America.

Conclusion: the nature of the sporting dividend

It is an ironic epithet for the Soviet Union that its level of commitment to producing sporting champions is one of the few policies which has been widely imitated and has outlived the Soviet state. In many countries throughout the world there now exist full-time sportsmen and sportswomen whose activities are not funded by paying spectators. They are neither amateurs or professionals in the old, contending sense, but state *apparatchiki* who exist to bring prestige to their nations and governments. They are products of a sporting *etatisme* which expects a 'medal return' for its investment, the political benefits of which are clearly located in domestic politics rather than in international relations. Indeed, in countries like the United Kingdom, where some 40 per cent of lottery money at the time of writing is diverted to elite athletes and France, where four sports have been 'cherry picked' as the most efficient investment targets, there are specific attempts to assess investment against medal probabilities.[45] The practice was much reinforced in the UK by the 'dividend' of eleven gold medals at the Sydney Olympics and there is every indication that future governments will continue investment.

Of course, the Soviet Union cannot be given the unquestioned causal credit for these practices. Assuming the counter-factual hypothetical that it remained aloof from 'bourgeois' sporting competition after 1945, we can easily imagine that the development of television, the increase in international competition and nationalist pressure displaced by national media on to sport would have led to governments treating sport very much as they have actually done so. It would only take one government to successfully reap a dividend from an investment in champions and surely many others would have followed suit. Few governments showed much concern for sporting prestige in the first half of the twentieth century (though both Nazis and Fascists showed some leaning in that direction). On the whole, they considered the matter either trivial, none of government's business, or both, but in the second half of the twentieth century they developed an active concern for prestige achieved through sporting success. This was complicated by an intermittent concern to host major sporting events which sometimes complemented and sometimes contradicted the desire to produce champions.

Of course, the political games which involve commitment to success in the real games must tend to be zero-sum. If all states intervene and invest to produce success none is any better off than if none did, except insofar as politicians claim credit that they would not have been able to claim otherwise and except, also, that different populations may weight the value of sports very differently so that a wider variety of countries may see themselves as leading sporting nations than would be possible with a single weighting. But to some degree sporting investment must now be 'factored in' to many states as a routine need to be seen to be committed to sporting success and in the hope of a relatively small dividend by way of a 'feelgood' factor. Nobody could now have the kind of expectations of the political dividend from sport which drove many of the communist and African countries to invest in producing champions the third quarter of the twentieth century. Nevertheless, investment is almost certainly rising, perhaps confirming 'neo-liberal' fears about the difficulty of actually rolling back levels of state intervention and confirming the belief that states have innate tendencies to intervene in new fields when they are thwarted in old ones.

3 Not for the good of the game

Crisis and credibility in the governance of world football

John Sugden and Alan Tomlinson

> When I became President there was hardly twenty dollars in the cash box and now it gives me great personal satisfaction to know that things have moved on from there. I will leave with the cash box substantially filled with four billion.[1]

In this chapter we consider the central question of the global governance of sport by looking at the role played by FIFA (Fédération Internationale de Football Association). Our main concerns are classic issues for political science and sociology and are to do with representation, responsibility, accountability, agency-structure and, above all, power and its abuse.

One of the defining features of the twentieth century was the acceleration in the range and extent of international government organisations (IGOs) and their non-governmental equivalents (INGOs). In 1909 there were only 37 IGOs and 176 INGOs (including FIFA), while by 1996 it was calculated that there were 260 IGOs and a staggering 5,472 INGOs. In part, the growth in the number and reach of IGOs has been a response to the dramatic expansion of INGO activity. Whether they be charitable organisations such as OXFAM, political lobbyists such as CND, or global organisations of criminals and terrorists, national governments have collaborated, through bodies such as the United Nations and its satellites, or the European Union, to monitor and exert a degree of influence over INGO's activities.[2] Hitherto, sport in general and football in particular, have been exceptional to this rule.

Drawing upon Archer's classification of types of international organisations,[3] the central thesis of our argument is that since its foundation in 1904, FIFA has transformed itself from an INGO (International Non-Government Organisation) into a BINGO (Business International Non-Government Organisation) and that, contrary to FIFA's motto, this is not 'for the good of the game'. As Morozov states, the aims and activities of an international organisation must be in keeping with the universally accepted principles of international law embodied in the charter of the United Nations and must not have a commercial character or pursue profit-making aims.[4] The governing body of world football grew throughout the twentieth century, from the initiative of seven European national football associations in 1904, to represent more than

200 at the turn of the twentieth and twenty-first century. As it has grown, in violation of Morozov's principles, FIFA's reason for existence has been increasingly profit-driven, particularly in the final quarter of the twentieth century. It has become a leading example of the professionalisation and commercialisation of modern sport, and of sport's emergence at the heart of the worldwide cultural industries.

Sport was conducive to economic and commercial exploitation in the context of international trade: in Miller *et al.*'s words, 'the high point of trade for imperial Europe was also its high point for setting in place the global governance of sport'. [5] Football as an international cultural phenomenon, alongside de Coubertin's initiative of the Olympic celebration of international competition, was a remarkably resilient and sustained case of the supra-national growth of the administration and governance of a cultural practice. The history of bodies such as FIFA tracks the increasing interdependence of the political (sports associations speaking for national interests, often with international aspirations) with the economic (cultural industries such as the international media forming more and more extensive partnerships with sports bodies and their corporate sponsors). As Miller *et al.* put it: 'What began as a cultural exchange based on empire has turned into one based on capital' (p.10).

We are not, however, minded to continue our scrutiny of these issues in an abstract or metaphorical sense by, for instance, prefacing our thoughts with a dissertation on globalisation, (post) modernity and related theories of international organisation and social change. To some extent we have already done this elsewhere. [6] Instead, we want to show what happens inside an INGO when the pursuit of profit overwhelms an ethic of service. To achieve this we present a summary of the findings of a detailed, embodied and empirical investigation into power and corruption at the heart of the FIFA family – as those who inhabit the inner sanctum of football's global governing body choose to refer to themselves. [7]

The crisis in world football

'Crisis, what crisis?' Joseph 'Sepp' Blatter, president of FIFA, might have said to the world as he surveyed the aftermath of World Cup 2002, 'the people's game has never been healthier'. The men's World Cup in Japan and Korea, Asia's first, was a great success: the high-tech stadiums bulged, the media coverage was massive and the blue-chip sponsors beamed. The women's World Cup had higher profile than ever before, particularly revered in China, the USA, Germany and Norway. On one level, then, world football was in rude health, booming, central to the initiatives and profiles of the international media industries. But on closer scrutiny, football was in crisis. Live attendances in national leagues were volatile and, mostly, falling, as were television audiences worldwide. Television and sponsorship monies provide a fragile basis for mid- or long-term planning. Media outlets over-expose the product and artificially inflate company accounts, allowing absurdly high sums of money to be paid

for the transfer of individual players, and to individuals for their playing contracts.[8]

Behind his smiling, sardonic countenance, as Blatter surveyed his empire in
2002, the Swiss knew that as a global business football was on the verge of
bankruptcy, and with it FIFA. Just beneath the surface things were beginning to
unravel. In the months running up to the 2002 World Cup FIFA was in trouble
like never before, and in the spotlight of the world media. The crisis was
precipitated by the collapse of trust in the inner circles of FIFA House, and
the challenge that was mounted by the European association UEFA, and some
of its allies, to the unbridled and scarcely accountable power of the incumbent
president, Blatter.

Crisis One: FIFA's finances

Ever since his controversial election to the FIFA Presidency in Paris in 1998
there had been a strong whiff of corruption about Blatter's regime. FIFA family
wars had been intensifying since the collapse of marketing partner ISL
(International Sports and Leisure) in the spring of 2001. Veterans of FIFA's
executive committee also agreed that Blatter wasn't the cleverest of diplomats.
He had fall-outs with the Asian confederation. He lacked the Havelange style,
the gait, the presence, the 'oomph', the gravitas, the charisma. Things began to
come to a head when ISL, FIFA's long-term partner, went bankrupt. We talked
to numerous ISL people in Lausanne as the company collapsed around them.
All denied responsibility, shuffling away from discussion and pointing towards
the culpability of the long-term bosses. Dick Pound, marketing maestro at the
International Olympic Committee (IOC) over the years, and about to contest
unsuccessfully the IOC presidency, said that FIFA lacked business credibility.
The IOC had already severed its links with ISL: 'We got out of our ISL relationship' a few years ago: 'they were way offside the core business'.

FIFA could hardly do this whether it wanted to or not. ISL had been long
known as the black-box bolstering FIFA finances. Blatter himself was of the
same generation as ISL top bosses, all inspired by the vision and style of the late
Horst Dassler of Adidas, whose brainchild ISL was. Some had left to form their
own outfits. ISL graduate Jürgen Lenz headed up TEAM, the company behind
the Champions League and UEFA's own preferred marketing agency. At the
time of the ISL collapse, the normally loquacious Lenz couldn't 'talk to you in
good conscience', choosing 'to abstain from comment'.

ISL's parent company ISMM had been ordered to start bankruptcy proceedings, by a Swiss court, in Aril 2001. Vivendi-Universal, a Paris-based media
group, turned down an invitation for a take-over rescue. ISMM collapsed the
following month, and arguments raged within FIFA concerning the financial
implications of the collapse, as ISL losses were put by the Swiss courts at a
monumental US$1.25 billion. Certainly monies went astray. Revenues due
from broadcasters in Brazil were diverted to a secret bank account.
Sponsorsip revenues of up to US$200 million were reported to have gone

missing. A hundred million US dollars of television money owed to FIFA was said to be hidden away in a bank account in Lichtenstein.

The scale of the ISL-based losses was at the heart of the debates within the FIFA committees and factions. Blatter was claiming that the ISL collapse had cost FIFA a 'mere' US$30–32 million, but as Agence-France Presse reported at the beginning of 2002, 'independent marketing experts suggested an extra zero could be added to that figure'. Later, a disillusioned FIFA general secretary Michel Zen-Ruffinen's estimate would be US$116 million.

Whatever the precise figure, FIFA needed to take out a US$420 million 'resecuritisation' bond from Crédit Suisse First Boston, to get its finances back on track. FIFA's business credibility looked to be at an all-time low when ISL's 'partner' KirchMedia itself went bankrupt in April 2002, though its creditors and FIFA agreed a deal to transfer the World Cup TV rights into a separate company, KirchSport. Blatter's 'Venetian night of love' in his 'sweet-heart deal' with ISL over the years – as a BBC *Newsnight* interview phrased it – had plunged FIFA into its most serious financial crisis ever. It had certainly been avoidable. Even FIFA's prodigal son Guido Tognoni recognised this:

> FIFA made with ISL a three-term commitment. Nobody was really challenging ISL in those days. Everybody knew that the links between ISL and FIFA are so strong that there was no chance and the links brought their status strong and there was no chance for another one, so you can make your own thoughts on that. ISL was the leading company in the world. They did a good job . . . Where I put the question mark on is the procedure. I think that everybody should have the same chance to bid for rights, and this is questionable that this is the case.

But Blatter hadn't got where he was without loyal deals. He had always been close to his old mentor Horst Dassler. Tognoni reminds us that 'Blatter was partly paid by Adidas in the early days because FIFA did not have money'. Blatter says that he only had his office in the Adidas building, this was while FIFA was building a new one. It would, of course, have been possible to hire an office rather than have the general secretary of FIFA operating from the premises of a sports equipment company. ISL had been Dassler's brain-child, and the long-established conduit for the less accountable FIFA-related monies. Blatter's loyalty was misplaced in the case of the over-stretched ISL, his faith in his Family not justified on this occasion.

On the initial collapse of ISL European football powers were incensed. After the 2001 Champions League final in Milan, UEFA officials announced that Blatter must explain. If he couldn't 'provide an explanation . . . he'd have to step down'. Blatter knew that only months later the FIFA congress in Buenos Aires would be a critical moment, vital for his survival if not credibility. The big European powers of UEFA had people in the wings, ready to challenge the shaky-looking Blatter in a presidential election in Seoul in 2002. Dr Chung, of Korea, President of the AFC (Asian Football Confederation) and a Director of the industrial giant, Hyundai, was one of these. His countryman 'Mickey' Kim had failed to win the IOC presidency, and this cleared the way for Chung to put himself forward, if called, for the top job in football. If not Chung there was the charismatic Cameroonian, Issa Hayatou, recently handed an IOC membership.

In Buenos Aires Blatter faced a vote of (no) confidence and UEFA president, Lennart Johansson, tabled a list of questions at the FIFA Congress in Rio de Janeiro.[9] It would be too distracting for the purposes of this overview to go into detail on all aspects of this list of charges. Suffice to say had a similar list of questions and allegations been laid at the door of the CEO of any other major global corporation, his chances of survival would have been extremely slim and even prison might have loomed.

Instead, Blatter performed an astonishing escape act, deflecting the questions in one of his classically stage-managed forums. He got delegates from Jamaica, and other small countries, to speak out and remind the big Europowers (England, France, Germany) of FIFA's crucial constitutional fact – one vote one country. The big powers might win the football and be First World leading nations, but they had no more power in FIFA than the tiniest member. Blatter moved quickly to call a vote of confidence. FIFA's general secretary Michel Zen-Ruffinen flapped, reminding him that there'd been no roll-call, no proper procedure. Brushing aside his top administrator, Blatter got his vote of confidence on a show of hands that made militant trade unionism voting tactics look like pure democracy. The Europeans were outmanoevred in classic FIFA fashion, a turning point for Blatter in his fight for survival. 'Pure Blatter, brilliant', conceded Franz 'Kaiser' Beckenbauer.

He might have lacked the presidential gravitas of Havelange, but Blatter was crafty. Chuck Blazer, General Secretary of the Caribbean, North and Central American Confederation (CONCACAF) has said that 'his predecessor was a better politician'. But the street-fighting skills of a lifetime in the business saw him through. UEFA retreated, licking its wounds. But as the scale of the financial crisis at FIFA escalated, and Blatter's leadership style became increasingly despotic, a challenge to Blatter's presidency was planned.

Questions over Blatter's salary had been another recurrent issue. One insider claimed that he was on a six-year deal worth 24 million dollars, a deal projected beyond the period of his four-year presidency. The head of the finance committee, Argentinean Julio Grondona, can be held responsible for this contract. The executive committee was never consulted on this. Chung took this up with Jack Warner, deputy chairman of the finance committee, in January 2002. This is a man who is born and bred to rule, scion of the Hyundai *chaebol*. He didn't mince his words:

> I would like to emphasize that the management of FIFA's finance is flawed and the lack of transparency is at the root of current speculations. It is of critical importance that we provide a clear and transparent investigation of FIFA's financial situation so that we could restore FIFA's honor and image in the world.

This is strong stuff indeed, and from a heavyweight global businessman. Chung focused on three points in particular: the inadequacy of audit company KPMG's review report on finances after the ISL collapse; the financial strategy, termed a 'securitisation scheme', a 'sort of loan arranged against the collateral of future revenues'; and 'the story I heard about the President's salary is . . . that it is more than 20 million dollars over 6 years, instead of 4 years'.

Chung's letter was one of numerous communications faxing and flying their way across FIFA's corridors of power between November 2001 and March 2002. Blatter wrote in early November to national associations, confederations and the executive committee, assuring them that the ISL losses would not exceed 51 million Swiss francs, and attaching a report of the auditors, KPMG. The review report of KPMG, on an interim balance sheet, was at pains to point out that a review is not an audit. It is hardly reassuring. Though 'nothing has come to our attention that causes us to believe that the accompanying interim balance sheet does not comply with Swiss law and FIFA's articles of incorporation', the ISL question was not settled: 'the overall implications of ISL's bankruptcy for FIFA may only be assessed once bankruptcy proceedings are completed'. The auditors also drew attention to FIFA's recognition of revenue and expenses 'on a cash basis', including 299 million Swiss francs of 'future income recorded in 2000 from existing marketing contracts (excluding TV-rights) for the 2002 and 2006 World Cups'. The balance sheet was conventionally well-balanced – 465,157,894 Swiss francs of assets; and exactly the same figure for the equity and liabilities. It balanced, but only with the help of the 24-hour cash placements clawed back from what was not yet earned. In December, thirteen (all the European, all the African, and Korean Chung) members of the executive wrote to express their overall dissatisfaction at the review report, and posed questions on the ISL losses, lost income from cancelled events, FIFA's relationship with Brazilian broker company Traffic (partly owned by Havelange and his son-in-law Ricardo Texeira), commercial contracts held by members of the executive committee, and the increasing profile of unaccountable presidential advisers.

'I am determined to continue to lead FIFA with policies of utmost transparency and open communication,' countered Blatter within days. Lennart Johansson, UEFA president, responded immediately on the financial question, the inner administration and conflicts of interest of committee members: 'Why do you oppose the setting up of an internal investigation group? What are you afraid of? We will come back.' On Christmas Eve, Jack Warner from Trinidad and Tobago wrote to Blatter to condemn the 'posturing and histrionics of some members', and their threat to Blatter's principles of 'solidarity and fraternity'. Warner looked back and forward: '. . . brokering and confederational politics take precedence over genuine discussion and debate and . . . the elections of '98 have never been over and are being fought in the FIFA Executive Committee. It will never be won at the level of the Congress'. Warner was reassuring Blatter that in any vote among the full FIFA membership, his loyalty base was intact.

Argentinean Julio Gondona, chair of the finance committee, joined the fray in January, to apologise for the late circulation of key papers, and to spout some

FIFA rhetoric on restoring 'a sense of security to the entire FIFA family'. FIFA's Scottish vice president, David Will, responded, scathing about the two-page auditor's review when he'd anticipated a 200–300 word document, and not letting go of the key issue of the riskiness of drawing upon future anticipated income 'to cover current costs without the direct permission of the Congress'. At the end of January the thirteen members reasserted their demands for the setting up of an investigation committee. Blatter conceded, following Will, proposing 'an ad hoc internal audit committee', and an extraordinary meeting of the executive committee in March, dedicated to financial matters.

The national associations heard from Blatter at the end of January, interested to learn that after the ISL collapse, 'I personally took charge of FIFA's financial situation ... and FIFA is in a position to keep up the benefits due to the national associations, competition organisers and commercial partners without any reductions whatsoever'. He also told them that the recalcitrant thirteen were acting out of line with FIFA statutes. This was too much for Chung, Johansson and Hayatou, who felt the need to also write to all the national associations, explaining their dissatisfaction with the 'drip by drip confirmation in writing of what we suspected already last year in June', that the ISL fall-out may be 500 million Swiss francs, ten times that claimed by Blatter. The three vice-presidents also wanted to know why ISL's bankruptcy administrator was not being pursued with reasonable claims, and why Blatter had not even referred to ongoing negotiations. In early February Blatter wrote to the executive committee, calling the reproaches in the letter 'erroneous, some of the accusations caluminous ... I can accept none of this'.

Crisis Two: out of Africa

At the same time that Blatter was fighting his critics about FIFA's balance sheet and his own finances, his presidency was re-engulfed in accusations about bribery and vote fixing at his 1998 election. There had been strong rumours circulating that money from the oil-rich Gulf had been used to secure the votes of a significant number of African delegates at the Paris Congress.[10] In revelations first made to the *Daily Mail*, Farah Addo, a CAF vice president, seemed to offer the first concrete proof of this when he claimed that he had been offered a bribe by Mohamed Bin Hammam of Qatar to vote for Blatter on the eve of the election. Addo has claimed that 18 of Blatter's votes came from African delegates persuaded to break ranks, helped along by bundles of cash dispensed in Paris's Le Meridien hotel on the eve of the election. If those votes had gone to Johansson, he'd have been ahead of Blatter by five votes in that first poll. In response Bin Hammam wrote to CAF's president, Issa Hayatou and in doing so, as the following excerpt reveals, lifted the FIFA family wars onto a new global scale:[11]

> Let me make a confession if we are going to start hitting under the belt, Mr. Addo has personally come to me in Zurich and claimed that you are in his pocket and you will do whatever he wants. He told me that he wants me to

run for AFC Presidency and he wants me to support you to become FIFA President while he would take over CAF Presidency. *He went on to say that imagine with three Muslims leading the global football confederations (FIFA) and two largest confederations (CAF & AFC) what power we will have in hand.* This shows you what kind of sick illusion and racism is in the head of this man. President, I told him 'Islam has got nothing to do with this and for me as far as Blatter is a candidate I will always be with him, only if he steps down I can think of an alternative and Issa is my favourite.

[Our italics]

An astonishing range of issues is raised by this item of correspondence: threats of revenge, world conspiracy theory, dictatorial government, personal sacrifice, the denial of corruption. By now the FIFA family was looking like a worn-out warring shambles of cabals and feuding factions. However, Addo was a relatively marginal figure in FIFA's corridors of power, a man not taken very seriously, even in his own African continent. But when the FIFA general secretary himself turned whistle-blower, many thought that Blatter's days may indeed be numbered.

Crisis Three: Zen-Ruffinen's dossier

Michel Zen-Ruffinen had been groomed by Blatter as his successor as general secretary. He had arrived in FIFA House, keen and ambitious, from a background in law, and experience as an international standard football referee. He came from Blatter's own region, the Valleé in Switzerland. Guido Tognoni, back in the FIFA fold until sacked as a consequence of the publication of our book *Badfellas*, talked to us after he'd been sacked in the New Year 1995 as FIFA's media and marketing guru. When he spoke of Zen-Ruffinen he spoke with bitter resentment: 'He came to FIFA and after three days he says that he wants to become general secretary, that is his aim, he is crazy. We were a bunch of people who were working together, we thought he is kinky'. Kinky or not, his rise was close to meteoric. Blatter told Tognoni '... "we need better organisation in FIFA House. FIFA House has also to work when I am not in". I replied "well, what happened during the last ten years? You were frequently away and the house didn't crash down, it worked fine". Then happened something very strange. All of a sudden, without consulting anybody before, Blatter said that they had a new "organisational chart".' This brought Michel Zen-Ruffinen in as deputy general secretary.

Tognoni didn't mince words: 'I was shocked, everybody was shocked in the management, everybody was shocked that Blatter took such a measure, taking the youngest one, the least experienced one and a lightweight, promoting him to deputy general secretary. I said to Blatter "can he give me orders?" and he said "yes" then I said "this I have problems to accept because he is not competent enough to give me orders, he has not the experience" ... I said "this creates a problem for me if this young chap has the competence to give me advice"'.

When Blatter became FIFA president in 1998 it seemed only natural that Zen-Ruffinen should succeed him as general secretary. But it did not take long for things to turn sour. In the four years of Blatter's presidency, the ambitious Zen-Ruffinen had been cut out of the loop of power, and could no longer stay silent on the manner in which Blatter was running FIFA. Blatter supporter Chuck Blazer, CONCACAF general secretary, claims that 'Blatter's administration is much more transparent' than that of his predecessor. 'More meetings; more information; distribution of committee chairmanships and positions, including his opponents. Financial information much more ample and available.' Zen-Ruffinen's view from the heart of the FIFA administration was a million miles away from Blazer's glowing testimonial.

At the FIFA executive committee of 3 May 2002, just weeks before the upcoming presidential election, Zen-Ruffinen broke his silence on what he called 'various turbulences'. Here is the rationale for this intervention, in the words of the former referee turned whistleblower himself:

> FIFA is flawed by general mismanagement, disfunctions in the structures and financial irregularities. I therefore decided to stand up for the good of the game; it has been too long, that I was loyal to the President. Many FIFA representatives from places all over the world encouraged me with their full support to clarify matters in regard of the various harmful occurrences taking place in and outside of the headquarters of FIFA. They felt embarrassed to be seen as 'FIFA family members' after all the recent news which damage the image of our organisation.

In his explosive document, Zen-Ruffinen asserts that Blatter took over both the administration and management of FIFA, against the statutes, working with a few select people in his inner group, the F-Crew, and 'manipulating the whole network through the material and administrative power he gained to the benefit of third persons and his personal interests. FIFA today is run like a dictatorship. FIFA is not a decent and structured organisation anymore. It has been reduced to the Blatter organisation'. Zen-Ruffinen describes a bloated family at FIFA House, 150 staff now rather than 50, plus 80 refugees from the ISL debacle, now located in FIFA Marketing AG. 'FIFA is in a bad shape today. FIFA is disorganised, the staff is dissatisfied, frustrated and the FIFA administration is governed by the President and a handful of people of his choice. The finances only seem to be in order. In fact, FIFA today lives from income of the future'.

The style of working of the F-Crew (the Führensgruppe, the leadership group), the inner-circle of four of Blatter's 'closest collaborators' – Champagne, Linsi, Siegler and Schallhart – was described to Johansson in Buenos Aires in June 2001 as 'merely an internal consultation body'. In reality F-Crew went way beyond such an advisory role, and began to deal with staff appointments, budget decisions and the like. The general secretary himself was nominally part of this grouping, but routinely found himself 'systematically circumvented'.

Zen-Ruffinen's document describes wide-ranging forms of maladministration, personal self-aggrandisement, conflicts of interest, financial irregularities and alleged cases of outright bribery and cronyism. The spiralling mess of the FIFA finances is plain to see. Zen-Ruffinen rubbished the president's public claim that FIFA had the highest ratings for its procedures, from established financial bodies: 'For 1998 and earlier, the years for which the President was responsible as General Secretary, no information is available anymore, even though documents must be stored for 10 years due to the law. Neither the former auditors of FIFA nor FIFA itself do have such information.' Zen-Ruffinen's summary of 1999, the first year for which he as the new general secretary had responsibility, shows the deep-rootedness of the escalating crisis. The strategy of borrowing against future income – what Chung called 'rather like the situation of a patient who extends his life by emergency aid' – was already in place:

> At the end of 1999, the liabilities exceeded the assets of FIFA, i.e. FIFA was overindebted in the amount of CHF 67.8 million. The situation could be improved since CHF 144 million were accounted as income out of TV-rights in the year 2000. However, what must be disclosed is that the balance sheet never appears to reflect a true and certain situation. Already in 1998 CHF 65 million were booked as income into the year 1998 out of TV rights regarding the World Cup 2002 to be recognised as income only for the period 1999-2002. The auditors (KPMG) have clearly criticised the respective accounting policy.
>
> (Zen-Ruffinen)

This borrowing against future assets – the 'securitisation concept' – was used with increasing desperation by FIFA, especially after the 2001 collapse of ISL. Regardless of this, the disillusioned general secretary goes on, Blatter, acting alone, could casually commit 250 million Swiss francs to the local organising committee for the 2006 World Cup in Germany, commit 12 million Swiss francs to McKinsey & Company and conduct numerous other dubious financial deals with individuals and outside bodies, with little or no internal accountability back in the general secretary's office or to the executive committee. Zen-Ruffinen's remarkable paper raised the stakes in the FIFA in-fighting, and provided the basis for what the following week was submitted to the Swiss prosecutor.

It looked as if this could be Blatter's toughest ride yet. The venom flying around the factions of the executive committee, and the stunning testimony of Zen-Ruffinen, culminated in the lodging of a criminal complaint by eleven members of the executive committee, on 10 May, just a couple of weeks before the Seoul Congress at which the presidential election would be contested. It was delivered by hand to the Public Prosecutor's Office in Zurich, 'filed on behalf of' individual members of the executive committee, writing from their residential bases: Lennart Johansson, Stockholm; David Will, Brechin, Angus, Scotland; Antonio Mattarese, Rome; Issa Hayatou, Cairo; Mong Joon

Chung, Seoul; Michael D'Hooghe, Bruges; Per Ravn Omdal, Eiksmarka, Norway; Amadou Diakité, Mali; Slim Aloulu, Tunisia; Ismael Bhanjee, Botswana; and Senes Erzik, Istanbul. This was the amassed forces of Africa and Europe pushing the FIFA wars to unprecedented levels of intensity.

The complaint concerned 'Suspicion of Breach of Trust' and 'Dishonest Management', as the charges are termed in the Swiss Criminal Code, which the complainants' attorney argued to be applicable as Blatter's activities were on behalf of FIFA, and the city of Zurich 'the centre of his professional activity as FIFA President'.[12]

This petition logs an extraordinary list of charges: vote-buying across the old Soviet satellites of East Europe, all of the Americas, particular parts of Africa; nobbling witnesses, shredding evidence; favouring insider contractors; stage-managing activities for personal aggrandizement; ignoring the board (the executive committee).

As the family at war uncharacteristically bared its feuds to the outside world, Blatter stuck to his guns. He knew where the grateful support would come from, and where the loyal votes lay. He had been planning for this for four years, and the key was his international schedule around the *Goal* development projects, a 'tailor-made aid programme', as Blatter himself put it: 'all about giving a chance: giving a chance to FIFA to channel the fruits of football's success back to the grass-roots of the game, and by giving those grass-roots a chance to taste some of that success'. Not a bad chance for Blatter, too, to remind the minnows of world football where their bread was buttered and they could certainly be relied upon to turn up at the Seoul Hilton and show their respects to the president.

Crisis Four: the Seoul Congress

'I am not a crook', said US President Richard Nixon, one grey November day in Washington in 1973. 'I am not a bad man', said Joseph 'Sepp' Blatter on stage in the convention centre of the Hotel Seoul Hilton, South Korea, the Wednesday before the weekend kick-off of World Cup 2002. In Seoul on this sweltering May day in 2002, the FIFA president sought to stem the tide of his own Watergate, with documents disappearing from the files at FIFA House, and integrity and credibility draining daily from the veins of the world governing body. 'Many, many thanks. You cannot imagine what it means to me having been during months accused by a certain press saying what a bad man I am'. 'I am not a bad man', he'd also stated at a press conference a little earlier: 'Look into my eyes'.

Blatter had just been re-elected as president of the governing body of world football. There'd never been a FIFA Congress quite like this one. It had come close in 1998, when Blatter won the presidency against European (UEFA) football boss Lennart Johansson. This time round Blatter faced a challenge from the boss of the African football confederation, Issa Hayatou, of Cameroon. The world media were hungry for this, and Blatter was splattered across the headlines of most of the world press, on news rather than sports pages:

all asking whether he could survive the serious allegations over his stewardship of FIFA. 'For the Good of the Game', FIFA's slogan, was looking like a laughing stock as Blatter reeled in the face of accusations of administrative malpractice, financial mismanagement and outright organisational deception and fraud. The English press, the *Daily Mail* in particular, went beyond a reliance on media releases and mere speculation, and relentlessly attacked the FIFA president and his network of cronies, crooks and charlatans who had made personal gains from their lofty positions. Much of the attention focused upon the question of whether Blatter was even fit to stand for re-election for the FIFA presidency. The media revelled in the dramatic atmosphere of charge and counter-charge as the FIFA edifice looked more and more shaky.

Havelange – the fittest 85 year old one might ever encounter – was in Seoul, observing the legacy of his presidency. The Big Man of the FIFA family, Havelange reminded his flock that the presidency demanded strong qualities. Hedging his bets, he didn't grant Blatter his total blessing as he gave his still-presidential nod, rather than taking the stage. His former protégé had made a mess of too many aspects of the family business, and was certainly incurring the wrath of his former mentor. But Havelange was still pretty sure that the smooth Swiss charmer would have done the business on the campaign trail.

Chuck Blazer was likewise smugly sure that Blatter would glide to a second term. We'd asked him, the weekend before the congress, whether his confederation could continue to deliver a bloc vote of its members on any issue, especially the presidential election. He confirmed the delivery of 35 votes for Blatter: 'It can continue to deliver block votes where a common interest is concerned. This is certainly the case in the Presidency and there are other issues as well, but this is one of the few which is voted on by the membership in full'. Blazer's boss, confederation president Jack Warner from Trinidad and Tobago, was looking confident and cocky as ever, despite press revelations of his dubious business privileges in FIFA deals in the Caribbean region.

Peter Velappan was there too, one of the men who'd turned against Sir Stanley Rous in 1974, casting his Malaysian vote in favour of the promises from Havelange. Velappan was now general secretary of the Asian confederation, 45 votes less easy to manipulate as a bloc. The FIFA executive committee member Dr Mong Joon Chung, from Korea, was one of the outspoken critics of Blatter's style and practices. But the man from the Gulf, Mohamed Bin Hammam Al-Abdulla of Qatar, was a key Blatter supporter. This was the same man alleged by Somalian Farah Addo to have offered the bribes for votes in Paris in 1998. Bin Hammam also facilitated Blatter on the campaign trail, with the provision of private jets to help him along in his busy schedule.

European associations were split down the middle, some big football powers, including England, supporting Hayatou, but many, including France, Germany and Spain, still hand-in-hand with Blatter. It was recognised, though only whispered, in the corridors of power of European football, that Hayatou was never in the running. Numerous football associations were for Blatter not just because of past favours and the spiders' webs of patronage and dependency. They were also adamant that no African – for this, read black man, and the myriad of alternatives to that term floated in some nations of Europe, particularly the newer nations in the east of the continent – could be contemplated as FIFA president. And it wasn't just at the heart of Europe where such prejudice was simmering. Delegates from South America, Asia, Arab Africa and the Gulf would not want a black African at the head of the FIFA family.

South America, Brazilian Havelange's original power base, was all the way behind Blatter. Julio Grondona from Argentina, chair of FIFA's comic-looking finance committee, was a long-term survivor of FIFA politics. Johansson had found South America a fruitless campaign trail in 1998. It was to be no different for Issa Hayatou this time round. Little Oceania was now well represented in the hall, a dozen member associations in a confederation only granted full confederational status in 1996. Adrian Wickham, for instance, from the Solomon Islands wouldn't waste much time listening to Issa Hayatou's case. He'd recently got on the FIFA executive committee, and a nice lump of cash from FIFA – US$668,000 – had just renovated and upgraded the Solomon's national stadium in Honiara. He liked Blatter's *Goal* initiative to help small footballing nations like his own. He wasn't about to waste all this good work and back calls for reform and accountability and the like.

The day before the congress, at an extraordinary congress at which Blatter planned to answer his critics, he'd looked vulnerable. The then English Football Association chief executive Adam Crozier called the Blatter performance an 'absolute disgrace from start to finish. There was no attempt at transparency in two hours of manipulation'. No opponents of Blatter were allowed to address the congress. Delegates from Blatter client countries such as Iran, Libya and Jamaica spoke fulsomely of Blatter's leadership, insulted UEFA president Johansson, attacked David Will and praised the president's financial acumen. The Libyan delegate, Muammer Al-Qadhafi Assadi, son of the dictator, was jeered as he tried to discredit African-based critics of Blatter. Scot David Will, FIFA vice-president, and chair of an internal audit committee set up to probe FIFA finances, was prevented from speaking, and confirmed that 'only one side of the financial information was given. Blatter just refused to let me speak and I'm very angry'. Korean Dr Chung was permitted to speak only in the form of a welcoming address on behalf of his home, host country, but did say that 'only one person is responsible for the division of FIFA'. Blatter was unapologetic, but defensive: 'I am not ashamed of what I have done. I don't always act according to procedures that are normally accepted, but I have done nothing against the Statutes of FIFA'. 'No peace in our time here', muttered one seasoned international journalist as the votes were cast.

But the dapper Blatter never quite lost his confident step. He knew that there was little chance of him losing the election. What surprised the parvenus to the FIFA scene was the margin of Blatter's victory. There were 197 national associations present in the hall and entitled to vote, and 195 valid votes cast. A two-thirds majority (130) was needed for an outright first-round victory. Blatter got 139, Hayatou a mere 56. The Cameroonian's supporters estimated that only 19 votes had come from the membership of his African confederation. Blatter more than doubled his 1998 winning margin, despite the charges of corruption and the extraordinary spectacle of the FIFA family feuds in headlines across the world. Media people in the hall gasped in shock at this.

Of course, for most of the vote-holders the election had little or nothing to do with principles of integrity and the FIFA delegates in the congress hall were less surprised at the outcome than some gullible media outsiders. They represented football's worldwide family, the more than 200 national football associations from FIFA's six confederations. In the year leading up to the election, Asia had 45 member associations; Africa had 52; South America had 10; the Central, North American and Caribbean confederation 35. Oceania (Australia, New Zealand and the South Pacific islands) had 11 full members; and the powerful European body, UEFA, 51. The bosses of the confederations were the powerbrokers of the FIFA family, seeking to mobilise bloc votes of their member associations. The presidents and their general secretaries and the men from the national associations themselves knew that Blatter was the master manipulator of FIFA's pseudo-democratic structure. In the FIFA congress, the delegate from the Cook Islands (population 17,000) has as much power and influence as the delegate from Germany, Brazil or the USA. Blatter had worked this system for over twenty years, first as general secretary, then for four years as president. In Seoul he demonstrated his mastery of the FIFA power game.

Vengeance

In *The Prince*, Machiavelli wrote that 'men should either be treated generously or destroyed' and 'it is much safer for a prince to be feared than loved'. In the weeks after his re-election Blatter, in the style of Machiavelli, moved swiftly to consolidate his power base. Clearly, Blatter had no intention of being bullied or, in his eyes, betrayed, by either his executive or his administration ever again. According to Tognoni, Blatter's problems with the executive were already well on the way to being solved. 'Blatter's stubborn at times', explained Tognioni. He had not exercised the authoritative and charismatic control of an Havelange over the executive. But at the last executive elections he tipped the balance in his favour by getting rid of Per Omdal (Norway) and Antonio Matarrese (Italy), two UEFA loyalists, and getting French football legend Michel Platini, his running mate from 1998, German Vorfelder, and Spain's Angel Llona on board – 'all his supporters', Tognoni confirmed. After his election victory the long knives were wielded as Blatter cleaned out his administration. The press release announcing the start of Blatter's purge was chillingly terse:

> Zurich 10 July 2002 – FIFA has yesterday and today parted company with seven employees. The decision to terminate or not extend these employees'

contracts comes as part of FIFA's restructuring process. President Joseph S. Blatter will present a proposal concerning the future structure of world football's governing body to the Executive Committee at its next meeting on 23/24 September 2002.

First head on the chopping block was that of Michel Zen-Ruffinen. 'If you have in your own house a traitor, this is bad', Blatter blurted to Jennie James of *Time* magazine, in the Glasgow Hilton on Champions League night: 'Have you ever heard of Brutus?' he continued, comparing Zen-Ruffinen to Shakespeare's assassin. This time it was Caesar who would wield the knife. 'Zen-Ruffinen is bad, not naïve and he's just not very smart' was the way Tognoni summed up the outgoing general secretary. 'Grondona got it right when he said, "I wouldn't put him in charge of a troop of boy scouts let alone FIFA. Now I feel I must apologise to the scouts!"'. As we've seen, Zen-Ruffinen had been the rising star in FIFA House when Tognoni was being shown the door and he still harboured resentment that the young Swiss lawyer and former referee had occupied the seat that he coveted for himself. 'I left FIFA seven and a half years ago because of Zen-Ruffinen's gross incompetence. No matter what he tells you, Zen-Ruffinen's charges against Blatter are a pack of lies and that is why they have been withdrawn from the Swiss courts'.

Loyal F-Crew members and other cronies were quickly moved into key management positions. Fellow German-Swiss Urs Linsi replaced Zen-Ruffinen as boss of the administration, and Blatter's former personal communications advisor, Markus Siegler, of Germany, made himself comfortable in the Director of Communications office, occupied across two successful World Cup cycles by the urbane Englishman, Keith Cooper. Then he turned his attention to FIFA's influential committees as fierce critics like David Will and Farrah Addo lost their positions of responsibility.

Next to go, for the second time was, Guido Tognoni, wrongly accused by Blatter of 'collaboration' with two English journalists in the production of a book that was critical of FIFA. The two so-called journalists are the authors of this chapter. We had talked to Tognoni on a number of occasions. Most of the information used in the book (and in this chapter) came from an interview with him in 1996, a time when he was outside of the FIFA family. This falls some way short of collaboration. Nevertheless, a confident and vengeful Blatter was taking no chances and Guido had to go.

With a tame executive and a loyal, Germanic praetorian-guard around him Blatter became increasingly despotic and invulnerable. He is, nevertheless, pledged to stand down in 2006 on the eve of the World Cup Finals in Germany. History suggests that things may turn out otherwise. Either way, with the Kaiser, Franz Beckenbauer, waiting in the wings, there would be smiles on the faces of officials of the Deutscher Fussball-Bund in Frankfurt. One can only wonder at what, back in Brazil, Havelange the Godfather must have thought of the Swiss-German cabal at the heart of his beloved FIFA. He may have mused that Blatter had learned well from his own Machiavellian leadership style.

The future for FIFA

If things continue as they are – FIFA run by Blatter and his acolytes – what does the future hold? In the final chapter of *Great Balls of Fire* we indulged ourselves by projecting what the future held for international football if it was allowed to continue along the course chosen for it by FIFA and its 'partners'.[13] In this vision we drew the logical conclusion that the commodification of the peoples' game would become total as national teams were replaced by teams representing trans-national companies – Team Nike, Team Adidas, Team Coca Cola, Team MasterCard etc – and the World Cup Finals would be played out annually between these teams in a permanent and purpose-built arena-cum-resort called Fifaland, in Las Vegas, Nevada. The rules would be changed to make the games more spectacular. The world's best players would be contracted to the companies, and certain performance-enhancing drugs would be permitted allowing them to extend their careers. Players like Ronaldo, Figo, Beckham, and Giggs would join an ensemble of ageing and aged rock stars and crooners permanently engaged in Vegas for the perpetual entertainment of an affluent global market and clientele.

Dream, nightmare, or vision of the future? In a classic case of life resembling art, shortly after we first penned this fiction, this dark fantasy came a small step closer to reality, thanks to Chuck Blazer when, in 1999 he sat next to Kirk Hendrix, president of Las Vegas events, who announced that the North and Central American soccer club championships would be held in the casino capital of the world. 'Our intent is to make this a success and bring it back on an annual basis,' Hendrix said. 'We would like to develop Las Vegas as a soccer destination. We think Las Vegas and the soccer community can be great partners'.

While Fifaland Las Vegas as described above may itself never happen, the wholesale transformation of football is more likely to come to pass. It is inevitable if the people – that is, all of us – passively accept that there is no choice but to allow the game to be driven by the bullish and ultimately self-destructive logic of big business. We cannot turn back the clock but we can still have a say in the shape of things to come. Either through incompetence, greed or vainglorious notions of pre-destiny, an earlier breed of football administrators – the league of gentlemen, the blazer and slacks brigade – forfeited their right to rule world football a long time ago. As former boss of the English FA (Football Association) Graham Kelly put it to us, 'The FIFA executive committee know they are part of a massively discredited regime, which, had it been in charge of a local Sunday league, would long ago have been subjected to the most rigorous inquiry and its officials banned from holding office indefinitely'. Should this come to pass, there is however a danger that their places will be filled by slick-suited chief executives or high flying commissioners, with scant regard for football's traditional culture. Jim Boyce, president of Northern Ireland's football governing body, asked, in the lobby of the Glasgow Hilton the night that Real Mardrid triumphed over Bayer Laverkusen, 'Who will clean up FIFA?' Before this question can be addressed, however, we need to understand what kind of reforms are necessary.

Conclusion: what is to be done?

After reviewing the state of the global governance of sport in general, Sunder Katwala, concludes that, 'it is difficult to find anything in the world quite so badly governed as international sport.' He goes on to say:

> Reform of international sporting governance is not inevitable but it is possible. Sporting governance is in a state of extreme disequilibrium – the tensions between the global revolution and unmodernised governance must eventually bring change of one sort of another. But change is likely to come from an uncertain combination of different forces – change from within, pressure from outside and change through collapse and crisis.

In 1998 and 2002 FIFA had a clear opportunity to 'change from within' and recover its position as the guardian of the world game. But, as the 1998 and 2002 FIFA presidential elections illustrated, turkeys do not routinely vote for Christmas. However, the democratising of FIFA may yet come about 'through collapse and crisis'. The bankruptcy of ISL in 2001 and the implication of senior FIFA officials, including the president himself, in this debacle, shook the organisation's foundations and renewed calls for democratic reform. Of potentially more significance than the alleged corrupt practices of individuals within or close to FIFA is the organisation's financial crisis. There is clear evidence that media and marketing interest in football, at least at the world level, has peaked or even gone into decline. Without the huge financial surplus that accrues to FIFA from such arrangements it is unlikely to be able operate on the same lavish scale in the future. Without the 'cash box' brim full and overflowing, the deals and alliances that have maintained FIFA as a fiefdom and kept the likes of Havelange and his protégé, Blatter, in power for nearly three decades, will no longer have this most important resource. If this comes to pass then calls for democratic reform, both from within and without, may become irresistible.

Hitherto, because of sport's mythical status as a politics-free zone, FIFA (like the IOC) has proven itself to be relatively impervious to pressure from the outside for reform. Up until now, the formal political presence of government in world football has been limited, usually, to token and largely ceremonial functions. Royalty, presidents, and prime ministers attending opening ceremonies of World Cup matches or the same people hosting lavish dinners for 'Fifacrats' and their retinues are among the roles routinely adopted by government representatives within the network. Interaction between national governments and FIFA tends to become more pronounced only when world football is perceived to have a bearing on the national interest. Typically this occurs around the bidding for and hosting of major international tournaments, particularly the World Cup finals. Mega-events in sports are staged for corporate profit, personal aggrandisement, and for state-driven national pride.

Otherwise, FIFA's engagement with state politicians usually only happens when it seeks to help one or more of its member associations prevent political interference into its affairs by its national government. Herein lies a clue that helps us to understand why up until now FIFA has operated largely beyond the reach of any international and democratically accountable legal framework. FIFA, like the IOC, was established by a class of people who thought themselves to be selfless, well-meaning, and right thinking gentlemen, who believed in the separation of sport from politics as a sacred principle. According to this view, politics and politicians could only violate sports integrity. People like Frenchman Jules Rimet, Belgian Rudolf Seeldrayers and Englishmen Arthur Drewry and Sir Stanley Rous felt duty bound to protect football from the overt interference of politicians, and the organisation that they helped to mould has continued to operate according to the same principles. This is a position that has, for the most part, been respected by mature democratic governments who rarely, if ever, meddle in the affairs of sports' governing bodies.

Of course, such a stance was naively self-serving from the outset, and is even more so now. It is a confidence trick that has been made easier to carry off because of the façade of democracy under which FIFA operates. As we have seen, when it comes to making major decisions, such as electing a new president, every member association has one equal vote. Thus, when it comes to the equity of representation, FIFA seems to occupy the moral high ground. However, often, those who cast votes are not themselves elected and neither are they accountable to any broader constituency. Furthermore, because FIFA elections operate a secret ballot, they can and have been rigged to ensure that those who are best suited to serve the business interests of big business are elected and re-elected. In this way, without any genuine democratic accountability, self-styled sporting aristocrats and autocrats secretly have manipulated and exploited global sport for their own financial and vainglorious purposes.

As Cable puts it, 'A culture of secrecy or perceived arrogance by international civil servants and policy elites can be seriously counterproductive. Opaqueness and secrecy are enemies of an open international system'. A big part of the problem is that neither INGOs nor BINGOs are subject to the same framework of international law as IGOs.[13] They have constitutions, members' voting rights, auditing procedures and so forth, but generally, accountability is an in-house affair. Cable observes that 'these [INGOs and BINGOs] may well create elaborately democratic structures of consumer and producer interests and provide for co-operation between regulators, but a necessary political dimension is often missing'.[14]

We would not by any means want national governments to run football. But at a domestic level democratically elected governments, should, through a legally constituted and independent agency, exercise a guiding, and if necessary, a restraining influence over the game. If, in many societies of varying political cultures, other important and formerly nationalised utilities such as gas, water, electricity and the railways have to be accountable to government watchdogs, then the same should apply to something as important to the national psyche as football.

At a regional level a similar arrangement could be worked out between, for instance, UEFA and the European Commission/Parliament, itself (in part at least) a democratically elected and representative body. At the least, such an arrangement would force these two bodies to come together and work out a sensible legal framework for the development and continued vitality of football in Europe, one through which the EC protected football from the business predators rather than helping them to feast at the top table. Similar arrangements could be worked out between football federations and regional IGOs in other parts of the world.

Finally, FIFA itself must be brought within the embrace of an accountable international organisation such as the United Nations, perhaps under the wing of this organisation's cultural framework, UNESCO.[15] Under such an arrangement, FIFA's off-shore financial status would have to end. All of its important decisions would be scrutinised by officials, themselves accountable to a broader electorate and within a wider legal framework.

What football needs at every level is transparently representative and responsible government. For this to happen the administration of football has to be rooted in accountable institutions and subject to the rule of law. We are not suggesting that politicians should run national or world football. A restructured and more accountable FIFA would continue to exercise authority over all member associations. But here it is important to distinguish between political control and political accountability. Control suggests uncontested domination whereas accountability alludes to representation based on transparency and the capacity for reform. In this regard, while FIFA is right to continue to protect its member associations from the political interference of those who would seek to control football, it is wrong to continue to protect itself from outside scrutiny and accountability.

'Why does this matter', media commentators have routinely asked us. It matters because supra-national organisations can gain for themselves unbridled power. Studying the practices and values of long-term survivors at the heart of FIFA's flawed system is important because the perpetuation of a system based upon cynical rhetoric and deeply ingrained hypocrisy can only in the long term undermine the more idealistic potential of sport and any claims that sport has a positive role to play as a form of trans-national global culture. Susan Strange has written of unavoidable ignorance, insignificant ignorance and 'the area of significant ignorance'.[16] 'The business of government', and 'what rulers and authorities need to know is a relative matter', she states. But 'good modern governments' need to know more and more. She argues that with a 'disordered monetary system', more things 'now lie ... inside the area of significant ignorance for national governments'. As politicians of the highest rank from some of the major national powers in the world continue to pamper members of sport's governmental bodies and elites, seeking the favours of bodies such as FIFA and the IOC, yet know little of (or refuse to look clearly at) the nature of future organisational partners, lack of knowledge of the politics of international sports organisations constitutes an acute case of significant ignorance. Strange wrote passionately of the need to combat the 'sorry state of the international financial system', not by trying to 'turn the clock back' or 'trying to muddle through'. Only radical reforms would suffice to deal with the extent of the global financial crisis, with the 'mad money' at the heart of 'casino capitalism'. Strange is right. Reforms remain tokenistic if generated from within. A political analysis of the organisation and governance of world sport is an essential premise for debates about the reforms that are necessary so that INGOs such as FIFA can really be seen to be working for the good of the game, rather than in the interests of those who have seen in FIFA, and other such organisations, an irresistible opportunity to benefit from a particularly lucrative BINGO.

4 Olympic survivals

The Olympic Games as a global phenomenon

Alan Tomlinson

In this chapter I do three things. First, I review some commentaries on globalisation and culture, and globalisation and sport. Second, I offer some selective reflections on the history of the Olympic Games, casting an analytical, periodising eye over the 24 (Summer) Games, warning against the analysis of the Olympics on the basis of a sort of boxed-off self-referencing history of the sport event itself. Third, I review projections and claims made for the Sydney 2000 Olympic Games, and then discuss why and how the Olympics continues to be such a prominent player in the global politics of sport.

In the first half of 2003 some of the world's major cities – London, Madrid, Moscow, New York, Paris – and other hopefuls such as Havana, Istanbul, Rio de Janeiro and Leipzig, lined themselves up for the competition to win the hosting of the 2012 Summer Olympic Games. In Prague, in June of the same year, over 100 delegates from the bidding cities of Vancouver, Salzburg and Pyeongchang accompanied their teams' last-ditch presentations, hoping to sway the remaining floating votes among the 100 or so IOC (International Olympic Committee) members whose whims and fancies would determine the decision as to where to place the 2010 Winter Games.[1] Top politicians, including prime ministers from Canada, Austria and South Korea lent their names to the bids, assuming obvious benefits should their city be successful. Such benefits, economic and/or symbolic, are notoriously difficult to identify in any precise fashion, and it is as much the ideological cant of the Olympic phenomenon that sustains its profile in the modern international world as any clear or tangible gains. This was reiterated in the rhetoric and style of the three presentations in Prague, where glitzy contemporary populism was mixed with pseudo-philosophical babble in tributes to the enduring values of Olympism. The eventual winner Vancouver went first, entitling its presentation 'The Sea to Sky Games', and lead man John Furlong talked of the Olympics as 'a powerful platform for building a better world through sport'. He recalled the words of the immigrations officer who'd greeted him on arriving in Canada from Ireland 30 years before: 'Welcome to Canada. Make us better'. 'To give is the Canadian way', he added, telling the IOC that 'The Olympic Winter Games will make us all better'. Hockey superstar Wayne Gretzky talked of the fulfilment of his sporting dreams, which included four Stanley Cup victories, then added that 'there's no greater honour than the Olympics because there's no greater movement than the Olympics', and stated Team Canada's belief in the possibility of a world living in peace through sport. Other Winter Olympians recalled their starts in sport. Catronia Le May Doan, speed-skating gold medal winner at Nagano and Salt Lake City, emphasised the limitlessness of the bid's vision of 'an Olympic dream of forever'. This would include 50,000 event tickets in an Olympic access programme for children who could not otherwise afford to attend any events, and an international youth camp populated by two children invited from every national Olympic committee. Furlong reappeared and pledged that if the decision went Vancouver's way, if the voters 'felt our passion', then we 'would distinguish ourselves in the cause of sport and humanity ... Our dream, like your dream, is a dream of forever'.

Salzburg was next, appealing to its small-town charm and its reputation for music and culture. Mozart, born in the town, dominated the soundtrack of the video clips, and the presentation was compered by Annely Peebo, a blonde opera singer with a potentially winning smile, who was soon to warble the title line of the bid, 'The Sound of (Winter) Sport'. The Austrian prime minister, Wolfgang Schussel, referred to the success story of the Olympics, stated an intention to get over 100 nations to participate in 2010, and praised sport's capacity to cultivate 'competition instead of confrontation', and to speak for peace. The head of Salzburg's music festival also emphasised the peace-stimulating dimension of cultural exchanges and intercultural understanding, beaming out her message that 'sport and art are like sun and moon', they are both 'the source of our well being'.

Pyeongchang's presentation was headed up by IOC member Dr Un Yong Kim, veteran sport campaigner for and boss of taekwondo, and chair of the association of international federations. Kim and the bid committee's chairman offered full government support for the extensive construction programmes that would be essential, support confirmed soon after by prime minister Kun Goh. Further presenters emphasised the projected venue's nickname, Peace City, and the universality of winter sports. The bid talked up the theme of a Games for all based upon fundamental principles of peace and humanity. Much was also made of the potential of the Games to further the process of the uniting of the two Koreas. Across all the bids ran a theme of dreams come true, grafted on to a commitment to peace and a form of humanitarianism in which Olympism could show the way forward beyond some of the most pressing problems of the age.

At every such presentation, ceremony and vote, it is clear that the appeal is never to simple economic benefits, or infrastructural upgrading, or national sentiment. Something else is claimed for the Olympics, something transcendental in relation to the grubby materialism of everyday life. A strange, spiritual sense comes to pervade the proceedings. At such moments, criticising the Olympics is akin to laughing out loud in church.

Global culture, global sport: the Olympic Games as a global cultural event

Sociologists and social historians of sport have long recognised the centrality of the Olympics in any historical narrative of the rise and spread of international sport. Miller *et al.* observe how as forms of televison-based popular culture, events such as the Olympics provide 'a crucial site where populations are targeted by different forms of governmental and commercial knowledge/power'.[2] They ask us to attempt to imagine such an event stripped of all the familiar cultural and political symbols that have become so familiar to worldwide audiences:

> No comprehensive media coverage, no national flags flying, no playing of national anthems, no politicians involved in the ceremonies, no military displays, no tables comparing national standings, and athletes competing in whatever clothing they desired instead of national uniforms.[3]

It is of course difficult to achieve this act of the imagination. A deeply entrenched and historically claimed symbolism of co-existing national rivalries, perpetuated alongside the commercially branded later cases of the corporatised Games, is one of the assumed dimensions of the mega-events of contemporary global culture. Maurice Roche locates this merging of the commercial and the political on the level of global consumer culture:

> Mega-events have had, and continue to have, an important role to play in the development of this global consumer culture through their long-established promotion of what I refer to ... as 'touristic consumerism'. They also contribute to understandings and experiences of 'one world' through their capacity to carry universalistic meanings and ideals. These include those associated with the benefits of peaceful cultural exchange between nations, ethnic and ideological communities (expos and Olympics), scientific and technological 'progress' (expos), human 'progress' and the value of personal and national achievement and recognition through rule-governed competition.[4]

Mega-events such as the Olympics are, for Roche, quintessential phenomena of global modernity, 'intrinsically complex processes' which combine the interests of political and economic elites and professionals from the increasingly supranational cultural industries. These interlocking elites operate on a number of levels, Roche goes on: 'within and between urban, national and international levels ... working together in a medium-term time-horizon both to produce the events and to manage their effects'.[5]

The Olympics are, of course, more than mere reflections of social processes and trends. They are formative as well as formed, pointing the way towards new cultural formations and as such important indices of change and cultural transformation. Maguire identifies the last quarter of the nineteenth century as a major phase in 'the international spread of sport, the establishment of international sports organizations, the growth of competition between national teams, the worldwide acceptance of rules governing specific sport forms and the establishment of global competitions such as the Olympic Games'.[6] In this list, it is the Olympics and the very grandeur of the scale of the conception of de Coubertin (the Renovateur), that constitutes a project of seriously globalising proportion and potential, ridden with contradictions rooted in de Coubertin's aristocratic, imperialist, patriarchal roots, but nevertheless premised on a vision of an increasingly networked, compressed and orchestrated global culture. As Maguire also notes, the Olympic Games continue to provide a stage on which can be played out some of the recurring tensions of global politics. The West 'still has hegemonic control in the global sport figuration' but for non-Westerners a 'main source of potential dispute may well be the Olympic Games'.[7] Miller *et al.* note the strong opposition of the Third World to the 'undemocratic ways' of the IOC's international Court of Arbitration for Sport.[8] And the Games have provided, case after case through their history, an opportunity for the expression of national identity. Bairner has reaffirmed how, on the level of the national, different statements can be made to a world audience, in the context of the Olympics, about what it is to be American or Canadian.[9]

The Olympics operate therefore as a focus for the articulation of serious national and global political dynamics, and as a giant billboard for the elite crop of multi-national corporations that are the preferred sponsorship partners of the International Olympic Committee. These political and economic dimensions are interconnected and serve the interests of what Miller *et al.* (2001) call the New International Division of Cultural Labour, which operates in the context of 'five simultaneous, uneven, interconnected processes which characterize the present moment in sport: Globalization, Governmentalization, Americanization, Televisualization, and Commodification (GGATaC)'.[10] Listing all these processes may be a disservice to crisp English prose, but it is an important reminder that the economic, the political and the cultural are not separate dimensions of phenomena such as the Olympics. Studying the global reach of events such as this requires an analytical approach sensitive to the ways in which these dimensions intermesh.

Recognition of the profile of the Olympic Games is well established in the scholarly circles of the historical and social scientific analysis of sport. The Games are not, though, always seen to be of great significance in more general approaches. In his analysis of the transnational capitalist class, one of Sklair's main propositions is that 'the globalization of the capitalist system reproduces itself through the profit-driven culture-ideology of consumerism'.[11] He makes no mention of the IOC, and the Olympic Games is mentioned only in footnotes, in terms of some of its policy developments around green issues and the environment,[12] and as an example of the increase in sport sponsorship of international sporting events.[13] Sklair's analysis is on the macro-level of the workings and reach of transnational companies and capital, which he sees as powerfully entrenched in their positions: 'No social movement appears even remotely likely to overthrow the three fundamental institutional supports of global capitalism that have been identified, namely the TNCs, the transnational capitalist class, and the culture-ideology of consumerism'.[14] The Olympics is in some senses, from this scale of macro perspective, just one example of the operationalisation of the practices and ideologies of global capital and the trans-national companies that dominate the centres of international capital. It is not surprising therefore that they are not acknowledged to be any more or less interesting or important than any other such exemplar. More surprising is the total absence of any discussion of the Olympic Games or international sports-media events in the work of John Tomlinson. Tomlinson's major themes are connectivity in a world characterised by 'a particular and exaggerated sense of proximity', aided by a form of 'high-profile globalizing technology', all with the potential to 'change the nature of localities'.[15] Central concerns in his book are deterritorialisation, hybridisation, mediated communication and its consequences for cultural experience, and the question, or possibility, of cosmopolitanism. Those of us working consistently on sport would find it hard to ignore the Olympics as a major example through which to explore such themes, and associated themes, derived from Anthony Giddens, of time-space distanciation and its implications for people's experience of place. Tomlinson cites shopping malls as examples of what Giddens has called the 'phantasmagoric' nature of modern places. Olympic villages and stadia, Olympic parks and sites could equally usefully be viewed as illuminating cases of such places.

Generally, although Olympic scholarship has generated extremely valuable histories, contemporary studies and critical interventions – far too vast a range of sources to be meaningfully listed here – a challenge remains. This is the straightforward challenge of re-locating critical analyses of the Olympic phenomenon within the context of debates concerning the nature of international cultural politics, the operation of the interests of trans-national companies and international capital, and the nature of international sport's relation to global consumer culture and international markets. Any such challenge should reconsider the balance of forces that have combined to make the Games, and the so-called Movement of which the Games are an embodiment, an international phenomenon of such profile, impact and longevity.

The Olympic Games 1896–2008

The simple facts of the growth of the Olympic Games are widely established, in an expanding line-up of events, participants, media personnel, media coverage and worldwide spectators and television viewers. But the story of the survival and eventual expansion into everyday global consciousness of the Games was not an even one. Early Games after the inaugural success in Athens in 1896 were linked to expos.[16] In Paris in 1900 and in St Louis in 1904 events with few spectators were peripheral aspects of great trade shows, celebrations of expanding international markets. As high-profile cultural events they were insignificant flops. London in 1908 recaptured some of the revivalist momentum of the de Coubertin project. The British Olympic Association had been created in 1905, allocated a seat on the IOC, and with its well-established athletics organisation in the form of the Amateur Athletics Association it could respond to a desperate IOC, looking for a replacement host city in 1906 when Rome had withdrawn just two years before the event. The Franco-British Exhibition of 1908 became the saviour of the Olympic idea. Though by the final day 90,000 turned out to witness the marathon race, spurred on by a media picking up on British-American athletic rivalries, the event was again a marginal appendage. It is interesting to look closely at some of the surviving documentation of the time.[17]

The programme for the 1908 Olympic Games featured no Olympic logos or signs, and had no mention of the Olympics at all on the cover, which featured a high-jumper clad in classic white athletic kit, in an insert inside a kind of pseudo-classical door or arch-way: the programme is headlined 'The Great Stadium, Shepherd's Bush, London – Franco-British Exhibition 1908 6d'. The Olympic Games and the '4th International Olympiad' are not billed until page 2, after a first page advertisement for Robinson's 'Patent' Barley Water: in the ad, a polo-player is served by a man-in-waiting, and horses are held by others looking on: 'For any violent exercise, "Barley Water" is the best *Thirst-Quencher* when properly made' from R's Patent Barley. The IOC and the BOA committee line-ups feature on the third and fourth pages. The athletic contests scarcely feature in the programme. The event was seized upon by a range of advertisers, with advertisements for a range of products: a Pear's Soap baby on the back cover, McVitie's digestives, healing balm called Zam-Buk, a raincoat, Bryant and May and Swan Vestas matches, Gamage's equipment, Piggott and Ward retailers, 'Read's Olympian Oils – The Marvellous Pain Reliever and Muscle Strengthener' at a shilling and 2/6, available from 90 Victoria Street SW, golf balls, embrocine medication ('An antiseptic and disinfectant spirit' that 'makes old people feel young'); and Schweppes Dry Ginger Ale and Lemonade & Soda Water. Already, we see associations between athletic competition and self-improvement consumer products. The financial potential of the Olympics was very much untapped in London's first Olympics, but the commercial dimension and potential of the event was clearly recognised.

Alongside this commercial dimension, in the promotional literature of the British Olympic Committee, an idealised rhetoric of Olympism claimed that the Ancient Games 'formed a bond between widely scattered members of the Greek race; they fostered throughout the Greek world a sense of kinship and a consciousness of common ideals which not even war was able to obscure', and that the revival of the Olympics could foster an adaptation of fruitful past 'principles of bringing together the chosen athletes of all nations in the strength of their youth and in the prime of their manhood to learn in the chivalrous and friendly rivalry of athletic contests that mutual respect and esteem, which are the only sure basis of International concord'. On this basis, the BOC desired 'that the celebration should be worthy of the Motherland of International Sport'. The 1908 London Games confirmed the fragile cultural and economic basis of the Olympics, and provided some basis for the consolidation of the project in Stockholm in 1912. The Games after the 1914–18 Great War (Antwerp 1920, Paris 1924, Amsterdam 1928) remained on a relatively modest scale, though the US presence was becoming increasingly dominant, and included powerful statements of athletic prowess by women athletes. In Amsterdam in 1928, G. Van Rossem, secretary general of the Netherlands Olympic Committee and compiler of the official report of the Games,[18] could write proudly that the press needs were catered for by setting up a Press Section. The Press Stand could seat 600. 'In front of many of the seats there were small folding tables on which a typewriter could be placed or notes made' (p.247). The account of the provision of the media facility conveys the modest scale of the event, yet also the excitement of applying the new communications tech-nology to the international sporting event:

> [Next to the] post and telegraph office a room was fitted out in which the journalists could prepare urgent reports and telegrams. The writing tables being partitioned off so that each journalist could work without interfering with the others ... offices were fitted out at the Heerengracht and in De Groote Club, where all communiqués could be found, where the journalists could work, where they could obtain all the information they desired, and where, thanks to the management of the club, they could take their meals ... Further, there were 5 telephone booths installed in the office at the Heerengracht. This measure was not necessary in the Kalverstraat office owing to its being in the close vicinity of the General Post office, where ample provision was made.

The national Olympic Committee was not averse to a little self-publicity either, and 'occasionally propagative articles on Holland in general and Amsterdam in particular with suitable photos were sent out for publication, and in this con-nexion much assistance was afforded by the "Society for making Holland better known abroad" and by the 'Dutch Touring Club'.

The Committee also took a stance on a case of competing media interests, at a time when the written press was still for many the first source of contact with news and information, and in this case the outcome of sporting encounters:

> At the request of the Association Internationale de la Presse Sportive, the Committee gave up the idea of broadcasting results of the events, as the Association pointed out that this would be hardly fair to journalists whose papers had gone to much expense and trouble to send representatives to the Games. If the foreign papers had not done this, there would not have been the propaganda made for the Games in particular and Holland in general, which there was undeniably, due to personal visits.

The official report catalogued the scale of communications activity. A total of 14,480 telegrams were sent from the Press Bureau in the Stadium. Athletics (1,166) and the Marathon (1,058) days generated most telegrams in the second period. Football (441) and hockey were the busiest days of the first period. You can sense the excitement at how these Olympics began to experiment with people's expectations of time and space:

> The excitement which prevailed in connexion with the results of the contests and the extraordinary energy evinced by the journalists in their efforts to report to their papers as quickly as possible caused a sort of sporting rivalry among the telegraphists at Amsterdam. It was due to this fact that messages regarding the match Uruguay-Argentine were cabled from Amsterdam via New York to Buenos Aires in about 40 seconds. This incident was unique in the annals of the telegraph service and therefore deserves special mention.

Three hundred and seventeen journalists were present during the first period of the Games. In the second period this increased to 1928 and 616 respectively. At times there was pressure on space. Smaller press stands at some venues limited the number of these journalists admitted. Only 261 could cover fencing, 138 wrestling and weight-lifting, and 196 swimming. Amsterdam 1928 marked the beginning of a transformation, with international communications demonstrating the potential to speak for the internationalism of the event itself, and the national interests of the host and participating nations.

If the first eight Summer Olympics Games were relatively low profile, politically and commercially, the Games of the 1930s were more overtly political and expressive of national interests. In this sense, the Games from 1932 to 1984 can be seen as more explicitly political projects, in the 1920s and 1930s matched by the Soviet experiments in the use of sport for display and propaganda. It was in 1928, the year of the Amsterdam Olympics and a year in which Joseph Stalin was manoeuvering his way to power, that 'the USSR produced its own large-scale international Olympic-type multi-sport event in Moscow, the first "Spartakiad", a combination of sport event and mass festival'.[19] The second Spartakiad was held in Moscow in 1932. For the next twelve Olympic Games – Los Angeles, 1932; Berlin 1936; London, 1948; Helsinki, 1952; Melbourne, 1956; Rome, 1960; Tokyo, 1964; Mexico, 1968; Munich, 1972; Montreal, 1976; Moscow, 1980; and Los Angeles, 1984 – the political stakes became higher and higher. This included the exploitation of the 1936 Games in the cause of fascism and Nazism, and after the Second World War the use of the Games to fuel Cold War rivalries, once the Soviet Union was permitted into the party. The Olympics also offered nations the possibility of rehabilitation into the world community (Italy, Japan and Germany). Across this phase of the Olympic story, the explicit political motivation of intensely national interests catapulted the Games on to a new level, once the survival had been achieved in the London 1948 Games. The Games represented the wider sport cultures of the nations that participated in them. In 1929 Mussolini sought to win the 1936 Games for Rome, and at Berlin in 1936 failed again in a bid to stage the 1940 Games. But this hardly stopped the fascist sport project established by Mussolini. His regime celebrated high-profile Italian victories in Europe's first football World Cup Finals in 1934 and 1938, but the general sports project was operative across a range of levels.

In a 1933 booklet on the 'International University Games',[20] we have access to a discourse on the young sporting body that combines the claimed idealism of international brother- and sisterhood with the fascist project of *Il Duce*, Benito Mussolini. The rhetoric and hyperbole of the booklet repays close scrutiny. On its front cover it features a downhill skier, on its back cover a rower (in very modernist, sharp and angular imagery, canoe in the water looking like the spout of 1970s supersonic aircraft *Concorde*). Inside the booklet, the photograph on the title page is of an obelisk of Mussolini, and the Italian national flag. The opening photograph in the booklet proper is of the Mussolini Stadium.

The text of the booklet begins with a paeon to Romantic writers, then asserts that 'there are many new things in Italy and one more important than the rest, Italy is today the youngest country in Europe, with young people aged 20 or under making up 43% of the population'. It reports the 'wonderful progress made by Italy in this field of human activity', sport – its profile in the 1932 LA Olympic Games, Grand Prizes in other countries in motor-cars, horse shows, football matches, swimming, fencing – 'it is the result of ten years of the Fascist Regime which places in the front rank the health and the physical improvement of the Italian race ... the spirit of the Italian masses has been physically changed ... and successful efforts made to give a sporting education to young men which will strengthen their muscles today and mould their character in the future'.

French writer D. Chappert is quoted, writing in a leading Paris newspaper, telling his country's and Europe's liberals that they shouldn't be afraid to recognise and admire Italy's sports development, for sport there has become as important as anti-TB campaigns, draining marshlands, building hospitals, roads and schools: 'it is animated by the same spirit that inspired the unearthing of the glorious remains of ancient Rome and the development of aviation; sport has today become the real means of national education and stadia, sporting fields and swimming pools are being everywhere and democratically placed at the disposal of Italian youth'. Chappert's hymn to youth becomes an apologia for the fascist project:

> Those entrusted with the direction of this great movement justly place university students in the front rank of the great mass of the young men they are training, almost as if they represented the real youth of the country. Youth, is in fact the title of a hymn that has become national, and it is considered as the inexhaustible source of new energies and therefore placed at the head of this renewed country.

The Duce perfectly realizes that he can fully rely on this group of keen and intelligent young men fanatical for the greatness of their country, its glory and its mission in the world.

It may be a case of collective enthusiasm, a Latin exaggeration or a Mediterranean microbe ... but all the same it implies a great material organization and a practical and moral work of preparation.

Youth's foremost place in national life in fascist Italy in the 1920s and 1930s led to the organisation of elite groups within the academy: Fascist University Groups (FUGs), 'initiated in 1920, side by side with the Fascist squads of action'. The latter were later incorprated into the National Party and then into the Regime, and the FUGs retained their university base, soon reaching 55,000 in number and acquiring 'the character, both as regards culture and sport, of the most complete National Union in Europe'. FUGs were promoted in their 'sporting education', lectures, travel, cruises, international exchanges and reunions – 'Italian University students have acquired the conscience and pride of their status and they are now united in a mass of disciplined energies, from which the State and the Party have already selected with successful results, men of inexhaustible loyalty to fill positions of trust'.

Youth were also inculcated into the Yearly Littoriali Sporting Competition, first held in Bologna in 'the X year of the Fascist Regime'. These were designed to create and reaffirm the sporting masses, and to award prizes according to numbers and discipline and not just first places, and cultivate 'sporting spirit as a whole', reinforcing too the achievements of the first ten years of the Fascist Regime, during which 58 stadia and 493 sporting fields were built, and 3,500 sporting associations organised. It was the second time that Italy was preparing for these International University Games, after successfully staging them in 1928. For the 1933 event, the construction of the largest stadium in the country was planned for Turin. In Rome, the Forum of Mussolini was constructed for athletic exercises, staged in front of 20,000 spectators, 'surrounded with large marble figures of athletes in repose each one representing a branch of sport. This harmonious construction recalls Graeco-Roman buildings of a similar character and its situation on the green hills of Monte Mario, is bound, even during sporting exercises ... inspiring them with the higher ideals of physical and spiritual beauty as was the case in past epochs'. These Games, held in Turin from 1–10 September 1933, were an encomium to the fascist project. All the youthful idealism in the world could not undermine the prime political project. Italy, the booklet concluded, was sure that the Games would generate 'that serene and sincere spirit of comradeship and that spiritual and sporting brotherhood which unite the youth of the entire world in a real and great "internationale" '.

Arriving from anywhere else in the world that autumn in 1933, you might have swallowed the rhetoric of the Italian state and authorities, have understandably seen yourself as a representative of a noble internationalist ideal. But from the acceptance of the invitation onwards, and certainly from the moment

you entered the Turin stadium, your sporting idealism was appropriated – 'arrogated', as I have often called this process with reference to the Olympic ideal.[21]
Your sporting body would be speaking for the apologists of the Italian political
project. Even winning would not change this. For all of Jesse Owens's gold
medals and dignity in 1936, it made no difference whatsoever to the momentum
of the Nazi project. In such cultural moments and spaces the body is an instru-
ment of the ideology on the basis of which the sporting practice has been
planned and produced. The Olympics inscribe wider cultural projects and ideologies. All the Olympic hyperbole in the world does not alter this. In the
explicitly nationalist second phase in the history of the Olympic Games, they
prospered primarily on the basis of their usefulness as a vehicle for the articulation of political meanings and national rivalries. But as the Olympic project
veered from crisis to crisis in the crisis-ridden 'M' years from 1968 to 1980,
rocked by political protest (Mexico City, 1968), terrorist incursions (Munich,
1972), unprecedented losses (Montreal, 1976) and major boycotts (Montreal,
1976, and Moscow, 1980), it was its combined commercial potential and political use as shown in the 1984 Games that secured its future as a mega-event of
the televisual age. It was fitting that the Games marking the transformative
point of these phases in Olympic history were both staged in Los Angeles.

Reporting US$225 million profits, based on restoration of facilities as much as
new provision, celebrating the values of the free Western world after boycotting
Moscow in 1980, and producing opening and closing ceremonies based on sheer
Hollywood razzmatazz, the LA Games marked a point of transformation in the
cultural staging and underpinning political economy of world sport. It was the
first Games held under the presidency of Juan Antonio Samaranch, and launched
the Games into a new phase of development hand-in-hand with television companies willing to pay unheard-of sums to cover the events, and economic partners
paying huge sums for their exclusive sponsorship status and rights in the TOP
(the Olympic programme) scheme.[22] From that point on, the Games were guaranteed a future as one of the most high-profile global commodities. The Seoul
Games (1988) carried on the political mission of host cities, but the cultural-
commercial-economic rebalancing of interests was best encapsulated in the cases
of Barcelona (1992) and Sydney (2000), sandwiched by the attempt of Atlanta
(1996) to reconfigure the worldwide audience's perception of US geography. The
Games of this third phase were immersed in a developmental cultural logic of
economic regeneration and global self-promotion of cities and states, justified
widely and recurrently on the basis of some amorphous spiritual value of benefit
to all of humankind. This logic continues to fuel the scramble to win the right to
host the Games, with four of the world's top cities – London, Madrid, Paris and
New York – lining up in 2003 to do battle to win the 2012 Games.

G'day: Sydney 2000

Sydney was desperate to secure the 2000 Summer Olympics, to claim the first
Games of the new millennium. It was clear in its bidding documentation as to

its motives.[23] The main features of Sydney's bid as outlined in the Candidature File were:

1 The concentration of fourteen sports in Homebush, plus press centre and village: 'Sydney Olympic park was to be the largest concentration of venues in Olympic history'.
2 Many sports in Sydney Harbour Zone, yachting on the Harbour, six sports in Darling Harbour area: 'the fifth largest Olympic precinct in history'.
3 All athletes in the one Olympic village in the park 'for the first time in Olympic history'.
4 All venues within 30 minutes of Olympic Park.
5 Focus on needs of athletes in all aspects of planning.
6 '... to overcome fears about distance, transport costs to Sydney for all athletes and officials would be met by the Sydney Organising Committee, in addition to free accommodation and meals in the Olympic Village'.
7 '... the freight costs of canoes and kayaks, rowing shells, yachts and all horses would be met by the Sydney Organising Committee'.
8 Sydney 'a low security risk with no known threats to the safety of the Olympic Family'.
9 '... a four-year arts festival program with a particular focus on Australia's indigenous and multicultural heritage'.
10 '... the sheer physical beauty, the warmth of its people and the temperate climate of Sydney were also highlighted as providing a perfect location for the Olympic Games'.

And Sydney's bid 'broke new ground in promising the most "environmentally friendly" Olympic Games in history' developing guidelines later adopted by the IOC as the standard for Summer Olympic environmental policies. Crucially, the bid committee devised a sophisticated and comprehensive programme of lobbying IOC members. IOC members made visits to Sydney to be 'briefed on the plans and to inspect progress', and 65 IOC members visited Sydney at the invitation of the bid committee, not counting delegates to the GAISF (the gathering of international sports federations) conference in the city in October 1991.

And the lobbying certainly paid dividends. On 23 September 1993, five bidding cities made final presentations of 30 minutes each with 15 minutes for questions. Berlin, Sydney, and Manchester started in the Monte Carlo line-up. Features of Sydney's presentation included: Olympic film footage; the score to *Waltzing Matilda*; Kevin Gosper, the IOC vice-president and Australian Olympic Committee member, speaking on the Olympics and Australia's unbroken attendance record and showing the commitment of the country in this third consecutive Australian bid. John Fahey, New South Wales president, 'committed the NSW government to financially guarantee the Games', and carefully illustrated the solid, modern infrastructure already in place in Sydney, and stated concern for the environment. John Coates of the Australian Olympic Committee stressed 'The Athletes' Games', emphasising in particular the great 'centre stage' of harbour sites, the centrality of the Park, and the scope of the Olympic Village. Kieren Perkins, Barcelona 1500m freestyle gold medallist, spoke on freedom, safety, comfort for athletes and 'a clean, healthy environment'. The fifth speaker was an 11-year-old Sydney schoolgirl, Tanya Blencowe: 'Sydney is a friendly city where it doesn't matter where you come from. We are all Australians together. We eat together, learn together and play sport together. And that's what the Olympic Games really mean to me. It's bringing the young people of the world together to celebrate sport and friendship'. Prime Minister Paul Keating made three main points: he lauded the Australian love of sport, freedom and democracy, claimed Australia as a representative of the Asia-Pacific region and reaffirmed the city as an ideal venue for a safe games. 'Annita Keating followed her husband to the microphone. Dutch-born Mrs Keating spoke as a representative of the 25 per cent of all Australians born overseas, and of the 140 cultures found in Sydney, which she described as a "welcoming community" with a spirit of "friendliness and fun". She repeated the final sentence of her speech in both French and Italian, a gesture to which the audience reacted warmly'. The last speaker was the leader of the bidding team, Rod McGeoch, who reiterated the key messages, cited the Olympic ideals and charter, and closed with a suitably oleaginous appeal: 'Mr. President, on behalf of our entire team, on behalf of all Australians, and on behalf of all the peoples of Oceania, we humbly submit the Sydney 2000 bid'.

IOC voting proceeded thus:

City	Round 1	Round 2	Round 3	Round 4
Sydney	30	30	37	45
Beijing	32	37	40	43
Manchester	11	13	11	–
Berlin	9	9	–	–
Istanbul	7	–	–	–

The Australian bid came from behind, helped by bribery and late vote switches, to win in the last round. No-one knows the real cost of winning this bid and staging the event. Rome might have pulled out of the 1906 Games with just two years to go, but now if you win the right to stage a modern Olympics you simply have to make it happen. Just weeks before the Games, organisers were requesting and getting hundreds of millions of dollars from the New South Wales Government.

Sydney 2000 was the bumper Summer Olympics. It welcomed more than 11,000 athletes, several thousand officials and coaches, and as the 16 days whizzed by estimates of the number of mediafolk in town reached 21,000, although official estimates had been initially put at around 15,000. Athens 2004 plans to cater for 18,000 media. The Main Press Centre at the Olympic Park was vast, and the International Broadcast Centre was dominated by US broadcaster NBC, which had paid US$705 million dollars for the rights, and mobilised a workforce of more than 2,000. More athletes, more sports, more professionals remains the apparently inexorable trend.

The International Olympic Committee claims that the vast majority of the world's population able to access a television will have watched the action and that the opening ceremony was watched by several billion – though such claims are beyond corroboration, and more reputable estimates by independent researchers have put the figure at rather less than half the one trumpeted by the IOC. But it is beyond dispute that the summer Olympic Games does claim one of the biggest television audiences of all time. Australians, and Sydneysiders especially, responded to the Games with passion and a determination to shout for and support their own competing hopefuls, and then in the 24-hour pubs of Pyrmont and the like to party through till dawn. Australian Gold was won by the scantily clad blonde women beach volleyballers at Bondi Beach, by the muscular concrete-pillar necked water polo girls in the Aquatic Centre, as well as by the beach bums of the swimming squads and the fated and feted bridge to Aboriginal/Australian reconciliation, 400-metre gold medallist and lighter of the Olympic flame, Cathy Freeman.

When the big hopes were competing, the venues were a sell out and the great live sites of Sydney – Circular Quay, Martin Place in the Central Business District, Tumbalong Park at Darling Harbour, Pyrmont Park, The Domain atop the Royal Botanical Gardens, Belmore Park at Central Station – were throbbing with nationalist enthusiasm. The home crowds were raucously supportive of their Australian hopes, and always ready with a jeer and a boo for the athletes from the UK and the US. If there was no serious Australian competitor in an event, the crowd cheered any compatriot it could locate. At the boxing, this gave a moment of celebrity to a number of Australian referees.

It was nevertheless enthralling seeing a nation of 20 million people chasing the USA and China in the medal table, and celebrating this by waving or being draped in a national flag dominated by the flag of the United Kingdom of Great Britain and Northern Ireland. The victorious side of the Olympics for the host nation quickly became a metaphor for both the reconciliation embodied in the dignified presence of Cathy Freeman, and the success of the new Australia of multi-cultural mix. The silver medal in the first-ever Olympic women's pole vault was won by a blonde beauty from Adelaide, with the most New-Australian of names, Tatiana Grigorieva. Many of the Australian women were blonde, leggy and en route to, if not already packaged up in, modelling contracts. Tatania had already got the 'glam shots' of herself, in far less than her pole-vaulting outfit, ready for the world press.

The organisers of the Games, the much maligned SOCOG (Sydney Organizing Committee for the Olympic Games) could claim an Olympic record in ticket sales, far above the sales figures for Atlanta 1996. But there weren't many sell outs for the women's soccer semis, or the softball preliminaries, or the Graeco-Roman wrestling, or the handball. In the bloated Olympic schedule you can always get to see something, be a part of the event. You won't get into the best hotels in town, even if you're a regular. Writer and expatriate Australian Clive James could not get in his usual hotel as the main hotels in Sydney were completely taken over by the IOC and its Olympic 'family'. Sydney 2000 has been widely hailed as a model event, the 'best Games ever' in the words of the outgoing Olympic president Samaranch. What can we glean from this picture of the Sydney bid and event, to account for the place of the Olympic Games in the global politics of sport? It is to this question that I turn in the concluding comments to this chapter.

Concluding comments

To understand in any adequate fashion the social and cultural significance of the Olympic Games it is necessary to conduct the analysis on a number of levels: the historical, the national/local, the international/global, the economic, the political and the cultural. In the three main phases of the Olympic Games a grand socio-political project with a modest economic profile (1896–1928) was succeeded by a markedly political intensification of the event at the heart of international political dynamics (1932–1984). In the third phase (1984 onwards) the Olympic Games have been fuelled by the global reach of capital, which has held hands with the pseudo-universalist idealist hyperbole of an Olympism as it has sought to penetrate new international markets and re-image cities and regions in the international economy of a global culture.

Close consideration of the effects of Olympic Games upon the host city and the nation remains curiously inconsistent. But Seoul and Atlanta have hardly emerged as tourist hot-spots. Sydney has projected figures for increased tourism, but they seem more dubious two years on, as people realise that the long-haul flights to Sydney from the lucrative tourist markets of North America and Western Europe are not so irresistible after all, despite the scenes from Sydney's super September in 2000. Barcelona remains the serious contender to explain in any rational way the continuing attraction of staging the Olympics. Sustained studies have demonstrated the swing from business towards tourism in statistical profiles of visitors. High-spending US and Japanese tourists fill the expensive rooms of top Barcelona hotels. Catalonian nationalists still celebrate the profile achieved by the 1992 event for their region of Spain, and for their wider political cause and ambitions. The Olympic Village is walkable from the squares and *Ramblas* of the city centre, contiguous to the Olympic Port. Here, nightclubs attract young hedonists and *vose* cinema screenings attract the international English-language movie fan. The beach and har-bour-side base of the Olympic facilities is a base for thousands of promenaders, *flaneurs* of all types, ages and nationalities on sunny weekends. The Olympic Stadium atop the majestic Montjuic Park stages rock concerts and regular Spanish football league matches. Barcelona knows it was worth it. Other cities convince themselves that it was, as they seek to reposition themselves in the global marketplace.

Understanding the significance of the Olympic Games in the global culture of advanced modernity is not so much about what is on the agenda of Olympic competition and activity programmes. It is more about the global profiling of places and the worldwide expansion of consumer markets. The Olympic Games, with all its ceremonial and ritual and tradition, its deference to youth and internationalism, its preservation of the pristine purity of the Olympic Stadium, continues to be significant in the contemporary world because of its unique blend of the all-embracingly international, the passion for the celebration of national and/or regional identity, and the regular celebration of a global consumerism that attracts the sponsors to keep queuing up to be associated with the five rings of the Olympic logo so jealously and greedily guarded by the beneficiaries, luminaries and lawyers of the International Olympic Committee and its bogus 'Family'.

The irrational motives that drive those still spellbound by the Olympic Games and its promises are based in the fascinating hold that the Olympics still has on the contemporary imagination, and are stimulated by the image that the Olympic Games can still convey of a world in which the most passionate national interests can be mobilised within a tolerant and inter-cultural internationalism. It is undeniable too that those feelings – manifestly exhibited in the avenues and passages of Barcelona, in the streets and places/squares of Sydney – are genuine and deeply felt. The Olympic Games may be in some senses absurd, cases of magnificent trivia in the light-entertainment schedules of a mediated global culture. But they continue to provide a focus for the articulation of both a sense of national identity, and an international cosmopolitanism rooted in consumerism. Peculiarly, persisting across all the phases of the history of the Games is the rhetoric of spirituality, the claim that the Games fulfil some important expressive function over and above the politics and economics of the day. They have survived and in some undeniable sense prospered despite the shifting agenda of the event itself, and the many ways in which sport has changed. They have also been exposed as amoral or corrupt, unaccountable in ways widely typical of International Non-Government Organisations, but claiming to put the guilty house in order and get back on the ethical track, expelling a few bribe-takers and establishing an agenda for reform. At the level of sport practice and performance itself, the Olympics has represented as many lows as highs in terms of moral aspirations; and, as many world sports organisations would claim, and championships would demonstrate, the Olympics is not a consistent pinnacle of technical achievement. Yet despite three such persistent critiques,[24] they have survived and expanded. The rhetorical idealism of the Olympic movement, ideal and the like have certainly been arrogated to good effect by hosts of the Games, for uses internal to the needs of a city, region or nation and for purposes of wider international self-promotion. But the global religiosity at the core of the De Coubertin vision is consistently re-peddled, institutionally and individually. We see this in early messianic tributes to Olympism, in individual lives forged by a commitment to its ideals, and in the worldwide thinking of contemporary figures. The first programme for the

1932 Los Angeles Olympic Games featured an article by the president of the University of California.[25] For him, the religious elements of the ancient Greek Olympics provided a parallel to the Games' modern mission: 'May they promote the love of play, the reciprocity of good will, and the solvent of good sportsmanship in which shall be washed away the immemorial feuds of mankind that now obscure the goal that is nevertheless so surely there and so completely attainable, the goal of "Peace on earth, goodwill toward men".' As on 2 July 2003 the three cities slugged it out for the IOC vote for 2010, the contemporaneous exhibition in the Olympic Museum featured Ella Maillart, a pioneer of sporting Swiss womanhood.[26] Born in 1903, the ill-health of her childhood was reversed by a strength developed through sport, particularly the outdoor activities of sailing and ski-ing. But the sports were not only sources of physical wellbeing. They represented a spiritual journey, an essential aspect of her search 'for her inner being, which she discovered in an ashram in Southern India when the Second World War had just broken out in Europe'. For Maillart, all her physical efforts on the mountain and the seas were a 'search for foreign skies', part of a quest integrating the physical and the spiritual. At an IOC education event during the Sydney Olympics, focused upon a review of the Olympic truce and a consideration of its potential for contemporary initiatives and interventions, the president of the United Nations, Kofi Annan, addressed the meeting on video. He praised the Olympics for the way it provided a sight of men and women of all types, a collection of human diversity and inclusiveness. Sport, he said, shares with world affairs more generally 'the shared goal of a culture of peace'.

Making sense of the Olympics is no straightforward task. Much depends on where you look, and I have argued elsewhere that the Olympic experience can be seen as comparable to the theme park or the Disney experience.[27] But the Olympic phenomenon remains underpinned by an enduring rhetoric of universalist spiritual idealism, and a persisting hold on the worldwide imagination. Combining this so successfully with an integrated powerful pull of the political, the cultural and the economic – as consolidated in the transformative phase after Los Angeles 1984 – the Olympic Games are likely to retain their extraordinarily prominent profile in the global cultural consciousness.

5 Alternative models for the regulation of global sport

Ken Foster

Historically, sport has been governed by management structures that were hierarchical and authoritarian. Their ideology, and often their legal form, was that of a private club. The commercialisation, and the later commodification, of sport put pressure on this legal form. Private clubs began to exercise significant economic power over sport. National associations of sport, which grew up to manage their sports, exercised monopoly control. International sporting bodies, as federations of national associations, in turn organised global sport. Increasingly there have been legal challenges to the abuse of this private power by those who consider themselves damaged by it. The autonomy that allowed self-regulation by sporting bodies has weakened in the face of legal intervention. The need for due process in decision making and the need to prevent abuses of dominant power within the sport were two important consequences of this legal intervention.

Sporting bodies have reacted to this juridification of their governance by trying to create a zone of private justice that protects some of these legal values, a 'rule of law' in sport, but through a system of private arbitration. This strategy has been energetically pursued, especially at the international level, and particularly through the IOC's encouragement of the Court of Arbitration for Sport. Additionally the nature and functions of international sporting federations as global organisations has made legal regulation of their activities by national courts difficult.

This dual difficulty of regulation, private arbitration in sport and the inadequate national legal supervision of international sporting federations, has led to other approaches. The basis of legal intervention however is partly dependent upon the nature of sporting organisation and upon regulators' perceptions of the values of sport. One approach is to treat sport as a predominately commercial activity and to apply a market model to its regulation. This for example has been the dominant approach in the USA. However, regional regulation by the European Union suggests another approach. This treats sport as a cultural commodity with unique social elements and can be described as a European model of sport. It preserves the traditional autonomy of governing bodies over purely sporting issues. It encourages an organisational separation of commercial and regulatory functions within sporting federations. Its regulation of commercial activities is modified because of the 'specific cultural' values of sport, such as national leagues, the need for a redistribution of income, and support for local identity.

Overall, the traditional structures of governance in sport have been altered by the dual processes of commodification and globalisation.

Commodification

Sport has always had some market relations between promoters, spectators, players and clubs. Players became professionals. Spectators paid to watch the event. Promoters of the sporting event gained revenue and hoped that the event made a profit. In this sense, sport has been commercialised for a long time.

Commercialised sport saw little legal regulation. When the law deals with internal market relations, it intervenes little. English law is reluctant to upset 'free' contracts even when they are one-sided. Players were tied to their club and had good reasons, like many workers, not to sue their employers. The legal form of football clubs was not designed for investment and profit.

Commercialised sport has become commodified in the past two decades, especially with the arrival of specialised sports television channels who have paid much greater sums for broadcasting rights than previously. Sporting events are now sold to other than their immediate consumer; they become a commodity. Sport is sold to television or used to sell other commodities. The commodity form creates an external relation with other capitalists. Commercial enterprises now sponsor events, teams and individual players. Corporate hospitality at major sporting events is big business. Football clubs have become public limited companies and are run for profit rather than sporting success. Business to business relationships are more typical of commodification and the more equal power of two businesses in itself makes litigation more likely.

Thus commercialised sport has internal market relations and values, but it is still a use-value, consumed for its own sporting worth. Law rarely intervenes in this realm where sport is produced. Commodified sport is an exchange-value that allows for the creation of surplus value in its external market relations. Law controls these external relations more readily in the realm of circulation. The commodification of sport has produced greater wealth, especially the most popular sports such as football and motor racing. This has caused a crisis in the structure of governance as a battle over these new revenues ensued.

Two contrasting patterns of governance have emerged. Historically international sporting federations developed to manage international competitions and to regulate their sport globally. Take FIFA as an example, for football is the most popular sport and FIFA has 202 members. From its foundation in 1904, FIFA was intended to be an umbrella organisation for international football. It has representatives from every national association of clubs. It is a federation. The scope of its jurisdiction is universal. Anyone in the world playing competitive football is ultimately under FIFA's rule, via their club, their league, and their national association. Its statutes are designed to harmonise playing conditions in each country. They also provide for mutual recognition of each association's authority. This means for example that a player suspended by one association is suspended by all and cannot play anywhere in the world. FIFA's statutes also rule on issues concerning players; for example a player cannot play under the jurisdiction of more than one national association and the sporting nationality of players is also determined by FIFA's rules. The sporting monopoly that international sporting federations control is an important cultural value. Most fans want one champion and rival organisations confuse the sporting quest to establish the best. So FIFA and its regional confederations are the sole promoters of international football and the sole accreditors of a single national league. Players, on pain of universal expulsion, are forbidden from playing in games organised by outside promoters for commercial gain. FIFA is self-financed. It is not funded by governments and it claims to be free of political interference. It operates as a private institution within international civil society.

The traditional governing bodies have struggled to retain control over these new revenues created by the commodification of sport. By using their monopoly powers to license competitions and promote sport, they have tried to restrain rival promoters of events. Out of the revenues raised by the sport, the governing bodies have kept a share for the general good of the game. The competitors have not been allowed to take all the profit. This is best achieved by a hierarchical and authoritarian model of governance. The elite within the sport can be coerced because the governing body is globally the monopoly controller of the sport.

An alternative model emerges when the elite performers try to retain all the revenues that they produce. To gain this financial control, they are prepared to breakaway and create a new organisation. This has a different form of governance to that of the governing bodies. The commercial imperative that usually drives breakaway organisation in sport leads to a more corporate form of governance. When the Premier League in England gained its independence from the Football League in 1992, it became a company with twenty equal shares. This is a legal form more suited to a joint commercial venture and very different from the existing management structure.

Globalisation

The process of globalisation has also contributed to the crisis of governance, especially at the level of international sporting federations. With more international sporting competition, so the power and influence of the international governing bodies of sport have grown. The globalisation of sport has moved the focus of legal regulation increasingly towards international sports federations.

Globalisation is an imprecise and contested concept. Following Scholte,[1] it is possible to identify several strands in sport.

1 Internationalisation: there are more international sporting competitions. There are also more nations. In team sports, the post-war expansion in the

number of nation-states has meant that there are far more nations able to compete in global events. There has been more global movement and migration of sportspeople. Players of sport, at least at the elite level, have become global vagabonds, performing as often as not outside their home country on a global circuit. International sports tourism is now also big business. Many fans now follow sporting teams abroad or travel to international tournaments, such as the Olympic Games.

2   Liberalisation: the removal of cross border restrictions on trade is less important in sport but cases such as Bosman[2] have allowed greater movement of players and fewer nationality quotas in team sports.

3   Universalisation of sport: this is a process of harmonisation and homogeneity. There are fewer sports that can dominate globally. To transcend local and cultural differences that are seen as barriers to global acceptance, the variety of sports that are capable of being marketed globally diminishes. A global sport, like football and basketball, needs to be simple in its structure and thus readily understood by those who have never played the game. There is global broadcasting of major sporting events. The television audiences for the Olympic Games and football's World Cup are huge. Some national sports leagues are marketed and seen worldwide. English Premier football and basketball's NBA league from the USA are two leading examples. These globally-seen sports swamp local sports, which are culturally diminished by not being globally broadcast.

4   Globalisation is often described as Westernisation or Americanisation. However this conflates and simplifies a complex process. Arguably there are three elements here. First, there is the *rationalisation* of games into sport as part of the process of modernity. Written rules are adopted. Leagues are organised so that the best team can be rationally identified. Scientific methods of training, timing and judging are introduced. Second, there is *imperialism*, as the *Westernisation* of third world sport. The pressures of globalisation and homogeneity have led to an exclusion of the 'third world' from the global sporting arena. Developing countries are excluded because they have fewer facilities, poorer training and their best athletes are poached to the 'first world'. Sports have altered their technical requirements to the detriment of poorer countries. Sports like motor racing require massive technical capital that excludes them. Hockey introduced artificial pitches, which are expensive and disadvantage developing nations. This shifted the balance of power in world hockey towards developed countries, such as Australia and Germany, and away from countries such as Pakistan and India. Third, there is *Americanisation*. It is sometimes assumed that, because globalisation creates global homogeneity, in late capitalism this means the predominance of American values. However, the dominant forces in global sports have historically been European and, to a lesser extent, South American. North American sport, especially in professional team sports, has developed a very different model. In sport, globalisation does not necessarily mean the cultural dominance of Americanisation.

5 De-territorialisation: Globalisation alters the spatiality of social dimensions. As Giddens describes, 'it diminishes the space-time dimension'. We have global broadcasting of sport and global fans. These fans are also consumers and are arguably more likely to 'shop around' the global sports market for a cultural and sporting identity. As Giulianotti says 'The next generation of rootless football fans may come to practise placeless forms of ... fandom that are promoted through the spectacular television coverage of the top teams.'[3] De-territorialisation has weakened local identity in sport. As Giulianotti argues, 'globalisation brings with it a disembedding of local social and political ties between club and community.'[4] Even national sides are made up more of global mercenaries and less of local conscripts, as the ties of national identity weaken. In international sport, nationality has been manipulated for commercial gain. 'Shirts of convenience' are chosen by players who may have multiple sporting nationalities because of their ancestry.

This final conceptual strand of de-territorialisation is central to the problems of legal regulation. Building on Houlihan's work,[5] it can be argued that there is a difference between internationalised sport and globalised sport. In internationalised sport, the 'the nation is the defining unit'.[6] Sports teams are defined by their nationality. International competition, as in football, is between national teams. In Olympic sports, athletes represent countries with a fixed number of competitors in each event. Globalised sport by contrast has rootless teams with multi-national or nationally ambiguous teams. These rootless, de-territorialised sports are often typified by their identification with commercial sponsors. Formula One racing teams are defined by their manufacturers, such as Ferrari. Professional cycling teams are named after their sponsor, such as Telecom. Racehorses are often named after companies.

Two models of regulation flow from this difference. One is based on the national, regional and international regulation of international sporting federations. They can be challenged legally through doctrines that recognise their monopoly control over an important economic activity, and because they exercise a public function. They are subject to regulatory oversight, at least in their overtly commercial functions. They have 'no privilege arising solely from their status as global sports organisations.'[7]

The second model of regulation is one of 'contested self-regulation' by a commercial promoter of globalised sport. Usually operating outside, or free from, any international sporting federation in the sport, they have no direct regulatory functions within the sport but are a profit-making organisation of elite sport. Commercial promoters, or elite teams organising a closed league, usually adopt a commercial legal form. This leaves them vulnerable to regulation as if they were any other capitalist venture.

The challenge within most sports is that they have inherited the first pattern but that the process of commodification and globalisation are moving towards the second pattern. Internationalised sport suits the traditional model of international sporting federations because it respects national-based patterns of sport and its governance. Globalised sport suits a commercial, self-regulatory pattern.

This simple dichotomy however needs to be used with caution. As sport has become more globalised, so the need for international codification has increased. The rules of a global sport need to be universal and applied everywhere. This global codification is supplied by international sporting federations. They create a hierarchy of rules and insist that national associations, on pain of expulsion, follow and enforce the global rules. Increasingly national associations of sport have their rule books written at international level. The international harmonisation of rules has delocalised sport and moved it towards a single global regulatory framework and governance. The IOC is a supreme example of global regulation of sport. It acts as a global legislator, trying to embrace all sports. This is especially true of drugs policy, where it has tried to impose the same regulations with the same definition of prohibited substances and the same penalties on all sports.[8] So international sporting federations are harmonising and becoming more homogenous because of globalisation. Nevertheless, their claims for self-regulation are conceptually different from those of the commercial promoters of globalised sport and need to be distinguished for the purpose of legal analysis.

Regulating international sporting federations?

The regulation and legal control of international sporting federations is thus a key issue in the global economy of sport. There are two main types of regulation that for differing reasons have proved ineffective in the control of international sporting federations. First, the traditional pattern of self-regulation of sport is incapable of resolving conflicts that arise from increasing commodification and globalisation of sport. This has led to increasing legal intervention. Second, legal regulation by states or by national legal systems is poor. States are unwilling or incapable of challenging the power of international sporting federations. By failing to control international sporting federations effectively, national legal systems have hastened the trend towards alternative approaches. There are several reasons why national legal systems cannot effectively regulate international sporting federations.

Challenging private governance

The existing patterns of global governance of sport have proved incapable of resisting the pressures of commercial interests. Governing bodies have embraced commercialism, professionalism and sponsorship. The interests of other stakeholders in sport have been ignored or marginalised. In part, this is because the traditional model of governance within international sporting federations has been that of the private club, with autonomy to manage its own affairs without legal challenge or supervision. This autonomy has discouraged transparency and accountability in managing sport, and failed to deter arbitrary or irrational decision making.

Private clubs and private contracts

The approaches of national courts have been an important element in this failure to regulate international sporting federations. They have viewed international sporting federations as if they were private clubs and therefore outside detailed legal scrutiny. Sporting federations are treated as voluntary bodies, which people are free to join as members and to associate freely with others. They are not publicly accountable and cannot be held to the same legal standards of fairness in their governance that would apply to publicly funded organisations. English courts decided in 1993 that a sporting federation could not be made legally accountable for their decisions by the public law route of judicial review because they lacked the status and functions of public bodies.[9] The US courts have consistently held that sporting federations are not state actors thereby freeing them from an obligation to operate within constitutional guidelines, especially those of due process and equal protection.[10] Linked to this notion of the private club, is the idea that the rules of sporting federations are private contracts.[11] National courts will accept the validity of contract provisions excluding their jurisdiction. Provisions in the rule books of international sporting federations that their decisions are 'final and binding' have been accepted by the English courts as binding on the athlete.[12]

A second method of avoiding legal scrutiny is for sporting federations to make it compulsory in their rules that disputes go only to private arbitration. This arbitration panel will usually be an 'independent' appeals body set up by the international sporting federation or increasingly the Court of Arbitration for Sport. Here the genuine independence of the arbitrating body as well as the compulsory nature of the arbitration clause are the legal issues.

A third way of avoiding legal scrutiny is by exclusion clauses. Athletes are now asked to sign agreements not to take legal action against international sporting federations as a precondition of taking part in international competitions.[13] Such waivers have been used at the last four Olympic Games.

Private justice

The intent of all these legal tactics is to create a zone of private justice within the sporting field of regulation that excludes judicial supervision or intervention with the decision-making process of international sporting federations. It denies athletes access to national courts and leaves them dependent on the arbitrary justice of the international sporting federations themselves. Athletes can claim redress only from an arbitration panel created and appointed by the international sporting federation itself or at best the Court of Arbitration for Sport, created by the IOC.

Arbitration is used as an alternative to litigation precisely because it is outside the scrutiny of national courts. The Court of Arbitration for Sport[14] was created in 1983 by the IOC as an independent authority to conduct arbitration in international sports disputes. It offered the usual advantages of arbitration. It was a specialised agency with a speedy and inexpensive procedure. A decisive change occurred in 1993. An arbitration award of the Court of Arbitration for Sport was challenged by an athlete. He appealed to the Swiss Federal Tribunal arguing that Court of Arbitration for Sport was not impartial and independent. The Federal Tribunal recognised the independence of the Court of Arbitration for Sport and thus effectively gave it a legal seal of approval.[15] Nevertheless it was critical of the numerous links between the Court of Arbitration for Sport and the IOC. The IOC had financed the Court of Arbitration for Sport; it could alter the statutes of the Court of Arbitration for Sport and the IOC president could appoint half the arbitrators.

Responding to this judicial criticism, the IOC reformed the organisation and structure of the Court of Arbitration for Sport, which aimed to give it greater independence. Under a new Code, the powers of appointment and administration were removed from the IOC and given to a new body, the International Council for Arbitration for Sport. There are now 150 arbitrators. Parties to an arbitration each choose their arbitrator and then these two choose a third to complete the panel.

These changes have led to a considerable expansion of the Court of Arbitration for Sport's role. Before 1994, it was used by a minority of international sporting federations and its jurisdiction was not imposed on athletes by federations. Since its reform many more international sporting federations have amended their regulations to make arbitration compulsory. There is increasing pressure from the IOC on the international sporting federations to standardise their procedures and to use the Court of Arbitration for Sport as the final court of appeal, especially in doping cases. It established *ad hoc* divisions to settle disputes rapidly during the Olympic Games, beginning in Atlanta in 1996. The law applied by the Court of Arbitration for Sport in appeals against a sports federation is that chosen by the parties or, in the absence of such choice, by the law of the country in which the federation is domiciled.[16] As many international sporting federations are domiciled in Switzerland, this will in practice often be Swiss law.

The Court of Arbitration for Sport is a system of exclusive private justice. There is no right of appeal to the courts, at least not to the Swiss courts who have recognised its independence and impartiality. For an athlete appealing against decisions of an international sporting federation based in Switzerland there is no further recourse. It is assumed that other national courts would also recognise the awards of the Court of Arbitration for Sport because it is a genuinely independent arbitration.[17] The IOC sees the system as part of its policy of harmonisation of rules and procedures within the international regulatory regime of sport. The consistent application and interpretation of these harmonised rules of international sporting federations by a single institution are seen as a considerable advance towards a global set of sporting principles. From the IOC's perspective, the Court of Arbitration for Sport is presented as an impartial external body that is a better alternative than international sporting federations settling disputes themselves, even by way of independent appeals procedures. For its supporters the Court of Arbitration for Sport represents the injection of the rule of law into the disciplinary procedures to which athletes are subject. Reeb argues that 'centralising the resolution of sports disputes within the Court of Arbitration for Sport should encourage the harmonization of certain major legal principles that are still applied haphazardly by the top sports bodies, such as the right to a fair hearing'.[18] This analysis suggests that the Court of Arbitration for Sport's jurisprudential function is to bring international sporting federations into a standardised application of the rule of law. As such it is an important and active agent of juridification, forcing rules to be more legalistic and to be more formally applied. Nevertheless, the acceptance by national courts that this is a system of impartial and independent arbitration removes such issues from their scrutiny.

Lex sportiva

A more wide-ranging argument is that the emerging jurisprudence of the Court of Arbitration for Sport is creating an independent set of legal principles applicable to the resolution of disputes with, and within, international sporting federations. This jurisprudence has been termed *lex sportiva*[19] deliberately invoking the concept of *lex mercatoria*, which refers to a set of legal principles used to govern international commercial arbitrations.[20]

This argument claims that as an international institution, an international sporting federation can by their rules and regulations create customary international law and this will therefore be recognised as binding by national courts and so be outside their jurisdiction. The *lex sportiva* is a stateless legal order that governs the activities of international sporting federations. It is a private contractual order that uses binding arbitration to settle its disputes. And as such, it is respected by national courts.

National regulation

These three elements – private clubs, private arbitration and respect for a *lex sportiva* – combine to remove sporting disputes from the regulation of national legal systems. The inadequacy of national regulation over international sporting federations stems partly from this concept of unsupervised autonomy for private institutions. But it is also inadequate because national courts generally have difficulties in taking jurisdiction over global organisations. There are three principal reasons for this second type of inadequacy.

First, there is an argument that international sporting federations are international organisations and as such they have a 'diplomatic' immunity from national courts. The status of the IOC as an international body, and therefore outside the jurisdiction of national courts, was implied by the US courts in litigation arising out of the decision by the United States Olympic Committee not to send a team to the 1980 Moscow Games as a protest against the Soviet invasion of Afghanistan. In refusing to intervene the Court said that:

> Congress was necessarily aware that a National Olympic Committee is a creation and a creature of the International Olympic Committee, to whose rules it must conform. The NOC gets its power and its authority from the IOC, the sole proprietor and owner of the Olympic Games.[21]

The clear implication was that the IOC was an immune organisation and that that immunity extended to the national committees.

There has been further debate as to whether the IOC has a legal status as an international non-governmental organisation. The classic definition of international legal personality has been the capacity to enter into legal obligations at the international level with other international persons such as nation states. The IOC undoubtedly satisfies this criterion. In addition, the Swiss Federal Council has granted the IOC, which is domiciled in Switzerland, a special legal status that recognises it as an international institution.

Second, there is an argument that global organisations, especially INGOs, are outside the jurisdiction of national courts because of their international functions and the character of their governance. For example, the US courts refused to interfere with the programme of the 1984 Los Angeles Olympic Games, when a complaint of sex discrimination was filed, declaring that:

> ...a court should be wary of a state statute to alter the content of the Olympic Games. The Olympic Games are organized and conducted under the terms of an international agreement – the Olympic Charter. We are extremely hesitant to undertake the application of one state's statutes to alter an event that is staged with competitors from the entire world under the terms of that agreement.[22]

Third, a further difficulty with making international sporting federations accountable before national courts is the issue of jurisdiction. This raises the question of what is the proper forum for a case involving international sporting federations. An example occurred in the case of Lewis v Bruno[23] where a dispute between two British boxers was held not to be triable by the English courts because it involved the interpretation of the rules of the WBA, who were legally domiciled in the USA. The increasing globalisation of sport will make such cases more likely and increase the likelihood of 'forum shopping' whereby international sporting federations locate themselves in legally friendly countries.

This interlocking legal framework makes it difficult to regulate international sporting federations. They are effectively outside the control of national legal systems, which treat them as immune and unaccountable, either because they are global in scope, or immune as international organisations. However, there is one form of legal intervention that has had some effect in controlling the activities and governance of international sporting federations and that is regional regulation.

Regional regulation and a European model of sport

The alternative to globalised self-regulation or inadequate national regulation that has the most potential for resistance to commercialisation and globalisation is regional regulation. Such regulation can directly help to preserve national identity in sport and resist the commercial pressures that globalise sport. The best example of such regional regulation of sport is the European Union.

The European Union had a short period that lasted from the Bosman judgment[24] in 1995 to the Amsterdam treaty in 1997 where it looked as if a purely commercial model would be applied to sport. Legal regulation, especially through the enforcement of European competition law, would treat sport like any other business and not recognise any unique character to professional sport. Part of the move away from a pure free market model was signalled by the publication of the policy document in 1998 entitled the European model of sport.[25] This argued that the European regulators should try to protect sporting and cultural values. By implication it contrasted an American model of sport that was more commercial and subject to a different style of regulation.

American team sports have historically been organised as single economic enterprises in which the success of the league as a whole is the prime purpose. The league is owned by capitalists who then franchise teams to compete in the league. Entrepreneurs buy these franchises and construct a team to compete in the league by buying in all the necessary factors of production, such as a stadium, management and players. The promoters of the league aim to maximise profits in an overtly economic enterprise. Revenues within the league are distributed relatively equally amongst the teams in the league to try and ensure sporting balance.

It thus differs markedly from the European model, which is said to have a distinctive pattern of organisation and governance. This pattern protects the specific and unique cultural values of European sport. These are non-commercial values that a regulatory framework should protect by exempting some sporting matters from its scope.

The key features of the European model and the principal differences from the American model can be represented in the following table:

European model of sport *vs* American model of sport

	European (socio-cultural)	American (commercial)
1 Organisational motive	Sporting competition	Profit
2 League structure	Open pyramid. Promotion and relegation	Closed league; ring-fenced
3 Governing body's role	Vertical solidarity; sport for all	Profit maximisation; promote elite stars as celebrities
4 Cultural identity	National leagues; local teams. Opposition to relocation of teams & transnational leagues.	Transnational or global leagues; footloose franchises
5 International competitions	Important for national identity	Non-existent or minimal
6 Structure of governance	Single representative federal body	League or commissioner

These key differences can be expanded:

The organisation of sport is not governed directly by commercial motives but by sporting motives

The European model of sport is a model of organic growth in which enthusiasts combine to compete against each other. The values are sporting and social; any profit made is treated as incidental not central. In professional football, for example, there were historically limits on taking profits out of football clubs, so making them unattractive investment opportunities. The legal form of most sports clubs in Britain is that of an unincorporated association, effectively a private members' club. This is essentially a non-profit making form. The primary purpose of a sports league or competition is to find the best. Commercialism is a necessary evil, in some sports still resisted, and which governing bodies believe should always be secondary to sporting values. Many professional football teams run at a loss and would be closed on ordinary business principles. As economic enterprises they are frequently worthless apart from their major asset, their ground. They nevertheless continue to function, dreaming of sporting success.

The American model is an outcome of commodity production of sport where commercial values predominate. Sport is sold as a commodity, especially to television broadcasters. They are the primary consumer with massive bargaining power. Rule changes are made to accommodate television. Franchises relocate to capture new and larger fan and viewer bases. Failing franchises, which do not contribute to the greater economic good through gate and other receipts, are ruthlessly pruned or moved to economically greener pastures. Whole leagues in the past have failed economically and become redundant. The overall model and ideology is that sport is the same as any other business venture.

The structure of leagues is open

The European sports league has an open, not closed, structure. There is a pyramid structure through which teams can advance on sporting performance alone. Teams rise and fall through linked leagues by promotion and relegation. The rich club can be relegated; the poor team promoted.

This fear of sporting and economic decline is absent from closed sports leagues, such as those that are normal in North American sports. Such leagues are a closed shop with entry controlled by the incumbents. There is a fixed number of teams in the league with no relegation. New teams cannot break into the closed shop unless the league decides that its overall economic health will be improved by expansion franchises. The economic risks of sporting failure are reduced and this makes capital investment in a team franchise more attractive.

Sports federations promote vertical solidarity

The governing bodies take part of the commercial revenues generated by the sport and use it for the overall good of the sport. Vertical solidarity refers to the techniques that are used by a single governing body in the sport taking a share of the sport's total receipts and using them to support the grassroots of the game. Redistribution can help youth development, wider participation and coaching. The elite, money-making clubs in effect subsidise the lower reaches of the game. Vertical solidarity depends on the exclusive jurisdiction of a single governing body that has the jurisdiction and authority to reflect this form of 'taxation'. This is why European regulators and policy makers have been so opposed to the threat of a breakaway independent league of the top European football clubs, fearing that the sport overall will be impoverished.

There is no vertical solidarity in American sports. The professional leagues do little to support the game other than to support their own farm teams that can be exploited for gain. Elite performers are exploited for personal and collective monetary gain. The business of sport is seen as much as about entertainment as about sporting excellence.

The preservation of national leagues is culturally important

The preservation of national leagues is culturally important so that teams and their fans retain a sense of identity. Local teams are supported by vertical solidarity so that fans retain a sense of local identity. As a consequence transnational leagues are opposed, especially the emergence of pan-European leagues.

There is little sense of local identity in the American model. In sports where the team can disappear overnight and move to a new location, the league's identification of its supporters is one of commercial customers rather than fans. The business can and will be moved whenever commercial considerations dictate, more like a supermarket chain than a sports team.

team competition is important

rnational sports federations share the European sporting ideology,
___ is where the overwhelming majority of them had their historical roots.
They organise international competitions to establish the sporting best. They
usually follow redistribution policies similar to those of national federations,
trying to develop their sport globally and supporting the poorer nations. There
is little international competition in American sports. Baseball has its parochial
'World Series'; football has its genuinely 'World Cup'.

Sport is governed by a single governing body

Another major and crucial difference between the American and European
models of sport is the structure of governance. European sports leagues are
usually part of a wider structure of regulation and governance within the
sport. National governing bodies are the constitutional regulators of the
sport, both amateur and professional. They approve and license the sports
leagues. Independent sports leagues outside the structure of unitary governance
are absent or short-lived because a separate independent league is seen as a
threat to be eliminated.

The closed league of American sports leagues is an independent capitalist
venture. The sports league governs itself; it is independent, autonomous and
exclusive. The governance of the league is not in the hands of a national
federation for the sport but in a separate commercial structure. The league is
governed as if it is a single economic entity with a board of owners of the
various brands. This is a model of governance much closer to a commercial
board of directors. It regulates itself by agreement among the partners, although
they often cede executive power in non-financial matters to a powerful single
Commissioner. The professional league is not part of a wider constitutional
framework of governance. It is not normally affiliated to an international sports
federation.[26]

This ideal type of the European sports model has limitations. In most team
sports, the open pyramid structure does not extend throughout the sport but is
restricted to the professional levels of the sport. The dream of taking the village
cricket team to the apex of the game is not available. The professional league in
cricket, the County Championship, is a closed league. The same teams compete
every season and there have been only two new counties admitted in the last
hundred years. Even sports that have a relatively open structure, such as football, have narrow entrance points to the higher professional levels. Only one
team per season has been promoted from the semi-professional Conference to
the higher reaches of the fully professional Football League, though the number
was increased to two in 2003.[27] The fear of economic decline amongst the
professional clubs means that the trapdoor down into the Conference is still
narrow.

Other sports have moved to an American model to a much greater degree.
Rugby League, for example, has created a 'Super League' with strict entry

criteria. These include economic criteria such as the potential gate revenues. The sport has tried to enforce rationalisation and merge economically weaker clubs. It has granted new franchises in towns without any history of rugby league in an attempt to make the sport attractive outside its narrow geographical limits. The European sports model is not empirically universal nor is it immune from the forces of economic rationalisation and commodification. The closed league is developing in many sports and the historical links to the grassroots of the game are being severed.

American regulation

The American approach to the legal regulation of sport has been markedly different to that of Europe. American professional sports have been regulated by the anti-trust authorities starting from the position that they are commercial enterprises. For this reason it is instructive to look briefly at the approach of the American regulators for it represents the best example of regulation in a free market context, in which there has been little or no recognition that sport has a cultural or social dimension. It will then be contrasted with the developing model of regional regulation within the European Union.

The three major issues that have been litigated under anti-trust law are:

1   free agency for players
2   breakaway leagues
3   franchise relocation.

1. Free agency

Historically, disputes about players moving were the earliest preoccupation of sports law in the USA. Players were restrained from freely changing clubs, partly to control wages but also to counter rival leagues who wanted to poach players for themselves. The most notorious restraint was baseball's reserve clause. All players had a clause inserted in their original contract that gave the club an option to renew their contract each season. At the end of the season each team listed players that it wished to retain (reserve) and claimed exclusive rights over them. Other teams in the league agreed to respect these reserve lists and not induce the player to move. The player's club could then exercise its option knowing that the player had no bargaining power; he could not threaten to leave. Players were effectively bound to a single club until the club chose to release them.

The 'reserve clause' was upheld by the Supreme Court in 1922 when it decided the anti-trust laws did not apply to baseball.[28] When other professional sports expanded rapidly in the 1950s, partly because of money from television broadcasting, they also used similar contractual devices. These were challenged and in 1957 the Supreme Court held that, unlike baseball, professional football was covered by the anti-trust laws.[29] Later decisions extended this judgment to other sports and baseball's exemption was declared to be an anomaly.[30] Even this exemption came under judicial attack in the 1990s when courts tried to limit it to the narrow issue of the reserve clause and so allow anti-trust laws to apply to other questions such as franchise relocation within baseball.[31]

Once the preliminary issue that anti-trust law applied to most professional sport was decided, there was a campaign on free agency for players. Anti-trust law was used to protect the interests of the players. In a series of cases the courts asserted a Bosman-type principle of free agency for players.[32] Whilst not achieving full freedom of movement for players, these decisions have modified some of the worst excesses of labour practices within American sport. The draft system in American football, where new professional players are effectively assigned to one club, has been regularly challenged and has been slowly modified under this judicial onslaught.

2. Monopolies and rival leagues

The professional sport leagues now have a monopoly. There is only one league in each sport. But historically they faced competition. Organised baseball faced many rival leagues in its early days. The American League and the National League agreed to form, in effect, a single structure in 1903. Other leagues were 'defeated' by their long-term inability to get players. The Federal League was the last major competitor and it folded in 1915.[33] The Supreme Court's approval of the reserve clause in 1922 undoubtedly made future challenges from other leagues difficult. The pattern of new leagues emerging to rival the existing league left a legacy in American sports. Raw competition in the free market was to be the solution to organising sport effectively.

Other sports have had similar histories.[34] In ice hockey, the National Hockey League had a rival, the World Hockey Association, which survived for six years in the 1970s before four of its teams were absorbed into the NHL. The National Basketball Association formed in 1949 but faced the American Basketball Association from 1967 to 1976 until an agreement between the two leagues brought teams into the NBA. In professional football the NFL merged with the AFL in 1966 with all the eight teams of the rival AFL joining the NFL.

The commercial model of sport that emerges from this pattern is one of takeovers and mergers with a gradual tendency towards monopoly with only one league surviving. Not surprisingly, the application of anti-trust legislation, which was designed to prevent monopoly, was now, apart from baseball, assumed. When the NFL and AFL merged in 1966, Congress felt it necessary to grant an immunity from anti-trust legislation to the merger.[35]

The tactics used to defeat rival leagues have been considered in several leading cases.[36] The jurisprudence emerging from these cases shows a balance being stuck between the illegality of anti-competitive behaviour towards rival leagues and the legality of maintaining single sports league as the preferred form of organisation.

3. The relocation of sporting franchises

Getting the best commercial opportunities goes to the heart of the closed league system of American sport. By controlling the number of franchises, the leagues can control the entry of new teams. By controlling the location of existing franchises, the leagues can control which cities have a sports team. All sports leagues require a unanimous vote of owners to approve a relocation. Legal challenges abounded in the 1980s as the major sports leagues spread their geographical wings. There was a broad move of franchises from the rust belt of the north-eastern United Sates to the sun belt of the Southwest and the Old South. However, the most legally high-profile case concerned the proposed move of the Raiders football franchise from Oakland to Los Angeles, which was blocked by the league, the NFL, but allowed by the courts.[37] The key legal question – was the league abusing its dominant market position? – depended on what constituted the market. The NFL unsuccessfully tried to argue that they were competing in a broad market; either the entertainment market or the market for watching sport generally. The courts held that the market was a narrow one – specifically for NFL football. With such a narrow market definition, the NFL were obviously a monopoly. They then were unable to show that the blocked relocation was reasonable. Three principal reasons emerge from the litigation. One, that there was no obvious need for the league to control the allocation of franchises in order to produce a successful product in terms of the league's overall economic well-being. Two, that there were no express and objective criteria, such as population size or regional balance of teams, for the decision to block the transfer. Three, that the decision was not clearly an objective business judgment but was tainted by personal animosity. The consequence of this period of litigation over relocation of franchises was that judicial scrutiny of decisions overrode internal league governance but the sports leagues were also driven to adopt and follow objective criteria in future decisions over franchises.

4. Exceptions

The sporting leagues have however been saved from the full logical consequences of a commercial model by two legal doctrines that limit the impact of a commercial model.

First, during the 1980s, the courts allowed sports leagues to use the 'labor exemption'. This doctrine was inserted into the anti-trust legislation to ensure that collective bargaining between trade unions and employers was not treated legally as a price-fixing cartel. The labour exemption provided that if there was genuine collective bargaining in the industry then the anti-trust legislation was inapplicable. Players' unions now regularly bargain with the leagues on a wide range of issues as well as salaries. They successfully argue that these aspects of collective regulation are outside the scope of the antitrust legislation and so many issues of sports regulation, especially free agency, have now been removed from judicial scrutiny.

Second, a legal doctrine known as the single entity theory has been successfully argued. Under this doctrine, a sports league is treated as a single legal entity, akin to a joint venture between the clubs, rather then a collection of individual legal entities. By virtue of being treated as a single entity, a sports league is thereby not combining, which is of course at the heart of the anti-trust legislation, to the detriment of the public interest. The most recent application of this doctrine has been to soccer. In the landmark case of Fraser v MSL[38] the courts have allowed US soccer to keep a system in which players are centrally contracted to the league and then allocated to a franchise. The complex reasoning in this case suggests at least that new leagues in minor sports, as professional soccer is in the USA, may gain some protection.

The history of anti-trust regulation thus suggests that sport leagues cannot avoid judicial scrutiny given their commercial ideology and structures of governance, but that if players' rights are respected, rational decision-making is employed, unions are collectively bargained with, and fledging leagues protected then the full rigour of competition law can be modified.

European regulation

History

Following the landmark case of Bosman in 1995,[39] there was a massive increase in the number of complaints about UEFA's activities by those who were subject to its jurisdiction, especially clubs and players, and by those who had commercial relations with UEFA, especially broadcasters. For a time it appeared that the Commission might take an extreme position and say that all decisions made by UEFA, and indeed other governing bodies of sport, were in principle subject to challenge under European competition law. If football was just a business, and UEFA was its monopoly supplier in Europe, then the anti-competitive rules of the Treaty applied without modification. The spectre of continual involvement and intervention by the European Court of Justice and the European Commission into the affairs and internal governance of UEFA was thus raised.

This extreme position, that everything UEFA does is legally challengable, was soon seen to be untenable. After its brief flirtation with the undiluted free market model[40] and treating football as if it was like any other business, the Commission began to search for another position. The Amsterdam Treaty in 1997 had a Declaration on Sport annexed. This spoke of 'the social significance of sport'. In a protocol it was declared that:

> The Conference emphasises the social significance of sport, in particular its role in forging identity and bringing people together. The Conference therefore calls on the bodies of the European Union to listen to sports associations when important questions affecting sport are at issue. In this connection, special consideration should be given to the particular characteristics of amateur sport.[41]

This was the first recognition by the European Union of the unique features of sport. It was followed in 1998 by the Commission's paper on the European model of sport, discussed above. This argued that sport has a social and cultural role and is not solely about money. This paper was followed in 1999 by the Helsinki Report on sport.[42] This stressed the values upheld by existing governing bodies of sport such as UEFA. The Report concluded by calling for a new partnership between the sporting federations, the member states and the European Commission, which would require that the Commission as the principal regulatory organ should 'take account of the specific characteristics of sport'. An informal council of European Ministers of Sport in Lisbon in May 2000 issued a Declaration on the 'Social Dimension of Sport'. This concluded, in idiomatic English:

> Being a precious factor of the development of a 'feeling of belonging' as an expression of social cohesion and warrant of community life and solidarity, and also being an element of socialisation of groups and individuals that cannot be ignored, contributing to the strengthening of civic society, sport ... wishes therefore to be respected in its specific aspects within the space of the European Union, and to that end the specific aspects of sport, namely its social function, should be taken into consideration in the implementation of community policies.[43]

This was followed by the Nice Declaration on sport in December 2000. This was entitled 'a declaration on the specific characteristics of sport and its social function in Europe'. It proclaimed:

> Even though not having any direct powers in this area, the Community must, in its action under the various Treaty provisions, take account of the social, educational and cultural functions inherent in sport and making it special, in order that the code of ethics and the solidarity essential to the preservation of its social role may be respected and nurtured. The European Council hopes in particular that the cohesion and ties of solidarity binding the practice of sports at every level, fair competition and both the moral and material interests and the physical integrity of those involved in the practice of sport, especially minors, may be preserved.[44]

This new approach, recognising the specificity of sport, has two principal elements. The first element distinguishes between the sporting and social functions of sport, which will be immune from regulation, and the commercial activities of sporting federations. The conceptual basis of this distinction distinguishes different functions for sporting federations such as UEFA. For example if UEFA are regulating the rules of the game, then this will be seen as a purely sporting function and the Commission will not intervene. If UEFA are selling exclusive broadcasting rights to football matches as a collective package, then they are clearly functioning commercially and there is no apparent justification for this function to be exempt from European law.

The second strand addresses the social and cultural character of sport. It now encompasses many strands, some vague and aspirational, such as 'strengthening civic society'. Key policies however include 'identity' by preserving national leagues and international competitions and encouraging the redistribution of income within sport, as 'ties of solidarity binding the practice of sports at every level'. The policy agenda, driven by the politicians, has a simple underlying message opposing the commodification of football: save small local clubs; prevent a breakaway European Superleague.

The Commission's current approach

Collective marketing of broadcasting rights

The collective selling of broadcasting rights to sporting events by the governing body is a key factor in promoting solidarity within the sport. Unless the governing body can control these valuable commodities, they will be unable to generate sufficient revenue to act as trustees for a redistributive mechanism. Collective marketing and selling is thus one area where the European regulators have been prepared to accept a sporting justification to modify a free market approach. Legally, the rights to sports events belong to the home club. At least this is the case if the home club is the owner of its ground. For what is being granted to a broadcaster is a contractual exclusive licence to enter the ground where the game is being played. The club will also promise exclusivity by denying access to any rival broadcaster. However sports leagues typically will only allow participation in their competition if each club assigns their rights to the league. This central pool of rights is then offered for sale as a single package by the league, usually on an exclusive basis, to competing broadcasters.

Central marketing is objectionable to a free market approach for several reasons. It is claimed that it distorts competition amongst broadcasters. Sport, especially football, is a key driver in developing television markets. It is a 'must-have' item that is indispensable for getting viewers to pay for coverage. By pooling all the fixtures into a single package, only the large and richer media groups can afford to bid for them. Smaller and new entrants to the broadcasting market, and poorer terrestrial broadcasters, are excluded.

It is also claimed that exclusive deals bar other entrepreneurs access to the rights for different media. If these were sold separately, other companies could develop new sports services through mobile phones and the internet. Collective marketing is also said to prejudice the consumer. Such deals limit the total number of games broadcast and so deny viewers a free choice of games to watch. The sporting authorities defend collective marketing because it allows financial redistribution in the sport. Individual clubs are unable to sell their games at a market price; if they could, the popular teams would get richer, and the less popular poorer. In sport, the rich tend to win. So collective marketing, it is claimed, equalises the financial strength of the clubs by foreclosing individual clubs from selling their games.

UEFA have always claimed the right to sell and market the broadcasting rights of the competitions that it promotes, especially those of the Champions' League. The top clubs have complained that collective marketing is an abuse of UEFA's dominant position. The clubs have no alternative but to agree to forfeit their rights despite the economic loss that they suffer. Broadcasters also claimed that they suffered because they were unable to buy single games from clubs but could only buy a collective package from UEFA.

In June 2002 UEFA and the European Commission reached a compromise agreement on the matter that gave UEFA most of the spoils.[45] The Commission allowed UEFA to continue to sell, as a collective package, the live and delayed television rights to Champions' League games. Some other media rights, such as internet rights, will however be jointly exploited by the clubs and UEFA. The Commission appears to have allowed this anti-competitive practice of taking the clubs' commercial rights away from them to continue because of the redistribution of the broadcasting income that UEFA proposed to implement. UEFA claimed that the new agreement showed that it was possible to reconcile the specific characteristics and nature of football within the framework of European law. It is a notable departure from normal commercial considerations and is an important recognition that the redistribution of income by UEFA is a key social purpose that needs to be legally exempt.

The Commission has also shown an interest in the collective marketing arrangements that have been entered into by national football leagues. The deals struck by the English Premier League and BSkyB have been under scrutiny, especially in relation to the exclusive element of these deals.[46] The current proposal by the Premier League for the upcoming bidding round is to offer three different packages of games. This clearly results from discussions with the European Commission and is designed to avoid the charge of selling an exclusive package.

Separation of regulation and promotion functions

The boundary between the Commission's regulation and sport's self-regulation has been redrawn by the Commission's approach to the governance of motor sports by FIA. The Commission laid down an important principle that a governing body of sport needs to separate its regulation of the sport from its commercial activities in promoting events and in maximising their commercial value; a governing body must not use its regulatory functions improperly to exclude its commercial rivals from the sport.[47]

FIA had used its monopoly position in running international motor sport to prevent rival promoters setting up rival events through various methods. They refused to license rival promoters, competitors and events. They banned drivers who competed in rival events. They insisted that circuit owners grant them exclusive use of their tracks, thereby preventing any other promoter from using these circuits. They concluded broadcasting agreements that penalised the broadcasters if they showed rival events.

After a long period of negotiation, the Commission secured modified regulations from FIA. They insisted on a complete separation of the regulatory function of FIA, as the governing body of the sport, and its commercial function of exploiting the broadcasting rights to all motor sports events under its jurisdiction. The separation is designed to prevent conflicts of interest. The Commission also limited the extent to which FIA, as the regulator of the sport, can take measures to prevent rival promoters of events competing with FIA's events. The Commission wanted to separate the function of the FIA in promoting events (and thereby gaining commercial benefit) from that of licensing events as part of its regulatory function. The role of a governing body, according to the Commission, is to act fairly and create a level playing field so that all promoters of events are treated equally fairly.

The Commission here, unlike its approach to UEFA's governance of football, is clearly using a commercial model. FIA is seen as the current monopoly supplier of motor sports internationally. Rivals who wish to enter this sport and promote alternative competitions need drivers, circuits and broadcasting income among other things, to be commercially competitive. Each of these necessary components was controlled by FIA and they used their monopoly position to block rivals. Drivers were blacklisted, circuits were tied up exclusively, and broadcasters penalised if they traded with rivals. None of these tactics were acceptable to the Commission.

The different approach by the Commission can be explained because motor sport is a globalised, rather than an internationalised, sport. It had a commercial structure of management and offered no cultural or social justification of its anti-competitive behaviour. As such it was subject to normal commercial criteria in its regulation. This example may be unusual in that there was an excessive intermingling of the regulatory and commercial functions within the governing structures of international motor sport. However, it indicates that regional regulation can be effective and that the fear that globalised sport can escape all regulation and be immune from legal intervention may be exaggerated.

Self-regulation on sporting issues

The general approach by the European regulators to the governance of sport has been to allow an area of self-regulation to sporting authorities. The Commission has declared its policy publicly. Commissioner Monti in a speech in 2001 outlined the Commission's approach said:

> The Commission is not, in general, concerned with genuine 'sporting rules'. Rules, without which a sport could not exist, (that is rules inherent to a sport, or necessary for its organisation, or for the organisation of competitions) should not, in principle be subject to the application of EU competi-

tion rules. Sporting rules applied in an objective, transparent and non-discriminatory manner do not constitute restrictions of competition.[48]

This is a clear statement, although the three final conditions, objective, transparent and non-discriminatory manner, need to be noted. This policy follows partly from two important cases before the European Court of Justice in 2000. In Lehtonen[49] the Belgian basketball association had rules forbidding transfers after a deadline late in the season. A Finnish player who signed after the deadline complained that the rule restricted his free movement, following the Bosman ruling. The Court held that as long as there was no discrimination between EU citizens such a rule was not unlawful as it had a clear sporting objective, to prevent clubs buying in new players for the end of season play-offs. In Deliege[50] a judoka challenged her non-selection for Belgium in international competitions, where there was a limited quota of places for each nation. Again the Court found that the rules did not hinder her economic freedom and that sporting associations were free to set selection criteria as long as they were not arbitrary and were objectively justified. These two decisions gave sporting associations a degree of autonomy but arguably left the court with a residual supervision. The Court clearly rejected the argument that sporting bodies had a total immunity even over 'the rules of the game' but they had to satisfy basic legal safeguards such as non-discrimination and rational criteria for decisions.[51]

Conclusion

The governance of sport by international sporting federations is in principle not beyond the regulatory scope of states, either through national legal systems or through international law. But the nature of international sporting federations makes regulation through national legal systems difficult. Attempts to use a zone of private arbitration by international sporting federations may only allow self-regulation to reappear. Therefore, frameworks of wider scope are needed to control their activities.

Regional regulation is suggested as the alternative. Because European sport has specific features, especially the protection of open leagues and the issue of national identity, regional regulation can help to support internationalised sport against the encroachment of globalised sport.

If the process of globalisation continues, what are the likely changes to the regulation of sport? The political economy of sport is now ruled by global capital. This will hasten the Americanisation of sport and lead to the development of a single model of globalised sport. The present system of governance, as represented to a large extent by the traditional governing bodies, will be dismantled in favour of elite sports managing themselves, especially in the key area of profit maximisation. Even the minimum level of regulation represented by the European Union's approach will be resented by capital and it will strive to recreate unregulated, autonomous structures. Law and regulation needs to rise to this challenge by subjecting globalised sport, and its commercial forms of governance, to the full legal consequences of its commercial logic. The attitude of the competition regulatory bodies is decisive here. The approach of European regulation has tried to protect what it defines as the specificity of European sport. This embraces the cultural values of internationalised sport and not those of globalised commercial sport. Globalised sport, with a purely commercial model, needs to be legally subjected to the full force of competition law. The approach of the anti-trust authorities in the USA is instructive here for they have dealt longer with self-managed, closed sports leagues. The approach of the European Commission to motor sport is encouraging; regional regulation can be effective, if only because the most commodified sports are played, watched and financed in Europe. Where cultural values and the protection of national identity in sport are key issues, European regulation has tried to give those values special protection. Whether this protection of non-commodified values especially can resist the rising tide of globalised sport remains to be seen. A breakaway transnational European football league may yet be the key test.

6 Sport and the nation in the global era

Alan Bairner

It has frequently been argued that the various processes that have come to be known collectively as globalisation pose a major threat to nations and to identities created and supported by the concept of the nation. The argument is perfectly straightforward even though it is commonly expressed in far from accessible language. Put simply, economic, political, cultural and ideological trends, supported by a pervasive and all-powerful global media industry, must inevitably destroy the distinctiveness upon which nations, nationalism and national identities depend for their very existence. For some this means the triumph, at least temporarily, of what Tom Nairn describes as 'the dissemination of a secular faith, the new monotheism of cure-all Free Trade, or market-olatry'.[1] For other commentators, globalisation understood in this way will culminate in something even more specific, namely the universal acceptance of a peculiarly American way of doing things – ironic given that part of the argument aims to prove that all nations are doomed. Others are more precise on this point and suggest that all nation-states and national cultures are in danger of being subsumed within a new global order accompanied by its own homogeneous culture. Indeed, John Urry has challenged the very notion that what has emerged has been a struggle between the national and the global with the latter being characterised as a new region. This 'territorial trap', as Urry calls it, ignores the fact that global systems are by their very nature entropic and challenge the very notion of the bounded region.[2]

Specifically in relation to sport, Miller *et al.* argue that the global exchange of sporting bodies 'has made it increasingly difficult for the nation-state to be represented by conventional corporeal symbols, as the spread of schooling, commodification, scientization, medicalization, and surveillance as part of the NICL [New International Division of Cultural Labor] has reorganized sporting bodies'.[3] Maguire *et al.* argue that 'modern sport is bound up in a global network of interdependency chains that are marked by uneven power relations'.[4] The consequence is a set of global power networks within which 'the practice and consumption of elite modern sport can best be understood'.[5] 'Given this growth in the multiplicity of linkages and networks that transcend nation-states', they continue, 'it is not surprising that we may be at the earliest stages of the development of a transnational or global culture, of which sport is a part'.[6]

Elsewhere, however, Maguire presents a subtler and altogether more seductive version of the globalisation thesis to argue that the concept describes a process in which there is considerable exchange of cultural values and modes of expression.[7] According to this interpretation, the nation as we have known it may well be about to disappear but it will do so not because of the triumph of a single and unidirectional tendency – e.g. Americanisation – but rather because all national cultures borrow and will continue to borrow from each other. For Maguire, the result is a world that is characterised by 'diminishing contrasts' but 'increasing varieties'. The point remains, however, that distinctive national identities, it would appear, will still disappear.

There is, of course, another approach that argues simply that the demise of the nation and the concomitant triumph of a global order have both been greatly exaggerated. As Anthony D. Smith points out, 'in the era of globalization and transcendence, we find ourselves caught in a maelstrom of conflicts over political identities and ethnic fragmentation'.[8] Indeed, it can be claimed that the forces associated with the idea of globalisation have actually created political and cultural space in which historically submerged nations and nationalities have been reawakened and infused with new vitality. According to Smith, 'only by grasping the power of nationalism and the continuing appeal of national identity through their rootedness in pre-modern ethnic symbolism and modes of organization is there some chance of understanding the resurgence of ethnic nationalism at a time when "objective" conditions might appear to render it obsolete'.[9] Developing arguments that I have already expressed elsewhere,[10] it is this latter approach that dominates the following examination of the links between sport and the nation in the modern world. Furthermore, the chapter questions the extent to which the resilience of the nation actually runs counter to "objective" conditions. Particular attention will be given in this regard to Irish sport and specifically to the role of the Gaelic Athletic Association (GAA) in the global era. The chapter begins, however, with a few more general comments on globalisation, specifically in relation to sport.

Sport, nationalism and globalisation

Links between sport, nationalism and globalisation tend to confirm the validity of claims that global processes are best understood as multidirectional flows. For example, it is undeniable that American influences had a major part to play in the fact that baseball became such a popular sport in Japan. In addition, 'lifestyle' or so-called 'alternative' sports, whilst resistant to traditional ways of playing and organising sport, are also characterised, as Belinda Wheaton reveals elsewhere in this collection, by transnational networks. Even where there is evidence of national or even continental resistance to global forces – for example, the general refusal of Europeans to exhibit any real appetite for either American football or baseball – the point must still be made that cultural pressures work in mysterious ways. Thus, Europeans continue to play and watch association football in preference to American sports but they do so in ways that are increasingly influenced by the American (or perhaps that should simply read the consumer capitalist) way of packaging sport. Critics of this approach have argued that I failed to take into account the power of both capital and of the media when arriving at what are somewhat benign conclusions. The criticisms are fair to the extent that I could certainly have said more about consumer capitalism and the media in relation to sport. Thus, Scherer is correct when he writes, 'while Bairner briefly mentions the power and flexibility of capital and transnational corporations, many theorists might wish for a more detailed consideration of the impact of the global economy on increasingly dismantled contemporary nation-states'.[11] Equally reasonable is Scherer's assertion that 'some scholars might wish for a more exhaustive overview of the media's role in producing imagined national identities and national heroes'.[12] It is true, for example, that Miller *et al.* have considerably more to say about such elements in the globalisation process as commodification, the role of the media and labour migration.[13] However, they do so, one might argue, at the expense of examining the ways in which individuals relate in practice to the collision of the global and the national. But, in any event, I do not propose to remedy my own sins of omission in this particular chapter. Instead, I intend to go even further and argue that, whilst global trends have clearly affected the relationship between sport and the nation, they have done so in such ways as to underline the extent to which ideas about nations and nationhood are at least as central to political discourse today as they have ever been. In addition, in the hope of pre-empting possible criticisms that this chapter again fails to take capital seriously, I shall argue that this analysis can be supported with reference to political economy. The resilience of the nation is not so much a victory of emotion over economic necessity but, in part at least, a rational response to the latter.

My feeling about some of the more extreme versions of the globalisation thesis is similar to thoughts I have frequently entertained about the more elitist assumptions both of orthodox Marxism and of postmodern cultural theory. According to both forms of social analysis, the individual is revealed as a largely passive recipient of false ideas courtesy of whatever opiate the ruling class has on offer at any given time. Gramscian influences did much to turn Marxist thinking in more constructive directions that indicated that hegemonic ideas could be contested although one could easily be forgiven for harbouring thoughts that in this respect the pessimism of Gramsci's intelligence is altogether more persuasive than the optimism of his will. In relation to the study of sport, I am mindful here of Stephen Jones's work on the British working class and its capacity to articulate resistance through sport. According to Jones, 'it is clearly wrong to depict the working class as impotent consumers, having little or no say in the form and content of the leisure product'.[14] Central to this chapter is the contention that even in the face of unfavourable global odds something similar can be said today about nations, nationalities and nationalisms. The relationship between sport and the nation is not inevitably doomed with helpless individuals looking on as local, regional and national cultures are sacrificed on the altar of global capitalism. Furthermore, attempts to maintain the relationship between sport and the nation should not be dismissed as essentially reactionary confrontations with the inevitable in a last ditch stand on behalf of the emotional and the irrational. It may be precisely the impact of global capitalism that obliges people to act rationally and self-consciously in order to maintain the links between sport and nations.

Definitions

I shall begin by describing briefly how I intend to use certain concepts in this chapter. Prior to discussing the relationship between sport and nationalism in Ireland, Mike Cronin offers a useful introduction to the different ways in which nationalism itself has been interpreted – by theorists whom he classifies as primordialists, modernists, statists and political mythologists.[15] Their various interpretations have a bearing on the discussion that follows. But it should be noted at the outset that seldom if ever can any category relating to the nation be regarded as self-contained. Nor should one imagine that rival interpretations are mutually exclusive. As a consequence, and in order to be in a stronger position to fully understand how the nation/sport dialectic operates, it is essential to go beyond Cronin and to comment on a number of basic concepts that are connected to nationalism but often in quite complex ways. The words themselves are all well known and are frequently used in relation to the social significance of sport. It is important, however, that we are clear about their precise meanings if we are to use them in such a way as to understand how sport reflects and simultaneously provides insights into the struggles between nations and global forces.

The first essential point is to distinguish *the nation* from *the nation-state*. As Allison comments, ' "Nation" and the concepts derived from it are among the most shifting and elusive in the entire study of society, not least because they arouse such emotion'.[16] Yet perhaps this no longer matters. Writing about the need for the study of sport to take globalisation into account, Rowe and Lawrence write, 'it is increasingly difficult for an adequate sociology or history of sport to take the nation state as its main ground or point of reference'.[17] That may well be so but what does this tell us about the status of the nation as opposed to the nation-state in such analysis? One need go no further than the United Kingdom in order to clarify what initially might seem to be a purely semantic point.

As Nairn observes, ' "Britain" is of course by definition a nationless identity'.[18] Nowhere is this demonstrated more publicly than in the world of international sport. With a single Olympics squad, four 'national' soccer teams and three 'national' rugby teams together with Northern Ireland's part share in the Irish team, the UK's sporting landscape is testimony to the complex relationship between nations and nation-states. When we refer to the prestige that nations can derive from sport it is important to think in terms not only of internationally recognised states but also of submerged nations (Scotland, Ireland, Wales,

Québec, Catalonia and so on) for which sport has commonly been one of the most effective vehicles for cultural resistance. Above all, sport provides athletes and fans with opportunities to celebrate a *national identity* that is different from and, in some cases, opposed to, their ascribed *nationality*. The two need not be mutually exclusive. It is possible to support both British teams and Scottish ones or to represent Wales and also the United Kingdom. It can be argued though that national identity is what takes priority in the minds of sports fans. Nationality, on the other hand, is what matters to athletes since this guarantees the right to compete on behalf of a nation. It is worth noting, however, that nationality rules have become increasingly flexible in sport as a response to labour migration.

The desire, particularly on the part of fans, to express their national identity in the realm of sport is clearly linked to *nationalism* in the broadest sense or, at the very least, to patriotism. Former member of parliament Jim Sillars dismissed the attitude of his fellow Scots towards national sporting representatives as 'ninety-minute patriotism'[19] and it is common to use sports fandom to illustrate what Billig meant by 'banal nationalism'[20] and Urry has located under the heading 'brand nationalism'.[21] One could also add a distinction between 'shallow' and 'deep' nationalism in this respect. As this chapter argues, Irish support for national representatives in global sporting activities is in most cases patriotic and, by implication, relatively politically shallow. The relationship between Gaelic games and Irish nationalism is on the other hand much more profound. In general, however, attempts to distinguish the passions aroused by international sport from 'real' nationalism miss the point. It is undeniable that expressions of solidarity for players and teams that represent one's nation are closely linked to *cultural nationalism*. Whether or not they are also bound up with *political nationalism* is a different question, the answer to which necessarily varies from one individual to the next. For many people, even ones whose national identity is associated with a submerged nation, cultural nationalism is enough. They may well feel that they could not become any more Scottish or Welsh or Catalan than they already are with the formation of a nation-state that would correspond to their sense of national identity. For others though, cultural nationalism is nothing more than the emotional embellishment of a strongly held political ideology that will settle for nothing less than national sovereignty. How this is to be achieved as well as the constitutional character of the end product will be influenced to a considerable degree by the interplay between two other nationalisms that require some comment.

Ethnic nationalism and *civic nationalism* are often taken to be polar opposites, whereas in practice they may overlap and feed upon each other to a considerable extent. In essence, the former places most emphasis of the biological lineage of those who constitute a nation whilst the latter is concerned to include everyone who lives within the nation's boundaries. They are seldom mutually exclusive but understanding them as distinct entities at this point is useful for the discussion that follows. With these definitions in mind, it is now possible to take the discussion a stage further. The discussion proceeds by saying something about the traditional importance of the relationship between sport and the nation, particularly with reference to the concept of 'national sports', before going on to consider why and how this relationship can continue to flourish despite the challenge of globalisation.

Sport and nations

According to Allison, 'whether we are talking about nationalism or patriotism or the development and expression of national identity . . . it is clear that a national dimension is an important part of sport'.[22] For Miller *et al.*, 'the sporting body bears triumphant national mythologies in a double way, extending the body to encompass the nation and compressing it to obscure the social divisions that threaten national unity'.[23] These claims can be amply supported by evidence drawn from a wide variety of countries and an array of different sporting contexts. For most sportsmen and women, even in an era when money is a major incentive for sporting success, representing the nation still matters. Of course, it is not inconceivable that they might represent more than one nation with neither ethnic origins nor even well established civic connections being necessary for a move from one to another. Mike Ticher refers to 'an increasing number of international players, across a whole range of sports, whose apparently "obvious" nationality conflicts with the country they represent'.[24] For the overwhelming majority of athletes engaged in international sport though the matter is still relatively clear cut. For fans, things are arguably even simpler. Following one's 'proxy warriors'[25] into international competition is one of the easiest and most passionate ways of underlining one's sense of national identity, one's nationality or both in the modern era. Needless to say, not everyone wishes to celebrate their national affiliation in this way, in most instances for the simple reason that they are not interested in sport, the nation or the relationship between the two. But just as for most active participants, for the majority of sports fans the choice is relatively straightforward. This is not to deny of course that in certain circumstances athletes and fans alike may well understand their nations in different ways. Furthermore, it is not only sporting individuals who demonstrate the contested character of most, if not all, nations. Sports themselves also do so to the extent that they become 'national' in the popular imagination for a variety of reasons.

I wrote in *Sport, Nationalism and Globalization* that 'national sports take different forms and, in so doing, they provide us with interesting insights into the character of particular nations'.[26] I would like to develop that argument here and in addition suggest that the concept of the 'national' sport not only provides insights into the relationship between the various terms listed above that are associated with the nation but also helps us to understand how it is that nations resist globalisation even in a global era. Some 'national' sports are peculiar to specific nations. Their 'national' status is protected by their exclusivity – echoes here, it would seem, of ethnic nationalism. One thinks of Gaelic games in Ireland (of which, more later) and shinty or curling in Scotland. One might also consider under this heading the claims of ice hockey and lacrosse in Canada or bullfighting in Spain. The same is true of traditional games that are played in Sweden and elsewhere in the Nordic area. Although they are played by declining numbers of people and are spatially restricted to specific areas, they say things about the region which no amount of fanatical support for global games is able to do. These activities need not be exclusive to particular countries. However, they are in some sense linked to the essence of the nations in question even though their actual origins, like those of Gaelic games and shinty, are pre-national or at least prior to the emergence of nation-states. One might think of these various activities as 'tourist board' national sports. Certainly they have acquired a certain ring-fenced cultural status which is not enjoyed by other sports, no matter how popular in terms of participation rates and attendance figures. They advertise 'the nation' even though it may well be the case that they have demonstrably failed to capture the interest of all of the people who constitute the civic nation and/or the nation-state.

It should be noted, of course, that those activities that are most likely to be ring-fenced because of their specific cultural resonance do not always find favour with members of particular nations' cosmopolitan elites who may well believe that the nation is better represented by sports that are both modern and transnational. As Carrie B. Douglass notes, 'for many Spaniards and Hispanists ... bullfights are a minor, unimportant nineteenth century survival, part of an arcane world view associated with General Franco and his supporters'.[27] Certainly the *corrida de toros*, the classic form of the bullfight, is not universally popular throughout Spain nor does it even take place at all in some Spanish regions. There are, however, alternative taurine festivals in most of those places and that is good enough for the advertising companies which ensure that the bull and the matador are used to sell a huge variety of Spanish products together with holidays to Spain. Hurling fulfils a similar function in Ireland although the sport itself comes a poor second to Gaelic football if popularity is measured in terms of the numbers of people who actually play and watch. Canadian ice hockey, on the other hand, might appear to offer conflicting evidence. Beloved by the marketing men and women, it is also hugely popular and additionally offers Canadians the opportunity to engage relatively successfully in international competition. But we should, at the very least, recognise that not all Canadians think fondly of hockey and that in any event, come the summer months, baseball – the national pastime of the United States – takes over. The other 'national' sports already mentioned face even stiffer competition.

According to Phil Ball, 'Spanish football is in a sense so wonderful that the country needs little else these days to sustain it'.[28] The comment is surely intentionally hyperbolic. But it does serve to put the status of bullfighting into perspective. Football is almost unarguably the 'national sport' of Spain. Yet, as Ball himself reveals in his study of club rivalry in Spanish football, at least as much as taurine activities, the game helps us to appreciate the extent to which Spain is at best a divided nation and, at worst, not a nation at all –

merely a nation-state. Similarly in Scotland whilst curling and shinty may look right on an advertising hoarding alongside a glass of malt, a smattering of tartan and a West Highland terrier thrown in for good measure, few Scots play or watch these activities. As in Spain the true 'national' sport is football. Yet it does not necessarily unite the nation. Like ice hockey in Canada, football is heartily disliked by many Scots. The national team unites the country rather more effectively than *la selección* in Spain. However, in Scotland as in Spain, football is also a major source of division – between cities, between regions and, most damagingly of all, between followers of Celtic and Rangers whose national identity has constantly been shaped by other factors rooted in their own personal biographies as well as in the theological history of the Scottish nation.

In Ireland, whilst hurling may well be the sport of choice in the eyes of Bord Fáilte or the executives responsible for selling a variety of Irish products, including stout and whiskey, the sport's popularity varies considerably from one county, and even one parish, to another. Gaelic football is more uniform in terms of the support that it receives throughout the thirty-two counties. Yet there are isolated pockets where it loses out to hurling. Furthermore, the right of any Gaelic game to be assigned 'national status' is considerably weakened not only because some Irish nationalists opt for other sports, such as rugby union and soccer, but also because the overwhelming majority of the Protestant community in the north of Ireland have resolutely turned their backs on the whole Gaelic games tradition. It might seem easy to dismiss this difficulty by simply taking these people at their word and accepting that since they do not consider themselves to be truly Irish, their sporting preferences need have no impact on what does or does not constitute an Irish national sport. But this would be to ignore the basic precepts of Irish republican ideology that has consistently sought to embrace not only Catholics but Protestants and Dissenters as well.

Games such as rugby union and soccer have some claim on the right to be called 'national' in the Irish context. Despite their British origins, they are played throughout the island. Moreover, although rugby tends to be played by Protestants rather than Catholics in Northern Ireland, both football codes enjoy considerable support from both traditions on the island as a whole. They offer Irish sportsmen the opportunity to represent the nation at international level. Indeed, rugby, unlike soccer, allows northern unionists the chance to acknowledge their sporting Irishness whilst retaining a political allegiance to the union of the United Kingdom and Northern Ireland. It should be noted, however, that regardless of any claims that either sport may have to be recognised as 'national', neither has escaped the influence of globalisation. The two Irish 'national' soccer teams have both fielded players whose ethnic 'right' to belong has been relatively weak. The same thing has happened in rugby union, which in recent years has witnessed a flood of antipodean coaches and players, some of whom have qualified to play for Ireland despite having accents that conjure up images of Dunedin or Durban, not Dublin or Dungannon.

Gaelic games have been less affected by the movement of people that is commonly linked to globalisation except in the sense that Irish migrants

have taken their traditional activities to other parts of the world, most notably
north America. This is not to deny that changes taking place beyond the shores
of Ireland have had an impact on the Gaelic Athletic Association (GAA). I
would argue, however, that the factors that have been most influential are best
understood in terms of modernisation and capitalism as opposed to the more
specific category of globalisation. Gaelic games, I shall argue, have been relatively unscathed by the latter. As a result, the GAA offers rich insights into the
processes whereby the nation has been able to resist the global in sport as in
much else.

Sport and the nation: the case of the Gaelic Athletic Association

As regards the relationship between sport and the nation, the GAA has arguably received more academic attention than any other sporting organisation.[29]
It has performed a central role in the reproduction of a particular form of Irish
national identity since its formation in Thurles, Co. Tipperary, in 1884 to the
present day, when images of hurlers promote a vision of Ireland, both real and
imagined, whilst simultaneously advertising beer. Today, according to
Humphries, 'three-quarters of a million Irish people are members of the
GAA, but that figure represents only a fraction of the Irish people who are
touched by the games of football and hurling in their regular daily lives'.[30] For
Humphries, 'the GAA is more than a sports' organization, it is a national trust,
an entity which we feel we hold in common ownership'.[31] In similar lofty tones,
Healey claims that 'the Association has become a national movement, a driving
force behind the people, a giant parental figure to the youth of the country'.[32] In
broadly cultural terms, therefore, there is no disputing the significance of the
GAA's historic and ongoing influence.

The GAA's influence *vis à vis* the construction of Irish national identity was
relatively straightforward in the years immediately after its formation with
debates between physical force nationalists and constitutionalists being the
only major area of discord. However, its role in relation to national identity
was thereafter considerably affected by the fact that Ireland itself became an
example of failed nation-state building, resulting in Gaelic games, organised on
a 32-county basis, being played from 1921 in two separate political jurisdictions.
In addition, most relevant in the context of this chapter, the Gaelic games
movement has been increasingly affected by socio-economic trends in Ireland
and also in the wider global economy. The impact on the GAA of socio-
economic change is by no means new. Industrialisation and urbanisation,
which were accompanied by the growth of soccer as a major sport for both
players and spectators, has been gnawing away at the rural roots of the
Association virtually since its inception. However, it can be argued that the
pace of change experienced during the past two decades has been greater than
anything known previously and the global and postmodern impulses which
are the result inevitably demand new articulations of Irishness which, in the

opinion of some, may have only limited space for Gaelic games and the construction of Irishness which is felt to be associated with them.

Yet the general influence of the GAA on Irish life remains undeniable. Today, the Association has a membership of around 800,000 with 2,700 clubs fielding approximately 20,000 teams. Although it is stronger in some parts of Ireland than in others, its influence is felt throughout the 32 counties. For many players in particular, the identity which the GAA forges is essentially a sporting one relatively free from political connotations. Thus in the 1999 edition of the *Irish Sports Almanac*, writing about the challenges which currently face the GAA, Liam Horan fails to comment on any of the issues discussed in this chapter, concentrating instead on the use of modern technology to help match officials deal with disciplinary matters.[33] Gaelic games have problems, according to this analysis, but they occur on the field of play and not at the level of intellectual discourse on nationality. At least as significant, however, is the GAA's symbolic role in the construction of the Irish landscape. Gaelic pitches evoke a sense of Irishness even for those who do not see them regularly as they go about their daily business. Thus, they are very much part of Ireland's 'imagined community'.[34] It should be added that Gaelic grounds are by no means unique in this respect. For example, in Northern Ireland, certain soccer grounds are important symbolic spaces that contribute to the construction of unionist and loyalist identities as well as Irish nationalist ones.[35] Established in an effort to democratise access to leisure activities in Ireland and to resist the process whereby a British cultural hegemony was being consolidated in sport as in other spheres of activity, the GAA quickly laid down roots particularly in the rural areas of nineteenth-century Ireland.[36] From the outset it embraced representatives of all branches of Irish nationalism, including the Catholic church which has consistently played an important part in the reproduction of Irish national identity even though this role has been greatly diminished in recent times. Despite the involvement of Protestant, and even unionist, members in its formation, in a relatively short space of time, the Association came to be regarded as providing sporting space for certain types of Irish people, mainly men and certainly Catholic and/or politically nationalist. This development was assisted in no small degree by a series of bans (1885, 1887, and 1905) which sought to prevent GAA members from playing or watching 'foreign' games, tried to ensure that GAA facilities would not be used for such games and barred members of the British security forces from GAA membership. The foreign games rules were removed in 1971 but Rule 21 which prevented members of the British armed forces, as well as the Royal Ulster Constabulary (RUC), from joining the GAA remained in force until November 2001, despite increasingly strenuous efforts by leading figures within the Association to have it rescinded. In addition to having to deal with competition from other sporting activities, together with wrestling with the quasi-political question of how to react to the crown forces, the GAA has been obliged increasingly to react to general changes in the way in which sport is organised globally in the direction of sponsorship, professionalism and, most recently, the labour organisation of players. In its responses to all of these issues the Association has revealed particular ways of representing Irishness whilst continuing to provoke hostile responses from those who believe that its representation of the nation is out-moded and inappropriate for the new, pluralist society which the GAA's critics believe is emerging.[37] As a result, one might be inclined to believe that its self-proclaimed role as the repository if Ireland's sporting soul, whatever its earlier credibility, is now impossible to justify.

Writing in 1994, Barrie Houlihan noted that 'while Gaelic sports continue to be popular, the last 10 years have witnessed a rapid increase in the popularity of soccer, helped by strong performances by the Irish team in the 1990 and 1994 World Cup competitions'.[38] Whilst acknowledging 'the capacity of the nation-alist Irish community to maintain a degree of autonomy within the global sports culture', Houlihan argued that 'while the symbolism of Gaelic sport is still acknowledged as a powerful demonstration of the particularity of the Irish nation, soccer is now able to fulfill a similar function before a global audience'.[39] There is of course a large degree of truth in this statement. However, it would be wrong to suppose either that the GAA's role is purely symbolic or that its contribution to the promotion of a distinctive Irish identity has been dimin-ished over time. The GAA is arguably as strong today as at any time in its history. Moreover, it can be argued that this strength is derived not so much from its symbolic representation of an older Ireland but rather from its capacity to respond to an Ireland that is changing, due in large part to global economic pressures. It might even be argued that the nationalism which associates itself with and is supported by the GAA is deeper than that which other sports inspire.

Conclusion

For the most part, political economy has tended to be invoked in support of relatively hard-line readings of globalisation that talk in terms of cultural homo-genisation and/or Americanisation. The figurational approach is more insightful in this respect because it takes into account the importance of reciprocal actions and unplanned consequences leading to a rather more complex if not quite entropic universe. Attempts to emphasise the capacity of the nation to resist global change appear to be more closely linked to the tradition of philosophical idealism. What is celebrated is the power of a largely irrational idea to confront brute economic facts. This is misleading. In reality, it is absolutely essential to adopt a perspective that gives primacy to socio-economic factors if one is to understand fully the reasons for the resilience of nations and nationalism in the global era.

Marxists have found the nation and nationalism notoriously difficult proposi-tions. Many have tended to view nationalist ideology, not unlike a passion for sport, as a product of false consciousness, except in circumstances where it was felt that national liberation might serve the cause of social and economic emancipation. In general nationalism has been regarded by the left as being at best antithetical to class politics and at worst downright reactionary. Modernisation theory, on the other hand, has tended to recognise the progressive impulse that lay behind the emergence of nationalism as a political force. But the approach is essentially historicist and denies all claims that nationalism has premodern roots and or that it can act progressively in a wide range of different historical conjunctures. The way is open, therefore, to the philosophical idealists who present the idea of the nation as something that has a perennial appeal. In political terms, this approach is most likely to find favour with reactionary nationalists – those who constantly look backwards with great nostalgia to a world of blood sacrifice and ethnic purity.

It would be easy to categorise the contemporary role of the GAA as a product of the idealism of nostalgia, now using 'idealism' in a slightly different way.[40] As a result, Gaelic games in the contemporary era are understood to be nothing more than reactionary strategies whereby disaffected people seek solace in outmoded forms of physical activity. It is undeniable that the GAA is an instinctively traditional organisation. Its popularity is still most apparent in rural areas and its subcultures can from time to time prompt thoughts of rural idiocy in the minds of even the most passionately Irish cosmopolitan urban dweller. It should be noted though that nostalgia has an honourable place in the construction of radical ideals.[41] In any case there is an alternative form of political idealism, which applies with at least equal force to the GAA – that is, idealism of the imagination. As the late Bob Berki observed, 'imagination is the dominant feature of radical thought in the sense that the radical thinker's major premise in all his arguments directed against existing arrangements is an "alternative"'.[42] For Berki, 'imagination means that the proposed desirable alternative is essentially, significantly new'.[43] On the face of it, it would seem ridiculous to regard the GAA as linked to a project that is in any sense 'new'. That, however, is to ignore the fact that the association is operating today in a context that is radically different from the one out of which it first emerged. As a result, simply doing the same things as it has always done and doing these things well allows the GAA to be seen as offering something not only different but new – new, that is, in terms of the changes that have accompanied the onset of the global era. It may well have reinvented itself as a mode of resistance not only to cultural imperialism, its first avowed aim, but also to all of the homogenising tendencies that accompany late capitalism. It is a paean to community life and to the worth of the real as opposed to the hyperreal. Resistance has not been totally effective as the packaging of Gaelic games reveals. Concerns must also continue to be expressed in relation to the ethnic exclusivity of the GAA. Nevertheless, and contrary to most academic analysis, I would argue that it is possible to defend the association as a progressive force once the true enemy of liberation has been correctly identified.

Irish nationalists themselves would claim that nationalism in Ireland has generally been inspired by a set of progressive political values even though, on occasion, these have been corrupted by certain organisations and individuals. Certainly, despite what its critics would say, at no stage in its history has the GAA as a whole acted in an absolutely reactionary manner. Indeed, today perhaps more so than at any point in its development, the association is now able to say that it has not only sought to remove traces of reactionary and exclusive nationalism but it has also come to offer, in sporting terms at least, one of the more enlightened models of how people can respond to global economics and the accompanying drift towards cultural homogeneity. Was this intended? The answer is surely 'no', if we are thinking purely in terms of conscious decisions made by people within the GAA to challenge the homo-genising tendencies that operate under late capitalism. The outcome was planned, however, to the extent that there has always been a widespread con-scious desire within the association to keep Gaelic games alive in a rapidly changing world whilst simultaneously embracing change whenever that has seemed advantageous to the promotion of Gaelic sport.

There is no doubt that many Irish people identify with national sporting heroes. They celebrate their triumphs and share their sorrow in defeat. To that extent, all of the sports that Irish people play, no matter how global in their appeal, provide avenues for expressions of national sentiment in the face of homogenising forces. Only Gaelic games, however, provide us with a window through which we can examine particular representations of Irishness at the beginning of the twenty-first century. This is because Gaelic games are linked more profoundly to Irish identity than those other sports, no matter how many Irish people play them and at what level. This is not to suggest that only Gaelic games are played by the 'real' Irish. It is to argue, however, that the relationship between the people and the sporting activities, in this instance, is less likely to be mediated by external forces. As a result, it is easier to discuss the link between sport and the nation free from the complexities that aspects of globa-lisation create for other sports. Much has changed over the years in the world of Gaelic games. It can be argued, however, that the experiences of players and fans alike suggest a large degree of resistance to global forces. Moreover, to understand more fully the place of sport in a global age, it is important that such experiences are not ignored.

Indeed, I wish to conclude with a rallying cry to those who seek to develop our understanding of the relationship between the global and the national in relation to sport. There has been an abundance of theory in the area. There has also been any amount of studies of transnational organisations, including those that are charged with running sport and those that seek to profit from sport if such a distinction can be said to exist in practice. Arguably, what we need most of all now are studies of how individual men and women are affected by and respond to the global-national nexus. Sport labour migration studies are excep-tional in this respect.[44] But they tend to focus on elite performers. But how is the hurler in Thurles, Co. Tipperary, influenced by globalisation on a day-to-day basis? What does the club footballer in Hilltown, Co Down, make of global complexity? For that matter, what does the rugby player in Dunfermline, the football fan in Burnley and the *aficionado* of the *corrida* in Seville make of it all? The answer in each case is that these people are certainly not influenced by the global era to such a degree that they are likely in the near future to abandon totally their sporting attachment to the local, the parochial and the national. It is ironic, given its commitment to traditionalism, that the GAA emerges from this chapter as a progressive force. On the other hand, there could well be a salutary and an emancipatory lesson to be learned from what might otherwise be too easily dismissed as a contradiction in terms.

7 The curious role of the USA in world sport

Lincoln Allison

Any assessment of the relation between 'Americanisation' and 'Globalisation' must revisit the problem faced by Alexis De Tocqueville when he wrote *Democracy in America*. De Tocqueville was ultimately more interested in 'democracy' than in America. He saw democracy as the destination of a set of tendencies which had been evident, in Western Europe at least, since the twelfth century and America as the place where these tendencies met with the least resistance.[1] Very broadly, these tendencies were a movement towards greater political and social equality plus a movement towards greater commercial freedom, the two tendencies being in inevitable and permanent tension. A particular aspect of that tension which naturally intrigued De Tocqueville was the survival and even revival of the 'aristocratic' principle, more often discussed by a later generation of writers under the heading 'elitism'.

'Modernity', as we might call it, and Americanism are thus intertwined. Some phenomena must be seen as democracy-in-America: they are best (or only) studied in the United States, but much of their interest lies in the probability that England or France will eventually demonstrate similar phenomena. But there are also peculiar features of the United states, arising out of local conditions. For example, the constant tension between constitutionalism and populism is one which all democracies will face in some form or another, but the particular problems which arise out of the existence of Indian tribes and slave states are rooted only in the soil of the United States.

At the heart of this chapter is the distinction between two kinds of Americanism and Americanisation and the complex inter-twining between them. The intention is to update De Tocqueville's framework and to apply it to sport. Even at a preliminary glance we can distinguish sporting versions of the two kinds of Americanism. For example, the power of television in sport is something which a Tocquevillian observer in the US of the 1950s and 1960s might have seen as a guide to all our futures, despite what now seem extraordinary degrees of resistance to it in other countries where the television industry remained dominated by the state. In contrast, there is no reason to suppose that the very particular and important role played by universities and colleges in American sport is going to spread elsewhere.

The two-way exceptionalism

We must begin with the near-universal perception of an American exceptionalism. As Eric Hobsbawm remarked, considering the twentieth century as a whole, in the 'field of popular culture the world was American or it was provincial' except in the unique instance of sport. What made sport so exceptional was the triumph of Association Football as the world's game, 'a simple and elegant game...the child of Britain's global presence'.[2] Markovits and Hellerman suggest that in 'soccer', 'Crudely put, America did not matter'.[3] Soccer, like socialism, provides an example of American exceptionalism: both are institutions which developed a major presence almost everywhere, but not in the USA.

Seen in this light the world of sport offers an ironic reversal of the generally dominant flow of cultural power. Because of soccer it is the USA which seems insular and provincial in world sport. A strong flavour of this reversal is offered at the beginning and end of *Offside*. In the preface, Markovits describes returning from Frankfurt to Boston during the 1986 World Cup Finals to face an almost posturing lack of interest in the event.[4] In the second appendix of the book the authors survey the reactions of the American press to the 1994 finals, held in the USA. As Ann Killion wrote in the San Jose *Mercury News*, 'We won't be allowed to simply enjoy the event... Too bad it comes with so many strings attached'.[5] Those strings include a supposed liberal agenda that America should give more credence to the world's game and non-liberal national reaction against that. This often showed itself in expressions of scorn against soccer by those who purported to have tried to watch matches, often emphasising the lack of athleticism and the absence of goals. Writers also stressed the record of hooliganism in the major centres of the game, rather gratuitously since this was not a problem during the championships. As Jake Vest put it in the Orlando *Sentinel*, 'This may be the world's most-beloved game, but the world has always been over-rated'.[6] A further element in the often vitriolic debate was a resentment that Americans were being expected to take an interest in soccer when the World Cup visitors were for the most part unashamedly uninterested in the sports of the host nation. In many respects, the kind of cultural conservatism stimulated in the 'antis' of this knockabout debate was the precise inverse of what many people in the rest of the world feel about America. In return for what Jean-Jacques Servan–Schreiber described in the 1950s as 'coca-colanisation' the 1994 World Cup was seen as an attempted soccerisation of the USA.

However, it would be quite wrong to be carried away by the brute fact of the absence of soccer as a real Major League American sport or by the passion of some reaction to that fact. The apparent antithesis between America and the rest of the world has to be modified by an acknowledgement of several complexities. One is that there are doubts and ambiguities about calling things 'American'. Another is that in some respects the sporting relationship between the US and the rest of the world does mirror the normal economic structure of power. In Lancashire, arguably the geographical cradle of working-class professional sport, the county cricket team in its one-day manifestation is now called 'Lancashire Lightning' while the most famous Rugby League club is 'Wigan Warriors' who play their traditionally winter game in the summer, ironically to create a global season in a sport which is played in fewer than a handful of countries. The name changes may be a trivial stylistic influence (though this is open to debate), but the season change in Rugby League is one of the major breeches of tradition in a British sport. All of these changes can be attributed to a form of Americanisation mediated through Australia. The arguments for them normally posit one of the two countries, if not both, as the example to follow in acknowledging the 'need' for sport to develop consumer-friendly, television-oriented forms in order to survive and prosper in an increasingly commercial society. Thus we can trace the 'Lightning' and the 'Warriors' as well as more significant changes to the fall of Singapore in 1942 and the consequent re-orientation of Australia's world-view towards a dominant USA.

It is also the case that if we broaden the concept of sport to that of leisure and conceive it as an industry then the relationship between Americanisation and globalisation seems more normal. The sports-goods industry is dominated by firms with power bases in the USA. Hollywood presents sports films such as 'Field of Dreams', 'Bad News Bears' and 'The Mighty Ducks' in an idiom the world can understand even if it is not the world's favourite idiom. A Martian who had access to cinema but to no other means of communication would come to the conclusion that American sport was also world sport. The new global systems of communication abound with anti-globalisation messages, most of them from young and Asian origins, which see their cultures threatened by a global-American package which includes fast food and rock music as well as basketball and baseball.

But I will be insisting throughout this essay that we must not equate America with Major League. Even in soccer the US looks a much more 'normal' society below the professional level, with its nineteen-million participants and domination of the women's game. Also we must question the extent to which the 'American' sports culture is actually American as opposed to being a conduit for essentially British ideas and institutions. The US imported the idea of the organised game from England. Two of its major sports, baseball and football, are clearly English in origin while ice hockey is Canadian. Only basketball is truly American in origin. Important minor sports, especially golf, tennis and track and field athletics, are also British in origin and to a greater extent than in the major sports have continued to imitate British practice. Of course, one should not attribute too much significance to mere origin; the perception of origin is usually more important. The continued success of soccer is not seen in the twentieth century as an 'Anglicisation' because the game is seen as a global phenomenon, shaped by global forces. Almost equally, cricket and Rugby Union have been internalised in South Asia and the Southern Hemisphere and their re-shaping owes as much to distinctive cultural traits in those countries as to their English origins. A New Zealand rugby fan or an Indian cricket fan is not likely to emphasise the 'Englishness' of their sport whereas they may well put greater emphasis on the American qualities of basketball simply because the US is identified as a source of cultural power.

Thus, the analysis of the relations between globalisation and Americanisation in sport involves almost every kind of conceptual difficulty. We are talking about influence, always a matter of conjecture and vagueness; to make matters worse it is a question of cultural influence. In any case, there are at least three senses of 'American' sources of influence. There are those which are American in the sense that the US experiences the consequences of some kinds of general tendency earlier than other societies. There are those which the US has taken from elsewhere (most often from Britain) and transmitted to itself and to other parts of the world with degrees of change which may vary from the essential to the superficial. And there are those which are peculiar to the US itself. In order to understand and evaluate 'Americanisation' in world sport it is thus necessary to analyse what is distinctive in American sport, the sense in which it is distinctive and from what it is distinctive.

The peculiarities and distinctiveness of American sport

In this section I intend to distinguish five important aspects of sport in the United States which, in different ways and according to variable comparisons, make it different from sport elsewhere. In doing so I will be invoking a wide variety of sources, but an especially useful source has been the work of those historians who have sought to explain the failure of association football and cricket to assume the kind of role in American society that they did elsewhere and were often expected to in the US.

Commercialism

By commercialism I mean a tendency for social arrangements to run according to principles of free markets and fair exchange combined with a belief in the propriety of those arrangements. In this sense much of the political history of sport consists of attempts to protect it from commercial forces thought likely to debase and corrupt it. I have argued elsewhere that the key episode in the history of British sport (also key, to varying degrees, in the Empire and an extended sphere of influence) was 'the establishment of an amateur hegemony' between 1863 and 1895, particularly the establishment of a set of ruling bodies ranging (in time) from the Football Association to the International Olympic Committee which were committed to the extreme mitigation of commercial forces.[7]

Of course, we would expect a greater degree of commercialism from the US. Writers from De Tocqueville to Antonio Gramsci have observed that the distinctive feature of American society is the absence of obstacles to the development of commercialism. Gramsci's account of 'Fordism' is of a political culture which uniquely accepts and admires a kind of capitalist brutality.[8] But a simple account of American sport as capitalist sport would be quite wrong. American elites absorbed and even exaggerated the British view of sport. Games were to be played to foster Christian decency and republican virtue, chiefly masculine virtue, not to make money. From John Mahaffy to Grantland Rice to Avery Brundage some of the strongest protestations of amateur principles are from American writers. I shall argue that these values are still present in American sport and embedded in many of its important institutions. But the crucial factor is that in the US space was left for the development of a purely commercial conception of sport. British and American sport developed along lines which were similar in many respects in the 1860s and 1870s; their paths diverged when baseball was allowed to develop freely as a set of competing (and often chaotic) commercial enterprises whereas national authorities were established in Britain to prohibit, exclude or limit the commercial principle.[9] Markovits and Hellerman are quite right to emphasise that one of the two most important differences between the US and other countries in sport is the absence of bodies like the Football Association and the Marylebone Cricket Club which had effective power to license and control clubs and competitions (the other being the lack of international competition in the principal sports). It was only baseball which developed in this space; until the television age professional football and basketball remained almost as marginalised in American society as Rugby League was in England. But the uninhibited development of baseball as the paradigm and exemplar of a Major League sport was immensely important and quite different from what happened elsewhere, as is illustrated by the fact that in 1930 the earnings of Babe Ruth, the most famous baseball player of the day, were more than twenty times those of Dixie Dean, the most notable English soccer player.

If the political space allowed for the development of baseball as a commercial sport in the 1880s was crucial to the nature of American sport, the continued existence of this space in the television age of the 1950s allowed the development of the Major League concept on a different scale. In retrospect, one of the most astonishing episodes in the history of sport is the absolute refusal of sporting authorities in most countries, including Britain, France and Australia, to exploit the potential of television as it became the dominant means of communication. English football all but banned the live televising of games; Australian cricket refused to sell to the highest bidder; nowhere were existing arrangements allowed to change substantially to suit the new medium. But in the US, television and Major League were allowed to grow symbiotically in the 1950s. At the beginning of the decade there were only 42 Major League franchises; by the end there were 101. By comparison, there were exactly the same number of 'first class' cricket counties and Football League clubs in England at the end of the decade as there were at the beginning. In 1950, it was estimated that less than 10 per cent of the population of the US in 1950 had ever seen major league sport. By 1960, more than 90 per cent of the population had some acquaintance with one or other of the Major League sports through the medium of television. The three major sports (or four if you include the more regionally limited case of ice hockey) developed in a network of intense capitalist competition between television networks, rival sports and rival leagues.

The development of Major League sport was unique in the world. The established civil authorities did not allow such a development in the countries in which sport was already established while in the Communist and post-colonial regions sport was controlled by the state for a variety of purposes, normally connected with nation-building and modernisation. The legacy of this control has lasted into the twenty-first century.[10] Major League sport is thus the unique paradigm for those who wish to commercialise and 'modernise' sport elsewhere. It is the principal dynamic of 'Americanisation' and a multiple source of debate about the reform of more traditional systems. However, the temptation to equate America with Major League in sport must be resisted. Much of American sport, including the vast majority of sports, lies outside the Major League ambit and it is as American to be concerned about the greed, unscrupulousness and vulgarity of Major League sport as it is to follow it. James Michener's famous essay on what is good and bad about American sport carries considerable resonance more than a quarter of a century on and the kind of arguments he invoked are still discussed a great deal more enthusiastically than are party politics.[11]

'Razzmatazz'

The word 'razzmatazz' came into being in the context of American popular music in the first half of the twentieth century, but it has come to be more generally used by outside observers of the US to denote a certain style of presentation, especially in sport. Bands, pom-pom girls, cheerleaders, wild celebration, the exploitation of every available commercial opportunity: these are the essence of 'American razzmatazz', frequently loathed by cultural conservatives but admired by modernisers in the rest of the world. Sometimes the worlds of English and American sport can seem like cultural opposites. In England we still expect a 'breathless hush', to use Sir Henry Newbolt's phrase, to dignify certain sporting moments like the last man going in to bat in the last over or the kicking of a vital penalty goal in a rugby match. Even in English soccer in the early twenty-first century crowds will diligently observe one-minute silences for recently deceased dignitaries or former players though they do not accord the same respect to a visiting penalty-taker as do rugby crowds. Meanwhile, in the US Major Leagues, the big moments are marked by the organ playing, the scoreboard flashing and the dancing girls dancing. American sport seems unequivocal about its status as 'entertainment' while British sport sells itself as a combination of pageant, tradition and expression of identity. It is possible, though, to find both styles within the same sport: the All-England tennis championships at Wimbledon are a pure case of the 'Old English' style, but the presentation of British home ties in the Davis Cup is copied directly from the (US) National Basketball Association and incorporates lasers and heavy rock music.

It is clear that these cultural differences have very deep roots. When cricket was at its peak in the US, in the 1850s, yet was beginning to attract some nationalist opprobrium, the game as played by Englishmen was often derided for its solemnity. For example, in 1859 Mortimer Neal Thompson, a popular humorist, described cricket as 'a solemn ceremony periodically performed by deluded Englishmen who think they are having fun.'[12] Even then it was customary to remark that batsmen raised in the US were much more aggressive than was either orthodox or wise. The counter-factual hypothetical suggested by Melville's research on ante-bellum cricket is that if Americans had been able to evolve and control their own form of the game it would have been modernised, shortened and Americanised and might well have come to occupy the space actually taken up by an intensified form of rounders.

Thompson's comment will ring true to most people who have played amateur sport in an Anglo-American context in the twentieth century. It is reminiscent of American Rhodes Scholars in Oxford rugby games embarrassing English public schoolboys by yee-hawing when the latter have scored a try. Or the sole American who has found his way into a village or college cricket team who whoops when an opposition wicket falls as the English captain apologises to the batsman, 'Bad luck, batsman. Sorry about that.' The differences of culture – or 'national character' as the Victorians would have put it – are long-lasting and profound, though ultimately inexplicable given the range of factors involved.

The transfer of sporting cultures to the mass media represented and magnified existing differences. Lord Reith's BBC discouraged a personality cult of commentators as it discouraged the camera crew for dwelling on the crowd for fear of encouraging 'showing off'. The objective was to present sport with dignity and avoiding changing what you were showing. Television was a poor person's poor alternative to real attendance. Roone Arledge's ABC took almost exactly the opposite approach, changing times to suit TV rather than live audiences, positively encouraging showing off by both crowd and players and creating the commentator as a star, beginning with Howard Cosell. Only in the 1990s did Arledge's assumptions about the televising of sport become the norm in Britain.

A Calvinist theology of winners and losers

Vince Lombardi, the coach of the Green Bay Packers who dominated the early Superbowls in the 1960s, famously said that 'Winning isn't the main thing – it's the only thing'. Paul Gardner transferred a business slogan to sport with his book *Nice Guys Finish Last*.[13] It is something of a cliché to say that American sport, particularly football, serves as a metaphor for capitalist life: both can be seen as a kind of Darwinist jungle in which you discover whether you are a winner or a loser. Or do you have the free will to decide? The ambiguity is parallel to that in Calvinist theology in which membership of the divine elite (the ancient past participle of the verb 'to choose' in French) is both predestined and meritorious. The most obvious symptom of the American obsession with winning is the unmarketability of the drawn contest. 'Ties' occur in only very rare circumstances in Major League sport whereas they are a substantial minority of results in both cricket and football in England.

But to accept the picture of Major League sport as a brutal struggle to find winners is to accept its sales hype rather than its realities. Because of the exclusivity of Major League sport and the institution of the draft the strength of teams is fairly even so everybody experiences victory and defeat on a fairly regular basis. Because the Major Leagues have organised themselves on sustainably commercial lines those involved are shielded from many of the harsher consequences of failure as they exist in British sport. There is no relegation to a lower league and under an arrangement specifically permitted by the Sports Broadcasting Act of 1961 TV rights are pooled. By British standards clubs have essentially sound finances and most are effectively subsidised by local government. All in all Major League sport is more like a cosy cartel than a ruthless capitalist competition. As Art Modell, the owner of the Cleveland Browns said of the National Football League owners in 1978, 'We're twenty-eight republicans who vote socialist'.[14] Not for the Major League competitor is the prospect of defeat which may mean not just relegation, but even the demise of the club. Nor do they have to face the extreme pressures of representative international competition where you may have to take a penalty on which your nation's hopes rest.

Yet mythology is also, of course, a social reality. The myth of a society of winners and losers with Major League football in particular as its sporting metaphor is an important element of American culture which is constantly transmitted abroad through films and television.

Athleticism and superlativism

The generic term for those who play sports and games in England is 'sportsman/woman'. In the US it is 'athlete', a term which in England refers only to 'track and field' athletes. It could be argued that this is a trivial difference in usage, but I do not think so. Whereas 'sportsman' suggests activities defined by sporting values such as fairness, judgement and dedication, 'athlete' suggests primarily a commitment to extreme physical achievement. And, indeed, if you suggest to a group of American football fans that their game is boring, over-specialised and lacking in the kinds of skill you need to play soccer or cricket (an experiment I have tried on several occasions), the reaction is normally to point to hard athletic facts which other sports cannot rival such as the existence of 300-pound players who can run the 100 metres in under eleven seconds. Major League sells itself as a place of superlatives, even – in the cases of football and basketball – as a kind of freak show. It justifies itself as the real location of the values of '*Citius, Altius, Fortius*'. As a spectator you are prepared to pay its prices because you are seeing the very best. In this respect its claims contrast quite sharply with those of domestic competitions in other countries whose appeal is much more based on partisanship and tradition and which do not portray themselves as the supreme level of competition because that accolade belongs to the international level of the sport.

However, it is clear that insofar as athleticism and superlativism distinguish the culture of American sport from the sporting cultures of other societies, they do so to different degrees. The contrast with Britain would be a much sharper one than the contrast with Germany, for example, where athleticism and super-lativism have been admired much more than they have in Britain. It is inter-esting to note that the perception of American athleticism has marked Anglo-American rivalry throughout the history of modern sport. In the early modern Olympics the American press was keen to point out that although their team did not always win the most medals they did win the more athletic events and they even published alternative medal tables which left out the more sedentary events which the British tended to win.[15]

The relationship between sport and education

The idea that what we now call sport (or sports) should be an essential part of a system of education, aiding the development of community and individual character as well as the health of children and young people is one which was imported in its entirety from Britain to the US. But it is an idea which took on wholly new forms and a life of its own on American soil. Nothing else in the world is comparable with the American system of college and university sport and relatively little is comparable with high school sport in the US. There are more than four and a half thousand institutions of higher education, the vast majority of which run sports teams and the majority of which offer sports scholarships. According to the National Collegiate Athletic Association more than 90 per cent of the paying audience for live sport in the US is for college sport and more than 99 per cent of athletes who perform in front of a paying audience are college athletes. Even on television the audience for the sum total of college sport is roughly equal to that for Major League.[16] The college system, just as much as Major League, is a typically and uniquely American institution. In the grandest of American universities, such as Stanford in California, the quality of facilities is such that an Olympic Games could be relocated there without further investment; World Cup soccer and professional football's Superbowl have already been held at Stanford.

Perhaps the most convincing way of demonstrating the rootedness of college sport in American life is by showing how it overcame considerable opposition to become what it is today. It is generally accepted that the early development of college sport, before the Civil War, was student-led and British-inspired. Even after 1865 most college authorities were either indifferent or hostile to orga-nised games, regarding them as an unscholarly diversion. The vestiges and legacy of this hostility have lasted throughout the history of college sport. Matters came to a head in the early twentieth century with the death of at least twelve college footballers in 1902; in the subsequent discussions and investigations college football was described in an extreme case as a 'boy-killing, education-prostituting, so-called sport' and it was 'touch and go' whether it would be banned. In 1905 the (Teddy) Roosevelt Commission recommended rule changes in football and in 1906 the Inter-Collegiate Athletic Administration (which developed into the NCAA) was established. College sport had begun to develop the vast culture and organisation which it now has. The opposition was never entirely eradicated: the 'Ivy League' of prestigious Eastern colleges opted out of the system, formally establishing a separate conference in 1956. In 1939, the University of Chicago opted out of formal sporting competition altogether. It is plausible to suggest that nothing like modern college sport might have evolved if the USA had remained as thirteen states (or even the twenty-four of the De Tocqueville period). It was in provincial America, in the Mid-West and the backwoods of the South that college sport took on new dimensions. States needed universities not only as channels for individual aspirations but also as a focus for local pride. Universities, in turn, became the torch-bearers for reason and progress in deeply provincial communities. College sport became a way of attracting the general support of the community to the university. It thus shares an historic origin in certain respects with the institution of tenure. One of its achievements, in my view, is that the inhabitants of Ohio regard Ohio State University as 'their' institution to a degree which is inconceivable in the relationship, for example, between the University of Warwick and the people of Warwickshire.

The college system remains the object of much cynicism and criticism. Arguably it is a system of pseudo-professional sport foisted on to higher education and its effects are to distort admissions, to undermine academic life and to exploit athletes. It may not be the direct 'boy-killer' it was a century ago, but NCAA figures show that well over half of Afro-American scholarship athletes neither graduate nor proceed to Major League and many of those are almost literally cast on to the streets having tasted the glories of large crowds, TV coverage and fan adulation. The system can simultaneously be accused of combining some of the worst excesses of professional sport with the exploitation of amateurs. Most European observers are likely to perceive it as a form of pseudo-professionalism, being aware of the draft system which feeds college players into Major League and of the status of college golf, for example, as a kind of 'junior pro' tour.

All of this is true, but a more balanced picture must acknowledge a wide range of contributions made by college sport to American life. The NCAA alone has more than 1250 institutional members and runs championships in eighteen principal sports. Many institutions, including most of the smaller and older colleges, are not members of the NCAA but are involved in sport to some degree. Many sports (including rugby and cricket) are not governed by the NCAA. College sport remains the heartland of the American sports fan. Geographically its tentacles extend to places hundreds of miles beyond the remit of Major League. Historically it has a permanence and sense of tradition precisely because its activities are dominated by sporting and communal values rather than by commerce. As they say in Indiana, 'The Colts (the Indianapolis football team which moved from Baltimore) may come and go, but Purdue versus Notre Dame will always be the Big Match'. Howard Nixon argues that sport is very much part of the 'American Dream', but it is college sport which best fits that role, allowing the local hero, the all-rounder, to progress from sporting victory to business and communal success.[17]

In certain respects the American system of college sport is the focus for sporting values and cultures in the way that professional sport is in England. It is also a system at least nominally founded on the ideals of amateurism and sportsmanship. The NCAA is an overtly amateur organisation (with a 17-page definition of amateur status in its regulations).[18] Its ideals are of the 'student-athlete' and of sport as an 'avocation'. It runs a system of awards for all-rounders who succeed in the classroom and on the field. Much of the appeal of college sport lies not in the superlative, but in the dogged support of the local. It is as much about romance as about the grinding out of excellence: the 'March Madness' basketball tournament allows for one-off acts of giant-killing which are anathema to Major League and more like the appeal of the FA Cup. The stout businessman who once played a whole five minutes as a substitute defensive end in front of 90,000 people and the TV cameras regards the experience as part of his success, whereas a five-minute career in professional sport would be a frustrating failure.

College sport is not usually given credence for its values; much of the debate about it concentrates on its spectacular excesses and failings, notwithstanding that these occur in a handful of sports and a minority of colleges. But it has remained amateur not only in the aspiration that all competitors be genuine 'student-athletes', but also, for example, in the strict confining of competition to undergraduates and to a maximum of four years and in the prohibition of financial incentives for sporting success. In some respects, like the abolition of athletic residential buildings, the hyphenated aspiration has been intensified. Above all, college sport remains the locus for debate about sporting values and ideals which are still in place in contrast to the drug-, strike- and crime-ridden milieu of Major League. Newspapers all over the US run stories and features on the issues of college sport such as whether the equality of women has gone too far or whether anything can be done to revive the 'walk-in' (the athlete who has no sports scholarship but wants to try out for a team place). These two issues are linked because it is the requirement to give equal facilities to female competitors under Title IX which restricts the space for additional squad members in the principal male sports. The assumption of these debates is that college sport still has a soul, culturally speaking, even if it is in constant danger of losing or selling that soul.

The ideas of globalisation and Americanisation

I have so far avoided discussing the contemporary conceptual debate about globalisation, largely because there is so much of it. Globalisation in its most general sense is the breaking down of boundaries so that the world tends to become a single system of society. One might imagine this happening on a planet which consisted of a set of roughly equal states which acted primarily as independent units but also in some respects as a system (a 'Westphalian' system as it is often called in international relations). As barriers broke down, as trade and migration increased and as regulatory bodies developed which covered the whole planet, we might witness an even and consensual globalisation. This would be a complicated and multi-dimensional process: trade, capital flows, institutional governance and culture might tend to move in the same direction as each other, but they might also rest or move independently or even inversely. Migration might be at a high level, for example, because of the strength of the Westphalian system and the consequent failure of economic opportunities and political rights to cross frontiers. Reactions to the growth of international trade may include attempts to protect and 'ring-fence' totemic cultural goods.

The issue becomes yet more complex on our real planet where the differences in power between states and the organisations based in them are enormous and where there has been since 1989 a sole superpower. Theories of the integration of the globe began the twentieth century as theories of imperialism developed by such writers as Hobhouse, Roy and Lenin. In the second half of the twentieth century some core ideas had been absorbed into the neo-structuralist theories of the United Nations Commission for Latin America, but also dependency theories and world systems theories which portrayed integration as a relationship between a 'core' (which gains and controls) and a 'periphery' which becomes increasingly dependant. These are a range of theories which greatly complicate the ideas of transfer and integration, turning them into accounts of power and imposition.[19]

It is at least possible that power and influence could exist as counter-flows, that Rome could absorb much from Greece, so to speak. But such influence tends to go unnoticed or not to be categorised as globalisation, certainly not in the adverse sense in which globalisation and Americanisation are often equated. Thus a room full of French children eating hamburgers and wearing baseball caps (backwards) is easily theorised as globalisation whereas a room full of mid-Western businessmen eating warm salad with lardons or deep fried camembert is merely sophistication, possibly globalisation, but certainly not Gallicisation. Although French influence in the US may be great and increasing (in some respects, and despite overtly anti-French prejudice) it is not normally understood as the consequence of a power structure, but of free choice. Jose Bove and his followers attack McDonald's in France, but nobody is counter-attacking the Frenchified restaurants of middle America. Yet it is also possible that free choices to mutual benefit may also occur in the context of cultural transfers from a powerful to a less powerful state.

All of which is intended as further notes of conceptual caution and as a framework for the concluding consideration of the extent of Americanisation in world sport. This will be done by considering three dimensions of the problem: first, by an overview of the main headings under which globalisation is considered and how they work in sport, second by assessing the main features of American sport in terms of their achievement and potential for transfer to the rest of the world and finally by asking the question of whether and in what respects a particular kind of cultural conservative might be concerned about American influence in sport.

The dimensions of globalisation

There are aspects of sports which make the US look like the 'core' of world sport in relation to a dependent periphery. In many kinds of sports goods the system of production is dominated by American capital even when the labour and the market are predominantly elsewhere.[20] In films, the world watches American sports film, but not vice versa. Arguably, basketball has an NBA core in relation to which the rest of the world is a periphery, aspiring to the standards and products of the American institution. A similar situation exists in (ice) hockey where Canadians often feel they have been peripheralised by a National Hockey League centred on the US.[21] But in some cases this is reversed: in the mighty case of soccer England feels like the core (along with Spain and Italy) with players from all other countries, including the US, aspiring to the prestigious European leagues and spectators throughout the globe (including an American minority cult) wanting to watch English games. There has been some cultural penetration by American sports in European markets: baseball peaked in the 1940s (and established a permanent place in Italian sport) and football peaked in the 1980s, but this process has been dwarfed by the American importation of soccer and rugby as alternative participatory sports. US interests are not disproportionately represented in the relatively powerful systems of global sports governance though that representation has certainly increased in the Olympic movement since the success of Peter Ueberroth in commercialising the games in his organisation of the Los Angeles games of 1984. In short, it is difficult to portray the US as exercising the kind of dominance in globalisation that it does in economic organisation.

Exporting the peculiarities of American sport

I have argued that the college system is the heart of American sport. It remains deeply rooted in American life and with some influence on individuals in the rest of the world through foreign scholarships, but it remains essentially a national phenomenon: its sartorial styles export easily enough, but its essence does not. A rare and minor example of imitation was in the news in 2002 when Team Bath, a soccer team of subsidised sports studies students based on Bath University became the first university team since the nineteenth century to reach the first round proper of the FA Cup where they lost 2–4 to Mansfield Town. The team had been established by a previous American vice-chancellor. However, it was widely commented that, whereas in a top American college football game you will see future stars of the professional game, Team Bath consisted of failed and ex-professionals. Soccer is still a game in which players are expected to start early, remain dedicated and skip university: Markovits and Hellerman show that of 132 players in the top six squads in the 1998 World Cup only two had been to university.[22] A great deal of soccer may be played in the American college system, but it has very little bearing on the global game.

An assessment of the culturally penetrative capacities of American athleticism must be more equivocal, not least because some other cultures – notably Slavic and Germanic cultures – also tend to value the purely athletic more than does British culture. There is also a difference between admiring the remarkable abilities of individual athletes like Muhammed Ali and Michael Jordan and wanting to absorb a more pure form of athleticism into one's own sporting culture. However, since the peak of the popularity of American sports in the late 1980s we can identify a number of factors which have led to a revival of soccer and a decline of interest in athleticism (including a drastic decline in the popularity of track and field athletics). Drugs are certainly part of the problem and a widespread public cynicism about their use puts more of a premium on games of craft and judgement. Race is also an issue with an equally widespread perception (however misconceived or badly theorised) that outstanding athletes tend to be of African origin. Thus, although it is a complex issue, there are undoubtedly considerable and growing obstacles to European admiration for the American totem of the 300-pound 11-second man.

Equally, since I have already dismissed the cult of the 'winner' as a kind of 'Sunday truth' (as Bertrand Russell would have put it) it is unlikely to have much culturally penetrative capacity. But one aspect of that cult is possibly more influential: the abhorrence of the draw as 'like kissing your sister'.[23] Draws have traditionally been a common and accepted part of both soccer and cricket while American sports fans have (uniquely) found them entirely unsatisfactory: they were part of the case against cricket even in the 1850s. It is true that as one-day cricket (and limited-over cricket at the amateur level) have become a larger proportion of the game draws are much less frequent and that in soccer many forms of cup game now incorporate arrangements to produce a winner at the first attempt (or the second in the case of the FA Cup). Whether these changes can be attributed directly to American influence as opposed to acceptance of other forces of change is impossible to tell.

Which brings us to the aspect of Americanisation which must be considered most seriously. Major League has set an agenda for world sport in two distinguishable, but overlapping ways. First, there is its style which has often been so appealing to people in more traditional (or, arguably, backward) societies. In the 1980s, especially, when English soccer had an image of hooliganism and semi-dereliction many of its administrators and commentators looked to the bright orderliness of Major League for their salvation. The dancing girls, the 'family' atmosphere, the purpose-built, all-seater stadia were seen as the only alternative if the game was to revive. Indeed, 'Premier League' does ape Major League in many of its essentials (including ticket prices and the removal of standing terraces) though in few of its stylistic details: cheerleaders are extremely rare and the cult of the pie has kept popcorn at bay. If Major League has set the agenda, though, it has met with vigorous debate rather than a nem. con. vote. There is a vast body of fan-writing which condemns these changes, normally on the grounds that the Major League atmosphere is bland and anodyne.[24] Premiership grounds remain contested territories in this respect as in others.

But more important than the style of Major League is its logic. American professional sport has established structures for a sustainable commercial sport. Elsewhere, sport has either resisted commercial forces and/or they have been unleashed on top of existing sporting institutions which are neither truly commercially viable nor do they have the means of adaptation. At the time of writing, for example, at least 90 per cent of English football clubs are insolvent in at least some sense. There is a far more urgent need to learn from Major League than mere admiration for a more commercial style. Real commercial logic applied to team sports in the early twenty-first century means very few clubs, operating at the highest possible level and oriented towards a televised market, preferably internationally. As far as the big money is concerned the rest of sport consists of support services. Another implication, outside the USA, is that international competition becomes increasingly important at the expense of domestic competition.

Consider two examples of arguments generated by Major League logic. The first concerns the issue of relegation in English Rugby Union which has been riven with disputes over fundamentals ever since it allowed payment to players in 1996. The question at issue is over whether the top level of the game (also called the Premiership) should be 'ring-fenced'. Protection of top status has been vehemently advocated by Rob Andrew, Director of Rugby at the Newcastle club and formerly one of England's top players. The argument has been put very clearly by Nigel Wray, the owner of the Saracens club, who compares living with the prospect of relegation to trying to manage a property with only a twelve-month lease. 'Promotion and relegation are the reasons why 95% of football clubs are financially shot to pieces ... (they) are alien concepts in Australia and America and, if we're honest, they're rather better at sport than we are ... Relegation leads to chaos. It leads to a lack of financial planning ...'[25]

The vast majority of people (according to an email poll conducted by John Inverdale) were opposed to this view. As Maurice Lindsay, chairman of the Orrell club, put it, all clubs must be part of a pyramid in which you can rise as high or fall as low as your playing merit dictates: 'Because sport is all about having a dream'.[26] Pyramid systems now exist in football, cricket, rugby and hockey. In cricket, the 'first class' level is ring-fenced, but promotion and relegation between two divisions were introduced in the year 2000. Ironically, pyramid systems are fairly new in English sport, largely a product of the 1980s. The sports authorities approved them because they were meritocratic and more in tune with modern sentiment than the supposed 'old boy networks' they replaced. Yet Wray's argument that they are incompatible with a genuinely business approach to sport is surely valid. As is Lindsay's argument that the Major League concept is incompatible with traditional English ideas about sporting organisation. One should perhaps add that for all the validity of Wray's argument it does not acknowledge that in the American model the league is a firm and the clubs are franchises, which is a very different structure from the norm in English sport where the club itself is a firm.

The parallel argument in football is that the traditional system of 92 professional clubs is not commercially viable. Peter Kenyon, Chief Executive of Manchester United, has said 'I don't think you can have four divisions of professional football any longer'. In reply Gordon Taylor, the Chief Executive of the Professional Footballers Association, cites our national pride in having the largest number of clubs of any country in the world and adds 'football's part in the social fabric is even more important – it brings communities together on a regular basis'. Once again it is much easier to find supporters of Taylor than of Kenyon, but it is clear that in football as well the logic of a truly commercial sport is incompatible with English tradition.[27]

Although the reformers of English sport often do look directly to America for their examples, they more often look to Australia, which in many respects mediates between the two. Much of the reason for this is that we have to play Australia, especially at cricket, and usually come off worse. As Michael Parkinson, a leading sports journalist and a strident moderniser, puts it, 'The basic difference between the way we and the Australians run cricket is that we still hanker for the past. We debate the merits of one-day cricket, coloured clothing, floodlights, covered wickets, technology and the county system. We are suspicious of change. Australians embrace it ... Consequently, while they have prospered, we have atrophied'.[28]

We can speculate as to the reasons that tradition has proved so much less of an obstacle to modernisation and commercialisation in Australia than it has in Britain. The country has a self-image of newness rather than oldness; its club structure is much smaller and less embedded; its media empires have been particularly dynamic and aggressive; it has been more positively oriented towards America. Whatever the reasons, the consequences have been a dynamic for change in Australia, which often apes American practice either intentionally or subconsciously. There is a 'World Series' in Australian cricket, the score boards offer amusing animation (such as a weeping, waddling duck to represent a player who is dismissed without scoring) and media presentation is much more American BC than BBC.

The test of cultural conservatism

In the 1980s there was, allegedly, something that amounted to a 'moral panic' in Europe about the prevalence of American programmes on prime time television.[29] The European Commission went so far as to single out the saga *Dallas* as the focus of its concerns. I confess to having been a fan of *Dallas* (to the extent of possessing books about the making of the programme). I appreciate the theoretical argument, later put by the French Government during World Trade Organisation negotiations, that the American product is expensively made, but that the marginal costs of its distribution are low so that it can in effect be 'dumped', crowd out the local products and thus undermine national cultures. However, I could not bring myself to regard *Dallas* as a threat to English identity.

In general, though, I would admit to a cultural conservatism which is incompatible with pure market liberalism. There are aspects of our culture which may be undermined by economic change and which we may seek to protect politically, I am here using 'culture' in Scitovsky's sense of goods which do not just give us 'pleasure', but contribute to our senses of meaning and identity.[30] These goods in my case would include aspects of the English countryside, pubs and theatre for example. It is typical of cultural conservatism in this sense that we are not content to enjoy such totemic goods, but seek to 'list' and preserve them 'for future generations' and that the failure to do so would undermine and even destroy present pleasure.

Some of these goods are sporting: the extent of English professional football, both in general and as a supporter of a particular club and the network of seven thousand clubs and a quarter of a million players in English amateur cricket. Some of the sporting goods are even less definable: the *spirit* of English amateur cricket, the *atmosphere* of major sporting events like Cheltenham and Wimbledon. Are they 'under threat'? It is a difficult question to answer: as with many evaluations of change it is hard to pick a path between arch-conservatism, which sees all change as destruction, and Panglossianism which refuses to acknowledge that change can ever be truly destructive of good. What are the sources of change which might be seen as destructive? One is an increasing commercialism which subjects more activities to market criteria than was previously the case. Another is the social dimension of commercialisation, meaning that people spend a higher proportion of their time on specific acts of production and consumption, leaving less time for the voluntary and amateur aspects which lie in between. In what senses can these changes be called Americanisation? They certainly involve the rest of the world becoming more like America, but one cannot attribute any intention to Americanise, nor can one prove an answer to the question of whether they would have occurred if the United States did not exist. We are back to De Tocqueville's problem of the relationship between 'democracy' and 'America'.

In its sporting dimension, as in several others, the US is both exceptional and influential. By offering a model of commercial sport, America sets the agenda for change. It would be wrong to blame America because its influence is neither intentional nor malicious. But it is not illogical to resent Americanisation in this sense, because its influence is hostile to many of the sporting values and institutions which have been held dear elsewhere.

8 Local heroes and global stars

Paul Gilchrist

On 9th January 2002 the American golfer Tiger Woods entered New Zealand's capital, Wellington, as a guest at a gala charity dinner. His presence in the country was owing to the latest tournament on the global circuit, the New Zealand Open at Paraparaumu. The preparations for his visit mirrored those of the arrival of a Head of State. Bomb squads, accompanied dogs, scoured the surrounding area for explosive devices and possible traces of terrorist activity. Police helicopters circled overhead. Fences had been erected around the landing site and Special Forces covered the perimeter by manning strategic rooftop positions. However, Woods flew into Queens Wharf amidst controversy. Waiting to greet him was an assembled mass of protesters who had decided to target the golfer as the centrepiece to their anti-globalisation demonstration. They were protesting about poor working conditions for workers in South East Asian 'sweatshops'. The cause of their protest was unjust pay differentials between Woods, who had signed a five-year endorsement contract with Nike worth US$100 million (roughly US$130,000 a day) for wearing a Nike baseball cap, while workers received a US$2 a day pittance. The demonstration was a lively affair, led by chants of 'Nike, Nike take a Hike!' and began with a street theatre in which child workers were wheeled out in front of an assembled panel of corporate fat cats and auctioned off. The irony being that 'Mr. Nike' bid the lowest price and wheeled off his new workers to the factory. Tiger, who confronted the protesters at one point, simply remained mute, beamed his brilliant white smile and looked slightly bemused by the whole affair.[1]

This chapter attempts to understand the sport star's response to political and ethical questions in light of tensions between community and individualism, performance and representation, which are at the heart of the idea of the sporting hero. Its premise is to argue that globalisation has agitated these tensions. To members of the sporting elite globalisation promises a 'borderless world' of an unrestricted cosmopolitan nature, where money, fame and trophies can be won in far off places.[2] Yet, to communities who register an emotional commitment to their sporting heroes globalisation appears as a threat, if those opportunities are carried to an extreme. There exists the danger of nomadism. Here the exercise of asocial individualism by the sporting hero results in a transgression of the relationship between hero and society, which releases malevolent political pressures. Our understanding of globalisation and the sporting hero therefore entails examining the *location* of sporting heroes within late capitalism, as corporeal representatives of broader collectives (most commonly the nation), and also as part of the global economy of sport. This understanding will be made easier if we draw a conceptual distinction between the sporting hero and the sport star. This task will be dealt with in the following sections and throughout. As a rejoinder and partial disclaimer I have not sought to focus explicitly upon the gender dynamics of this distinction and the problems and opportunities the globalisation of sport brings to this dynamic. Such a topic, I believe, is worthy of more attention than this chapter can provide.[3]

The idea of the sporting hero

In the mid-nineteenth century we witnessed how the industrial revolution paved the way for profound technological and social change. One of its impacts was to transform local geography, at one point causing Wordsworth in 1844 to castigate the arrival of the railway by the banks of Lake Windermere, and protest, 'Is there no nook of English ground secure from rash assault?'[4] In contrast, the writer Henry Thoreau could be seen to reject the parochialism and pre-modern sentimentality of Wordsworth, and embrace the imminent possibilities borne from change. He expressed, sitting by the banks of Walden Pond, that he felt,

> . . . refreshed and expanded when the freight train rattles past me, and I smell the stores which go dispensing their odours all the way from Long Wharf to Lake Champlain, reminding me of foreign parts . . . and the extent of the globe. I feel more like a citizen of the world.[5]

The above views express two instances where individuals have come to terms with the broadening of their horizons from the local to the global. They are also indicative of alternate readings of the same process, in this case the coming of the railway into sedate countryside. Globalisation therefore is not just about benign and liberating possibilities accorded to us by a more cosmopolitan social environment, but about the conflict of values, interests and ideas, the very stuff of politics, which renders our experiences of global flows heterogeneous.[6]

When consideration is given to the sporting hero a similar ambivalence arises, which produces a complex reading of globalisation. However, in order to excavate the nature of this ambivalence, some conceptual clarification is needed. I stipulate that the idea of the *sporting hero* is a *totemic* construction, it carries a *totemic logic*. In order to unpack this claim, one needs to grasp the nettle of the essence of the concept of totemism. This concept has a lineage within anthropological and early sociological studies of primitive cultures and was used to denote a relationship between a kinship group toward a sacred and representative object of that group.[7] The relationship carried acute social significance and was one of mutual beneficence, where, as J.G. Frazer wrote,

'. . . the totem protects the man, and the man shows his respect for the totem in various ways'.[8] There are three important sets of interrelated ideas underpinning the concept. First, the totem, the material object accorded with at times a superstitious and mysterious reverence, expresses and idealises social divisions existent between classes of people in society. These divisions are subjectively understood and felt by members of the group. The classic example drawn from anthropological studies is of a group that identifies with an animal, a plant or a force of nature (e.g. the wind or rain) who construct a totem to reflect the distinctiveness of their group identity. Second, this relationship is part of a religious or quasi-religious and social system. The bonds of association between members of the group and individuals toward the totem are ones of mutual respect, often bathed in an idea of tradition or ancestry that is expressed, at certain junctures, through public and ritual ceremony. Third, these relationships carry moral and political implications, alerting members to the presence of threats to the collective's way of life and its identity. I would concur with Wundt, however, in stating that these features are of shifting significance, where 'some of the meanings may recede, so that totems . . . frequently become a nomenclature of tribal divisions, while at other times the idea of ancestry, or perhaps also, the cult of significance, predominates.'[9]

The point about conceiving the idea of the sporting hero as totemic is that we understand and recognise more fully the uniqueness of the social group; the importance of a representative to legitimating and expressing a collective's identity and way of life; the public and ritual nature of the celebration of achievement within a system of shared understandings; and also the potential threats posed to the group. The presence of other totems or heroes of sport who hold an allegiance to a rival community, for instance. A 'totemic' view, therefore, writes Allison, incorporates 'the wholesomeness of Arcadia, edged by the threat of the wild wood, linked to ourselves by the particular ties which make it our tribal totem'.[10] In this instance the sporting hero exemplifies the purity of achievement in a distinct cultural location, a representative of what is publicly valued by the community – hence the granting of hero-status rather than other forms of accolade. They figuratively represent a range of virtues and excellences which only hold public value for a specific group of people.[11]

This view is more explicitly recognisable when we consider postcolonial societies and disenfranchised communities. Sport offers a range of cultural forms in which their community can be given a history, be it embodied and imagined.[12] As CLR James made clear in *Beyond a Boundary*, the subaltern struggle has been intimately related to the search for sporting heroes, a cultural form to be imbued with a distinct meaning and value.[13] This is amplified by intransigence of other forms of expression and reform, especially at an institutional level, where the political power of the community evaporates. In the case of the West Indies the success of Constantine and the 'Three Ws' sent a signal to the world of a vigorous and ambitious set of islands that no longer tolerated the yoke of colonial rule. They had found the cultural form in which to signal their arrival to the rest of the world and to forge a new history more resonant with their subjectivity. A more recent example is that of the heroics of the athlete Cathy Freeman at the Sydney Olympics who claimed victory in the 400 metres under the weight of national and international expectation. Her perfor-mance symbolised a politics of recognition and reconciliation of the continent's native and immigrant communities: her Aboriginal kin could now have their own flesh and blood totem. This idea of the sporting hero may sound rather emotional and dramatic but it is drawn from precedent thought on the subject. In the sporting literature, the conceptualisation is to be found mainly in socio-historical accounts. Holt and Mangan write, sporting heroes 'reflect [society's] values, aspirations and ambitions ...'[14] where 'Each nation ... interprets its sporting achievement according to its own intellectual traditions'.[15]

Sporting heroism, therefore, is not a universal category of intelligibility. It is certainly unclear, for example, whether the reception of Sir Henry Newbolt's poem 'Vitai Lampada' would be translatable to other contexts. As an ode to self-sacrificial forms of manhood which fundamentally requires strength of character (bravery, courage, 'guts' and 'bottle') in the service of imperial ambition, it intuitively appears at odds to Germanic or American forms of physical culture, which, in the main, stress physicality and excessive bodily performance.[16] The view of 'Englishness' has often traded upon a cultural stereotype where qualities of character imbue the social construction of its sporting heroes. There is some truth to this. The English tend to express a strong cultural preference for the 'underdog' or the 'little man', who is able to overcome conditions and competitors to emerge as a champion. Yet, to a degree the interplay of culturally defined narratives surrounding heroism and masculinity is paradoxical. We can admire virtues of hardness and the extremes of muscular performance, yet, we yearn for the underdog to triumph. A classic example taken from British sporting history would be of bespectacled insurance clerk Don Thompson, who having collapsed in the heat of the Melbourne Olympics, prepared for the Rome Olympics by creating a steam-room effect in his bathroom (using kettles and heaters) and walking up and down the bathmat. He managed to capture the gold medal in the 50 km walk, despite differences in resources when we consider his American and Soviet counterparts.

Global sport lends itself to this particularist model of national and cultural identity in two ways. First, it is organised to accommodate a meeting of national communities, represented by sporting elites who symbolise traditions, values, roles and virtues of their respective homelands. In a benign sense the meeting of communities in the arena is also an interpretive space where we discover unique forms of life, embodied by and possessing social ideals and a rich tapestry of tradition, which carry depth and meaning. Second, the sporting hero adds himself to the sum total of the expression of the community as a cultural object, along with language, dress, architecture, customs, song and law. Sport and sporting heroes, therefore, are essential in terms of representing an image of the nation to the rest of the world and, internally, play a part in the socialisa-tion of the young and the formation of a culturally specific subjectivity.

The idea of the sport star

Sporting contests are important on a global scale because they are typical of dramas of valuation that structure equivalence, by offering the material upon which cultural differences can be shared, even though doubts can be cast on the extent to which difference is understood or even tolerated. The totemic construction of sporting heroism sensitises us to difference, as champions are forwarded into the arena of sport to deploy the body in motion (often accompanied by mental cunning and qualities of character) in order to bring the prize of the contest back to their homeland, to the adulation of the community. This idea rests upon an intimate connection between the work of the individual, in displaying heroic (typically masculine) qualities, such as strength, courage, tenacity, endurance and the ability to sweat and toil, on behalf of a larger constituency. There is also a sense in which the narrative of difference, of nation and community within modern sport is submerged.

The spectacle of modern globalised sport demands that athletes perform in heroic style, with the heroic act as a secondary consideration.[17] Heroism, according to the conceptualisation above, tends to be more local in nature, rooted within performance that requires 'heroic qualities' for their completion. This broad and necessarily open-ended conceptualisation applies equally to officers who police inner-city streets, fire-fighters, and fishermen who trawl the seas in bad weather. Such activities, along with sport, carry a narrative of risk and achievement which is conducive to the construction of an heroic status. The spectacle of the sporting event or mega-event (World Cups, heavyweight title bouts, the Olympics) requires no such phenomenon for their success. Heroism is largely replaced in significance with stardom, which brings to the fore different qualities of meaning and association. The idea that heroes are local in reach, socially and culturally specific and hence only carry meaning for some people is partly methodological. My childhood heroes, the darts player Eric Bristow and cricketer Ian Botham, although having won renown through captivating feats of sporting prowess, could hardly be said to be heroes common to other Englishmen, or Englishwomen, or even to those based within my sociocultural location. Processes of adulation and celebration of heroic achievement, although mediated through channels and discourses that draw others to bestow and acknowledge a similar feeling of attachment, remain fundamentally personal. On the other hand, in today's media saturated public culture sport stars are unavoidable, they permeate our experiences of the everyday: from bar-room discussions of Beckham's latest hairstyle to the image of Tiger Woods beaming his ivory smile from roadside billboards to the melodramatic histrionics of Gazza having a night out on the town and to the tabloid-induced daydreams of Kournikova's buttocks.

Sport stars bewitch; their spectre haunts popular culture. But the plethora of ghosts invoked by discussing modern commercialised sport do not owe their presence to the process and construction of heroism, in the sense as outlined above. Rather, a different process of the creation of fame and renown occurs, one based upon the power of the media and the interests of corporations within late capitalist society. The often quoted work of Daniel Boorstin, *The Image: A Guide to Pseudo Events in America*, made the claim that the concept of the true hero, the individual who serves as a role model and exhibits moral leadership, is being replaced by the concept of transient celebrity. A celebrity is a person well known for being well known, a creation and puppet of the media. The element of performance, merit and achievement rooted within a display of individual talent has disappeared from the construction of fame.[18] The sadistic, but highly popular, panopticon of the television show *Big Brother* takes this distinction to its extreme and a host of British sport stars at the end of their careers have sought to use such vehicles in order to remain within public culture. (The boxer Nigel Benn, cricketer Phil Tuffnell and footballer John Fashanu on *I'm a Celebrity ... Get Me Out of Here!'* and boxer Chris Eubank on *Celebrity Big Brother*). Their appearances within this television genre highlights the extent to which the cult of celebrity pervades the popular imagination and it appears that the seemingly unlimited supply of 'stars' is equally matched by audience demand.[19]

The idea that sport stars have a bewitching and magical presence underpins a variety of associated concepts. Glamour, for instance, a word often used in conjunction with discussions of stardom and celebrity, until the early twentieth century, was associated with the occult. It denoted an attractiveness, allure and charm which centred around an object or a body – an attractiveness too power-ful to be real. Sport excites the boundaries between what is traditionally con-ceived as the empirical (real) and the transcendental (ideal) realms. Sport, which allows the dialectic between the real and the ideal to be played out routinely provide the conditions for heroic achievement. This dialectic is expressed in classical sociological thinking. For Durkheimian, sport has a reli-gious character; it contains a distinction between a sacred world in opposition to a profane realm, men are elevated to a sacred level through forms of collec-tive action that symbolically represents the community.[20] The real is counter-poised to the transcendental. In a similar vein, Max Weber makes the distinction explicit in his work on the charismatic hero, as a man who possesses 'a certain quality of an individual personality by virtue of which he is set apart from ordinary men and treated as endowed with supernatural, superhuman, or at least specifically exceptional qualities'.[21] This idea is applicable and arguably congruent with our understanding of what constitutes a sporting hero. Both the sporting hero and the sport star carry a 'sorcerous mystique', though they diverge on the modes through which this mystique is conveyed.

Stars are iconic. Indeed the common media parlance used to denote the social and cultural importance of sporting personalities is 'icon', often coupled with the prefix 'media'. The term carries meaning which is not too distant from the religious manifestation of its usage, where an icon is a symbol, often a pictorial representation, of something that no one has ever seen. An icon stands as a sign for something that is exclusive and a wonder to behold. Hence, it can be deployed to regale the 'godlike' achievements of figures from the world of competitive sport, or activities that carry a sporting aspect. The achievements of Edmund Hillary and Tenzing Norgay in being the first humans to successfully ascend (and return from) the world's highest mountain can be considered iconic. In the same vein it can also be used to denote the shadow that records, achievements, and triumphs cast in the popular imagination – as a symbol of the adventurous and progressive spirit of mankind. The term 'iconic' therefore also manages to blend the empirical and transcendental. Everest, like individual or collective heroic achievement, can be given a sensuous and visible presence, recordable through pictorial representations and other forms of media technology, which now saturate our image culture, but is also invested with a spiritual, invisible meaning that is difficult to comprehend.

Furthermore, the notion of icon carries advantages in explicating the globally mediated, visual and public world of sport and sporting personalities. To repeat a now over-worn banality, the images of sport stars play a part in our everyday cultural experience. However, one should add the rider that such experience is increasingly loaded with a plethora of commodity signs, indicative of the extent to which the 'projection' of the presence of social actors is increasingly intertwined with economic activity, embedded in consumption. One can go so far as to state, uncontroversially, that the primary mode of everyday attachment to sport stars, particularly by youth subcultures, is consumerist.[22] Packaged as commodities, sport stars prostitute themselves, selling their bodily space and privacy in order to hawk around, like highly mobile clotheshorses, the latest products, brands and merchandise of their corporate paymasters. Increased market presence is rewarded with wages that often outstrip those gained solely by sporting performance; our relationship is to be seen in terms of the rate at which we buy into their products, and hence the global cultural presence, of sport stars. For the corporate and media interests of the sports industry, attachments to sporting heroes through the nation is just one possible avenue in its marketing strategy.

The broader implication, put by Jameson, is that the market and the media are now symbiotic, the 'products sold on the market become the very content of the media image', hence it may no longer be possible to forge a distinction between 'consumer culture' and 'media culture'.[23] The characteristic demanded of the sport star is to possess *personality*, for they are part of a multi-media, multi-market sales campaign. The campaign's primary purpose is to earn revenues and decrease production costs and it achieves this through translating fictive hermeneutic codes of sport into 'saleable' narratives ('the virtuous hero', 'the dastardly villain', 'the role model', 'the clown', and 'the beautiful heroine'). Perhaps the best sociological conception of the sport star is provided by Mauss' notion of 'persona'. The star is a compound character, with a corporeal public presence, where the persona is a 'a mask, a tragic mask, a ritual mask'.[24] The commercial imperatives of the sports industry requires athletes to be performers, able to don masks and fashion an individual style, to provide a 'new take' on endlessly repeated acts. Sport stars need to be entertainers, they need 'to possess the actor's skills of presenting a colourful self, to maintain allure, fascination, and mystery', as Featherstone writes.[25] Their lives are theatrical. Stars are required to display control over and recognise the significance of their gestures, actions, movements and behaviours. The photo opportunity is their currency. And within this frame symbolic management and the positioning of the body is all important. One event from 2003 captures this brilliantly: the meeting of England football captain David Beckham with the former President of South Africa, Nelson Mandela. This publicity event was designed to promote South Africa's bid for the 2010 FIFA World Cup; yet, it captured an important difference between the hero and the star. Peter Conrad playfully wrote of this stately affair that 'The martyr of conscience met the fashion victim, the grizzled statue shook hands with the gilded totem pole, the man with the scars chatted to the man with tattoos'.[26] For Mandela, his quiet endurance through years of imprisonment for a cause in which he resolutely and unwaveringly believed mark him with heroic qualities and provide him with a sacred mystique. Beckham, on the other hand, although redeemed through his set-piece accuracy on the field of play, is actively aware that his magic or media presence is dependent upon his beauty, artifice and style.

To conclude this section, I contend that the crux of the distinction between the sporting hero and sport star is provided by literary theory, in the difference between classical and neo-classical dramatic forms. Whereas the classical protagonist's heroism is assured simply by appearing on stage, by the displaying of heroic virtues or enacting of bodily feats, the neo-classical protagonist is conscious that his heroism must be mediated from a periphery.[27] The distinction is captured perfectly by Shakespeare in Coriolanus. The irony of the story concerns the intransigence of the hero to acknowledge the need for his deeds to be recounted to the masses. Coriolanus and his Volscian counterpart Aufidius ably enact this tension between performance and representation. In the play, the latter cedes a cynical acceptance that 'our virtues/ Lie in th'interpretation of the time'.[28] While the former rejects Rome's offer of money and the rituals of Consulship (sealing the path to his tragedy) by telling the gathered patricians and crowd that honour is 'a quality of action/not the actions effects'. Coriolanus fancied that it is possible to stand 'As if a man were author of himself/ And knew no other kin'.[29] (These thoughts certainly seem anachronistic when we consider the importance of sports management groups, like the late Mark McCormack's IMG, in the management of image.)

The sport star and global political economy

The growth of the media and the process of commodification underpin and infuse globalisation and have served to strengthen the reliance upon mediation, and hence the power of cultural intermediaries. Its effect has been to marginalise the need to produce heroics, where individuals aspire to a purity of physical performance in the service of a community. To gain entry to the public stage members of the sporting elite now only need to carry concern for image, glamour, fashion and style. Depth has been replaced by depthlessness.[30] This situation has been predicated upon a growth in the range of institutional mechanisms through which we receive representations of heroic effort. Such *supply-side* features include technological invention and innovation which has given us the radio, television, film, the Internet, print media and the photograph. We are bombarded with a range of information and images about the sporting and non-sporting lives of heroes and stars. Their lives are seen as newsworthy, and hence, as news is circulated through discussion, forms part of our everyday lives. The media is also cannibalistic. It feeds off itself, through speculation, rumour and gossip, so that we also witness a secondary circulation of stories. The content of the public sphere is now so saturated with the lives, loves, tears and tantrums of 'personalities' that we commit a *non sequitur* to say that we live in a 'celebrity culture'.[31] This process has grown so intense, argues Whannel, that its effect is like a 'vortex' – sucking in various media, where it becomes impossible, for a time, not to pass comment upon a 'seismic' event (like September 11, Princess Diana's death or David Beckham's marriage).[32]

The commercialised nature of modern sport also bears a requirement to produce heroes in order to be economically viable. It has been written in *The Economist*, for instance, that 'the most important [aspect] is personality: a sport will attract neither crowds not TV cameras unless it can first offer heroes.'[33] As the profit motive is transferred on to cultural forms, the range of artistic products turned into a 'species of commodity ... marketable and interchangeable like an industrial product', increases.[34] Sport almost predestines this process. It provides the institutional and hermeneutic criteria for sporting heroes to emerge. The nature of contest will fashion winners and losers, records will be broken, sublime pieces of skill will punctuate the routine match; heroes and villains will emerge. Sporting heroes therefore offer themselves as products of the 'culture industry', to be fashioned into sport stars. Their presence is ceaselessly repeated while at the same time their form is individuated, offering novelty and originality, through fashion, glamour and other marks of distinction, to be mass consumed.

The modern sport star, therefore, is to be understood as both cultural product (as a brand to be sold) and process (part of the chain of advertising and brand or product endorsement) that underpins the regime of capital accumulation within late capitalist economy. They are deeply implicated in global political economy. The broadcasting of major world sporting events, which includes the Olympics, World Championship athletics and the FIFA World Cup, has been estimated to have been received by nearly 200 countries by the early 1990s.[35] Sport has developed to be 'everywhere ... all encompassing and instantaneous ... right there beside you from cradle to grave', in the words of Nike's Chief Executive, Phil Knight.[36] This makes for incredible commercial opportunity, which has been exploited by major worldwide companies, as they seek to sell their wares and expose their brands to dormant, emerging and developed markets.

Through these links sport stars are able to combine their popular cultural presence with lucrative economic contracts. Of course, to suggest the association of the sporting hero with commercial advertising is a novel feature would be wrong. In the 1950s Denis Compton was the *original* 'Brylcreem Boy'. His popular cultural appeal, which linked sport with beauty and glamour preceded David Beckham by over half a century. Both on-field performance and his natural good looks were part of his appeal for post-war Britain. While, thirty years prior to Compton the archetypal amateur hero, English cricketer CB Fry, regularly featured on advertisements for Plasmon Cocoa, Craven Tobacco, Marsuma Cigars, Perrier Water and Sanatogen tablets.[37] The synergy between commerce and sport is also witnessed in tennis heroes from the 1930s, Fred Perry and René Lacoste, who, respectively, launched the world's first lines of sports leisure wear.

However, the association between sporting heroes and products were managed locally, and intended for a native audience. It was an introspective affair. Theorists of globalisation are keen to stress that the novelty arises from the intensity of the (unequal) exchange of ideas, technologies, images, capital, people and commodities between nation-states.[38] The demise of the Soviet system, which led to the end of the Cold War, marked the genesis of a new world order in which states signed up to Neoliberalism, no longer refusing to bend the knee to liberal democracy and the market-based economy.[39] The picture we gain of the international terrain is now one hued with the affairs of transnational corporations (TNCs), supported by an international regime of organisations and agreements (WTO, IMF, G7, World Bank and GATT)[40] in the search for new markets, cheap labour and, ultimately, increased profitability.

The image of sport stars therefore plays a significant part in the desire of predominantly Western companies to gain a market share in local economies. Prior to the FIFA World Cup 2002, for example, a marketing campaign was launched which linked the image of David Beckham with the 'high performance' associated with British Petroleum's Castrol engine lubricant. In one advertising campaign Beckham's body was fashioned into a well-oiled, slick and burnished motorcycle. Transnational corporations like BP, Nike, Reebok and Adidas attempt to foster emotional ties between stars and products, which justify the huge sums paid out in finding and retaining celebrity endorsers. This is not only done by harnessing global sport stars such as Beckham, Jordan and Woods, but also through local heroes.[41] The intention is to foster a good company image and a pre-eminence of brand and product awareness at the expense of other competitors. In Beckham's case the marketing of Castrol motor oil traded upon the ability to transfer meaning from the star to the product (for example, strength, reliability and invincibility), which creates a positive commercial image.

On the other hand, there is a potential for commercial interests to lose out when stars under-perform at global sporting events. Before the FIFA World Cup 2002 Roy Keane signed a £500,000 nine-month endorsement with PepsiCo's 7Up soft drink, the highest paid amount in the company's Irish marketing strategy. However, by the time the advertisements were launched Keane was able to view them in his native country after his mysterious sending home following a row with the manager, Mick McCarthy, before the Republic of

Ireland's team had even kicked a ball. Similarly, Thierry Henry was signed by French car manufacturer Renault to promote its Clio hatchback. Yet, in the second match Henry found himself on the receiving end of a red card. Subsequently the defending champions exited the tournament in the first round after a series of lacklustre performances in which they failed to score a single goal![42] There is a real danger and susceptibility, then, of associations between 'trusted' brands and fallible humans.

Closely interconnected to the intimate relationship of star and brand are the legal issues pertaining to personal endorsement contracts, the holding of official sponsorship rights for tournaments and the intellectual property rights of players. There has been increasing and widespread concern among sport stars over 'ambush marketing', the commercial exploitation of their image by other companies and businesses. The issue is now so pertinent that in 2003 the young 17-year-old Everton and England football prodigy, Wayne Rooney, publicly expressed his unease as a pub opposite Goodison Park changed its name to *Rooney's* without his permission.[43] In the world of cricket this issue has been particularly notable. A sponsorship row over the use of players' images came to a head in the lead up to the ICC Champions Trophy in Sri Lanka in 2002 and the ICC Cricket World Cup in South Africa 2003. The International Cricket Council (ICC), the game's ruling body, expressed fears prior to the tournaments to the official sponsors and to the Murdoch-owned Global Cricket Corporation (GCC), who held the exclusive television and marketing rights, that it would not be able to honour the contracts as players sought to protect their personal endorsement rights. Players, such as Ganguly and Tendulkar of India, claimed that the contract contravened legal rights, liberties and entitlements and acted as an unfair restraint of trade. Furthermore, the GCC was quick to remind the ICC that its contract contained a clause stating that the countries must send their best players to the tournament. A furore emerged between some of the leading players, such as Sachin Tendulkar, and the ICC over his being asked to sign contracts forbidding any personal endorsements which might conflict with World Cup sponsors. The sponsorship row lead to a stand-off. It was eventually settled through a negotiated settlement between the players and the ICC. In response for players requesting to personal sponsors not to air commercials featuring them during the tournament and for 17 days afterwards, the ICC agreed to place funds accrued from the World Cup into trust rather than pay any moneys to the constituent boards. This funding arrangement was deemed appropriate in order to protect the ICC from legal action for claims of compensation by companies aggrieved over the inability to exploit the images of their stars at the most profitable sporting moment.[44] The resolution, however, was inadequate, piecemeal and *ad hoc*. It failed to permanently settle conflicts between sport stars, international ruling bodies and individual transnational corporations as they all jostle to find the most profitable relationship from the game.[45] However, it did have a further implication. In order to protect their right to profit from the use of their names, images and signatures the world's leading players have unionised, under the Federation of International

Cricketers Association. It remains to be seen what pressure this body can exert in the melee. As these examples reveal, stars are part and parcel of the economics of the media-sport production complex; mechanisms of control, management and regulation over their images are intensely bound with the economic drive for profitability.

Consumption, image and resistance

It should be clear, therefore, that the location of the sport star as part of the global political economy of sport is different to the relationship between the sporting hero and his native community. Stardom brings distance and dislocation between the community and its heroes. Without hesitation we can endorse Rojek's sentiments that the 'mass-media constitute the prime channel of contact' between audiences and stars.[46] The social effect of mass-mediated culture is arguably universal. A capitalist division of labour exists; on the one hand, a global class of specialists inhabits the mediascapes, ethnoscapes and ideoscapes of transnational cosmopolitan culture and, on the other, exists a public whose primary role is cultural-consumer.[47] The audience is distanced from participating in culture, towards treating culture as a consumer good. Sport stars exist as commodities: objects to be viewed, bought, played with and then discarded when a newer and brighter model comes along. In a subtle way, we are all in the same boat. We have the freedom to express our difference, but only with the codes and objects the industry provides.[48]

However, as the opening paragraph to this chapter highlighted, the global political economy of sport generates immense wealth, yet, it also raises questions about the type of society that generates it: its values, commitments and ethics. While the media has the power to shape the image of the sport star and of TNCs it cannot control how we cognitively receive and interpret that image. Growth and technological innovation in the mediating sphere has also facilitated the circulation of ethical questions regarding the practices of global actors. New media outlets and forums, such as the Internet, have the potential to be a free realm of deliberation, close to Habermas' conception of a 'public sphere'. A space where citizens can 'deal with matters of general interest without being subject to coercion; thus with the guarantee that they may assemble and unite freely, and express and publicise their opinions freely'.[49] Coalitions of mutual interest can be brought together to exchange ideas and information relatively unencumbered. New social movements have harnessed it as a site of dissent and resistance. It has played a prominent part in the recent anti-globalisation protests that have surrounded the meetings of global political, economic and bureaucratic elites. It has also helped not only to document forms of political participation (as a register of social history) but also operates as an arena where inspiration for new types of radical agency is provided,[50] and a radical political subjectivity is cultivated.

Globalisation, therefore, does not wholly concern the affairs of states and markets and the actions of the transnational capitalist class (as its representative elite);[51] it involves spurious and diverse actors from civil society who contest, dissent and actively resist perplexing features of neoliberal global restructuring. 'Globalisation-from-above' is met by 'globalisation-from-below'.[52] What is significant about this resistance is that it can be diverse in its form, often advocates public and tribalistic forms of protest, that it tends to be grounded locally but almost always has a transnational dimension, and that it tries to combine knowledge with politics. Citizens across many societies now increasingly dare to 'think for themselves', quite according to Kant's motto of the Enlightenment: *sapere aude! –* Dare to Know![53] The result is the creation of a technologically empowered deliberative public culture, where citizens are informed by propaganda and counter-propaganda.[54] Its effect, argues Urry, can be seen in a media culture which places individuals and social institutions under the spotlight, open to a process of ritualistic 'shaming'.[55] Information is used to render the reputations of states and TNCs untrustworthy. The most notorious British case in recent years being the attempted disposal of the Brent Spar oil platform by Shell UK which was sanctioned, after intense lobbying, by the British government. Arguably, this positions sport and the actions of our sporting heroes in a new light. The image of a boxer connecting with an opponent for a knockout blow, of the winger making it to the corner flag, or the beauty of a well-placed cover drive appear more stable and pure forms of meaning and interpretation.[56] We are able to trust our eyes in most cases.

However, as the sporting hero is distilled into its commodity form a good reputation becomes a prized asset. Sport stars become brands; they are subject to a heightened level of trust between consumers and the product. There is a prerequisite to put on a 'good show' and endorse products that can offer quality. A degree of dependency is placed upon this commercial relationship which makes sport stars more susceptible to negative media images if they are to retain good market presence. This relationship can work both ways. As seen above, companies can suffer when 'heroics' are not delivered. Likewise, the reputations of sport stars can suffer when their corporate masters undergo 'shaming'.

Michael Jordan's sporting career, for instance, was dogged by negative accusations made against the Nike sportswear he endorsed. One of the consequences of his association with Nike was to amplify the social importance of owning a Jordan-endorsed commodity, particularly among urban youth cultures. In the late 1980s it was reported that a number of American teenagers had been killed for their 'Air Jordan' shoes. This caused one judge to exclaim 'It's bad when we create an image of luxury about athletic gear that it forces people to kill over it!'[57] (This certainly seems to register a negative verdict against commodity fetishism and its management through media, advertising and marketing). Jordan's response was to tell reporters he'd 'rather eliminate the product' than be associated with crime and gangsters.[58] This did not stop the endorsements continuing however, and in 1990 Nike launched its US$60 million '*Just do It*' campaign, using Jordan's image. A second issue arose in the mid-1990s as Nike's entry into foreign labour markets brought human rights issues and the treatment of workers on to the political agenda. It was claimed that the major sportswear manufacturers (Adidas, Reebok and Nike) exploited Indonesian workers by paying young girls 15 cents an hour for an eleven-hour day. In the West the shoes regularly sold for US$70 and upwards, while LaFeber writes that, 'Jordan's $20m endorsement fee was higher than the combined yearly payrolls of the Indonesian plants that made the shoes'.[59] Jordan's response in this case, like that of Woods, was to remain quiet. Both Jordan and Woods, to protect their media reputations, neatly manoeuvred into self-titled 'apolitical' or 'non-political' positions. It is in these cases, where media and corporate interests conflict with the need to take an ethical and/or political position that we find the greatest expression of the persistence of the 'myth of autonomy' – the idea that sport and politics should not mix.[60]

For some commentators this situation is troubling: bell hooks, for example, mourns Jordan's acquiescence to protecting his media image and his inability to deliver a radical form of politics. This, she writes, is endemic of black male capitulation to neo-colonial white supremacist patriarchal social structures.

> Appropriated by market forces, the subversive potential of the Black male body is countered. This has been especially the case for Black male bodies whose radical agency is often diffused by a process of commodification that strips those bodies of dignity.[61]

Following a similar line of inquiry Jennifer Hargreaves explores the underlying imperatives of the sports industry. For her, these forces have constructed a masculine notion of competitive sport, which, in its quest for further commercial penetration and high-figure TV audiences, creates a need to produce beautiful honed bodies capable of performing an aggressive, muscular high-octane spectacle. Its effect for elite female sport performers is cultural masculinisation, where sporting heroines, she writes, are 'modern-day . . . manufactured clones of each other'. We should not expect these figures to serve as good role models, or the result as a step forward for the feminist movement. Heroines of sport, she contends emerge from the everyday, routine endeavours of women who struggle daily against social structures which challenge their efforts. We should not be seduced by a system operating according to underlying economic necessities which 'consistently induces them to abuse their bodies, tempts them to use unsporting and damaging performance-enhancing agents, and produces them as sexualised commodities'[62] for consumption by a global audience.

These responses share common threads, which typifies the current approach to theorising and excavating the nature of the sport star in society. They forward an explanation which sees the sport star as complicit in global capitalism. Kellner's reading of Michael Jordan is typical.[63] He regards the ubiquitous basketball player and corporate American interests as symbiotic. Jordan is the embodiment of the values of American capitalism – materialist acquisition, conspicuous consumption, excessive greed and ruthless competitiveness. His public presence is apolitical in order to maintain his reputation and so as to not alienate potential consumers from the range of associated products bearing his image. The tone of opposition against this feature often laments a failed chance for perhaps the highest profile individual in the world to connect with collective struggle. As Toure writes, 'Couldn't the world's greatest endorser have sold us something besides shoes?'[64]

Loyalty and location

At one level the explanation that sport stars seek to retain a good media image because their image is their currency is appealing. This thesis can be substantiated when we consider the development of a global sport mass media that possesses a highly controlled and detailed management of its product (sport stars) as the spectacle of sport is sold to audiences far and wide.[65] However, there is a deeper set of questions that oblige us to work at a level of abstraction in order to understand the normative nature of the idea of the sporting hero, the affront that globalisation makes toward it and the political reactions it creates.

The acquiescence of sport stars to take a stand on political or ethical issues, I contend, relates to the moral demands made upon them by other communities they inhabit. The above section highlighted the need to locate sport stars firmly within the operation of a global political economy, in the service of capitalism and the affairs of transnational corporations. If we consider the members of these institutions and organisations then it is possible to place sport stars within what Sklair terms the *transnational capitalist class*. This is a collection of global elites who work to sustain the dominance of capitalism as a social system, which includes a 'still-evolving' class of global actors, divided into four factions: TNC executives, globalising bureaucrats, globalising politicians and professionals, and consumerist elites.[66] I believe it is pertinent to envisage sport stars as, at the least, enmeshed in the affairs of this elite, and where most developed, as part of the transnational capitalist class. When we consider the slippage between Michael Jordan's sporting role as a visible endorser of Nike and his current business role as head of a division of the Nike Corporation this relationship becomes clear.

The globalisation of sport therefore renders a complex, more ambiguous, picture of place, loyalty and allegiance for the sport star, arguably because they are now implicated in distinct 'communities' beyond the nation-state. We can include here: *territorial* communities (city, region, nation, supranation), *non-territorial* communities (profession, family, religion) and *transnational* communities (sport, corporations). The problem for the sport star is one of relativism, requiring an ability to manage and reconcile conflicting claims made upon them. This idea provokes us into recognising the sport star as a complex social self who is defined, according to Friedman, by '*various and variant* identity constituents'.[67] This is captured well in the following poem, John Manifold's *The Recruit*.

> Pried from the circle where his family ends,
> Man on his own, no hero of old tales,

Discovers when the pose of lone wolf fails
Loneliness and, miraculously, friends,
Finds how his comradeship with one depends
On being both from London, say, or Wales,
How with the next a common job prevails,
Sport with a third, and so the list extends.

Nation and region, class and craft and syndicate
Are only some: all attributes connect
Their own with this kind, call him to vindicate

A common honour; and his self-respect
Starts from the moment when his senses indicate
'I' as the point where circles intersect.[68]

Although Manifold is writing about his experiences as a wartime soldier it is relatively easy to refer its message to the sport star. The poem illustrates the intersection of several circles of social, political and moral concern that informs the identity of the heroic individual. Yet, its overall tone and direction reminds us of the importance of loyalty and honour grounded within patriotic nationalism as a means to the intelligibility of his actions. These tensions are inherent in the globalisation of sport stars. On the one hand, media-corporate interests require stars to be mobile, transportable and translatable to other contexts, to respond fluidly to cosmopolitan opportunities that arise as new markets are sought. While, on the other hand, the star must manage their sense of self through forms of allegiance that are less transnational in their scope. This understanding of the sport star comes close to what Giardina calls the 'Global Hingis' paradigm, where the star has a flexible citizenship 'grounded within particular structures of meaning about family, gender, nationality, class mobility, and social power which vary from place to place'.[69]

The idea of the sport star promotes an idea that members of the sporting elite can be 'citizens of nowhere', where loyalties are ephemeral, transient and temporary. In terms of migration patterns sport offers unprecedented freedoms of movement to its stars. Ageing former England footballer Paul Gascoigne ('Gazza'), for instance, signed, in 2003, for second division side *Gansu Tianma*, in the Western reaches of China. Patterns of global migration, as Bauman reminds us, are polarised between those privileged classes who hold the right passport, have the right profession and affluence to exploit the situation. Others, predominantly from the global South, face displacement through warfare or hunger, seek to escape persecution and destitution, to find better lives for themselves, but confront a living reality of nation-states hidden behind barbed wire, watchtowers and machine guns.[70] A 'borderless world' for all people is therefore a fallacy but it appears the reality for sport stars.[71]

Nevertheless, the idea of flexible citizenship contained in the 'Global Hingis' paradigm is also a reminder that without the psychosocial sustenance groups provide individuals will inevitably experience an alienation of the soul. The

nineteenth-century German writer Herder noticed this same point. He disavowed the cosmopolitanism of the Enlightenment project and embraced plural
diversity and innate cultural distinction. The fundamental thing about humans,
according to Herder, is that they belong to groups. The marriage of the individual to the collective, through the sense of a common political and cultural
identity is the foundation of a healthy political society.[72] Sport, perhaps more so
than other cultural forms (e.g. music, theatre, radio, film and art), is more apt at
expressing such diversity on a global scale. A cosmopolitan and homogenised
cultural, political and economic order can be disavowed and rejected through
the persistence of real and felt attachments of the individual to community – its
traditions, history and heroic legacy. In this sense the local provides an affront
to the global.

The forms in which we express such diversity may be undergoing pressures so
that now it is common to talk of 'diminishing contrasts' and 'increasing varieties',[73] but the idea of innate and embodied cultural distinctions remains
powerful nonetheless. I think its power can be demonstrated when we consider
our sensitivity to threats against cultural traditions. Threats of change and of
'the Other' motivated by a view of globalisation as a homogenising or univer-
salising force. Of the former, sport, by virtue of its centrality to popular culture
and hence to notions of what constitutes the public realm, offers a powerful and
visible platform to legitimate or deligitimate processes of change. As stated
earlier, in the West Indian experience cricket offered the means by which a
history of the peoples of the islands could be created, it provided a social space
in which to conceptualise the birth of a postcolonial national identity. Yet the
feeling gained from reading James' work is one of a post-facto and teleological
mythologising of the Caribbean's cricketing characters, told from an author at
the forefront of a political and social movement for independence. What is
most telling is how James communicates the story of heroes who lived up to the
social and political expectations to succeed in the international arena, and
hence to legitimate at one level, the West Indies' maturation from the colonial
yoke (Constantine, Worral, Weekes, Sobers and Gibbs). While the story of
Wilton St Hill is told as a fallen-hero who failed to carry the burden of expectation of the West Indian peoples, by losing against the English.[74] These figures,
however, remain largely passive within this drama; they were to demonstrate
their political commitment through their sporting prowess.

In contrast, there have been examples of sport stars who have been willing to
actively confront processes of political change. The victory of the French football team in 1998 legitimised the notion that France could be imagined as a
multicultural or hybrid nation, where the triumvirate of revolutionary appeals
to liberté, fraternité and égalité could be extended to all its citizens.[75] The
president, Jacques Chirac, exclaimed on the eve of their success, 'This is a
France that wins and is, for once, united in victory'. However, four years
later the momentum gained by the team's World Cup victory and subsequent
European Championship success in 2000, was potentially unhinged. Jean-Marie
Le Pen, the leader of the far right National Front, attracted considerable support

for his candidature for presidency in spring 2002. His campaign centred on a radical agenda which charged France's political elite with propagating moves toward political and economic liberalism at the cost of the distinctiveness of the (racially homogenous) French character. Staple issues of the National Front, concerns over immigrant workers, unemployment and law and order, remained prominent throughout the campaign. The central question he posed was how could governments wedded to free-market globalisation reduce its corrosive impact on the social fabric of personal and local identity? This was an emotional appeal formed by suspicions of an integrationist European agenda motivated by the interests of big-business toward economic liberalisation. Le Pen's campaign found an accord with those who became disempowered or feared disempowerment, typically small businessmen, the metropolitan unskilled working classes and suburban youth. Nevertheless, it was an appeal wrapped up in a political rhetoric of racism; counterpoising the sanctity of France's rural and white identity against a political, cultural and economic malaise caused by the presence of (non-white) immigrant communities.[76]

Into this context stepped the French football team who had won the World Cup in 1998 whilst composed of eight non-indigenous players. Among them Zinedine Zidane, born in Marseille of Algerian parents, Lillian Thuram, from the West Indian island of Guadeloupe, Patrick Viera, who is Senegalese, and Marcel Desailly, who was born in Ghana. The team, upon Le Pen's success in gaining enough support to enter the second round of the French presidential election, used their high media profile in conjunction with the build-up to the 2002 tournament to warn the public of the dangers they faced if Le Pen were to become President. Robert Pires laid down an ultimatum: Le Pen as President or France's presence in South Korea and Japan. He stated, 'It'd be an impossibility to play [in the Far East]. We play for France because we're French, but the team's roots are from everywhere so if France is governed by the extreme right it makes it an impossibility to play for your country'.[77] Likewise, Zidane warned, 'People must vote, but above all they must think of the consequences that could arise if they vote for a party which does not correspond to French values'.[78] The implication being that French values are to be understood as cosmopolitan and multicultural values, rather than the isolationist and racist values harbored by the National Front.[79]

This ultimatum, which was not carried through owing to Jacques Chirac's re-election, raises some important questions. First, it highlights the position of public status and responsibility that sporting heroes are required to live by. As this episode illustrates, the question of 'who speaks for the nation?' was paramount. A collective of international, globe-trotting footballers, with the ability to speak from various indigenous and non-indigenous subject-positions, were deemed to be an appropriate assemblage to comment upon the concerns generated by the rise of the far right. They were regarded as representative of modern French values, located arguably in the most visible public arena, and hence were called upon to speak on behalf of similar communities whose social locations leaves their sentiments inaudible. They were called upon to speak because France and the world would listen.[80] Second, despite being multi-millionaires with lucrative commercial contracts, these French sporting heroes intervened, using a global sporting event to send signals through the media of their opposition to Le Pen, which confirmed the authenticity of their own (multi) cultural political identity. The question is whether the cultural and political implications of such an intervention are independent from their public moral position? One could posit the case that the practices they participate in provide a strong foundation for moral patriotism. On one level loyalty to a political community is a virtue born from deep-seated (and totemistic) bonds of attachment.[81] However, if we hold onto the idea that the sport star is a complex social self with different loyalties to be balanced then one can posit that the survival of the French nation-state, in its current form, is a logical necessity of their position owing to the national organisation of sporting competition at the global level. Moral concern with the state of the nation is coterminous with the interests of the stars, whose trade is built on this edifice. The issue is one of realpolitik.

Melnick and Jackson's recent work on young audiences and 'reference idol selection' in New Zealand is a prime example of the second threat, of the 'Other'.[82] They trace the psychosocial effects of globalisation-as-Americanisation in terms of young individuals' attachments to sporting heroes. The survey research conducted as part of this study instructed adolescents to consider whether they identified with a public sporting hero in any sense and to name the most important individual in their lives at any one moment. The results were interpreted in terms of cultural penetration of American cultural forms through the 'media-sport production complex'.[83] Individuals who associated with American sporting icons, such as Michael Jordan, were set against others whose primary identification was with indigenous heroes or heroines. The outcomes of the study found that 'Kiwis [accounted] for approximately one-third of the heroes/heroines named', causing Melnick and Jackson to conclude, '. . . the choosing of local, popular athletes may represent, however indirectly, a form of cultural resistance against American hegemonic sporting practice by New Zealand youth'.[84]

The significance of this research is its subtext. It trades upon a distinction between an '*authentic*' postcolonial national identity, where national sporting heroes inform individual subjectivity, and laments '*inauthentic*' attachments to American icons, taken to be indicative of New Zealand's growing dependency upon American popular culture. Implicit in this approach is the totemic logic of sporting heroism discussed earlier, which may explain for the amplification of the threat posed to local cultures by the influx of foreign (predominantly American) stars and associated cultural products. But there is a weakness inherent in such thinking. Despite an admirable intention to reveal a complex interplay between the global and the local in terms of popular culture, Melnick and Jackson reduce our understanding of globalisation to the spread of cultural objects. This line of thinking is common to a burgeoning literature dealing with how communities absorb, subvert and adapt cultural objects and invest them with a new meaning more resonant with local social, political and economic conditions. Recontextualisation of American sporting heroes is given as evidence of resistance to globalisation.[85]

However, there is a greater threat posed by globalisation, which brings into sharp relief the relationship between the global and the local, the community and its heroes: the danger of *nomadism*. In order to detail this threat the idea of heroic endeavour needs to be unpacked. There is a sense that sporting heroes 'act out' liberal individualism.[86] Their autonomy is predicated upon an ability to abstract themselves from relationships. The primary attachment is the quest for goals, records, accomplishments and glory, which requires 'heroic' virtues of strength, bravery, fortitude, courage and discipline. However, the abstraction of the heroic individual from the community carries a danger of unrestricted social authority, which contains the possibility of socially undesirable consequences. To return to Shakespeare, this is arguably the moral of the story of Coriolanus.[87] The more the hero identifies himself with communal ideals, virtues and tradition, the more he or she begins to speak as a representative of these elements, the more distant they grow from society. The process of embodiment acts as a separating motif and a source of ambiguity. On the one hand, we affirm the idea of what is of communal importance. We declare that sporting success and heroic achievements are valuable. On the other hand, the individual is distanced from society, the idea becomes mobile and portable, nomadic and anonymous. There exists the inherent possibility that the sporting hero could, as Barker states, 'walk away with the national idea, indifferent to those who feel they have the most affective and original claim on it'.[88] Autonomy is exercised and realised, the sporting hero becomes a nomad, displaying skills and excellences for another community. On the surface, therefore, this demonstrates the limits of conceiving of the community in human form.

The controversy surrounding the America's Cup in 2003 is one example of the danger of nomadism. Yachting's most prestigious prize saw the entry (and victory) of *landlocked* Switzerland, under the financial muscle of 37-year-old billionaire Ernesto Bertarelli. Bertarelli composed the Swiss 'Alinghi' team of world-class yachtsmen and women who had competed for other nations. It included former America's Cup winners Russell Coutts and Brad Butterworth from Team New Zealand, who were lured away by multi-million dollar contracts. Coutts and Butterworth, who had been part of the champion teams of 1995 and 2002, were instantly turned from national heroes to anti-heroes. '*BlackHeart*', a fanatical supporters group of the New Zealand team, launched a campaign against them with the slogan 'Country Before Money'. The new crew of Team New Zealand decided to emblazon their yacht with the new motto, 'Loyalty', so as to show their disgust. The rescinding of the relationship between heroic individual and their constituent or native community therefore carries distinct political pressures. The scale of the threats over Coutts' and Butterworth's defections apparently led to a similar deployment of New Zealand police resources in order to protect the Swiss team and route out potential terrorist activity against the defectors.[89]

The globalisation of sport burdens the modern sport star to comprehend and to take account of questions of wealth and status, migration and identity, honour and ambition, history and remembrance, fame and fortune. But to rescind the relationship with the constituent community is clearly troublesome. In a way, the response of Jordan and Woods to questions of politics and ethics, of where their loyalties lie may be the most appropriate for this day and age. Why upset the apple cart and the riches it provides? All you need to do is just smile and wave. Sports historian Richard Holt is correct when he writes that the new 'celebrity heroes' pursue money, fame and fortune with such verve that the old categories of 'amateur hero' and 'professional hero' now seems redundant.[90] One implication of the presence of stardom and celebrity is that our previous conceptualisations of sport may need to be reworked. The communitarian political philosopher Alasdair MacIntyre conceives sport as a culturally valued social practice that upholds a rich and unique form of life, embodied by and possessing social ideals and a rich tapestry of tradition. Sport is more than a set of rules to be followed in order to attain a set of goals, its norms, standards of conduct and virtues help to form its broader ethos and appeal.[91] It would be interesting to see, through further research, whether this notion of sport is either one that is recognisable to the sport star, or desirable for elite sporting athletes when the stakes are so high given the power of cultural intermediaries in according status and wealth. A further implication is whether this notion of sport holds a normative appeal in the fight against crass instrumentalism and the atrophy of community and tradition, virtue and heroics.[92]

Conclusion

Fundamentally, the globalisation of sport agitates differences between the 'heroic' community, in its culturally particular and spatially defined sense, and the sporting community, which is now transnational in scope. It is hoped that this brief analysis has made us more aware of the individual and often moral choices that sport stars have to make in negotiating a path between these communities. Often this is handled successfully. Nomadism does not appear as a threat and the potential to exercise asocial individualism is reined in. In normative terms, the commercialised, transnational and 'depthless' world of modern sport encourages the ability for selfish individual behaviour that in turn undermines the existence of strong and healthy communities which provide depth and meaning. The task at hand, therefore, is to rectify the moral failings of excessive individualism and to counteract its corrosive effects on social relations. This demand is not new to our thinking. It resonates from the concern with the erosion of traditional community structures as the result of socio-economic change. Tonnies provided us with an early statement of this sentiment when he wrote, 'the domestic *Gemeinschaft* or home life with its immeasurable influence upon the human soul has been felt by everyone who ever shared it . . .'[93] The normative structure underlying the totemic notion of the sporting hero requires an individual capable of recognising his social origins, of valuing the bonds and attachments without which they would never have entered the public realm. Media and corporate interests may have dislocated and distracted elite sportspeople from understanding the primacy of these allegiances. As stated earlier, a concern for image has replaced concern for performance on behalf of community. Yet, there is a sense in which the experience of performance on behalf of a community is emotive and lasting (think of Terry Butcher's bloodied head, Denise Lewis limping to victory at Sydney, Denis Compton's cricketing feats despite the removal of his knee). It would be a sad indictment of our society to think that our grandchildren, fading away on their deathbeds, on drawing their terminal breath, could only remember the products and not the presence, magic and wonder associated with sporting heroes.

9 Selling out?

The commercialisation and globalisation of lifestyle sport

Belinda Wheaton

Introduction: the 'alternative sportscape'[1]

There is now a body of academic literature examining the 'phenomena' of what has been variously termed 'extreme', 'alternative,' 'lifestyle', 'whiz,' 'panic,' 'action' and 'new' sports.[2] Such labels encompass a wide range of participatory and made-for-television sporting activities, including residual cultural forms such as climbing and snowshoeing and emergent activities such as wake board-ing and BASE jumping.[3] While commentators have differed in nomenclature, many are agreed in seeing such activities as having presented an *alternative* and *potential* challenge to traditional ways of 'seeing', 'doing' and understanding sport.[4] In this chapter I will introduce readers to the alternative sportscape, focusing on the type of activity termed lifestyle sports. I discuss firstly what these activities are, and their significance in contemporary sporting culture. I then examine what is arguably one of the main themes in their development, their increasingly global reach and concurrent commercialisation, particularly co-option by international and transnational corporations.

Lifestyle sports

Lifestyle sports are a specific type of alternative sport, including both established activities like surfing and skateboarding through to newly emergent sports like kite surfing.[5] While each lifestyle sport has its own history, identities and development patterns, there are nevertheless commonalities in their ethos, ideologies and increasingly the national and transnational consumer industries that produce the commodities that underpin their cultures. Historically, as Bourdieu has observed, many of these lifestyle sports originated in North America in the late 1960s, and were then imported to Europe by American entrepreneurs.[6] With their roots in the counter-cultural social movements of the 1960s and 1970s many have characteristics that are different to the tradi-tional 'dominant' institutionalised, Western 'achievement' sport cultures.[7] Unlike some alternative and extreme sports, lifestyle sports are fundamentally about participation, not spectating, either in live or mediated settings. Participants show high commitment in time and/or money and a style of life that develops around the activity. They have a hedonistic, individualistic ideology that promotes commitment, but often denounce regulation and institutionalisation, and are often critical of, or ambivalent towards, commercialism and formal 'man-on-man' style competition. The body is used in non-aggressive ways, mostly without bodily contact, yet they embrace and fetishise notions of risk and danger. The locations in which these sports are practised are often new or re-appropriated (urban and/or rural) spaces, without fixed or delineated boundaries. Theorists have represented the emergence of these sporting activities, and the subcultures and lifestyles that develop around them, as a new phase in the development of sports, characterised by some as 'postmodern'.[8] It is certainly undeniable that the emergence of these sports and their associated lifestyles is related to wider issues around changing contemporary Western society. In these sports we can see some of the central issues and paradoxes of advanced capitalist or late-modern societies, such as the expression of self-identity as increasingly 'mobile, multiple, personal, self-reflexive, and subject to exchange and innovation',[9] and the 'individualisation and privatisation of the act of consumption, even in seemingly public spheres'.[10] In the emergence and evolution of lifestyle sport activities what is being sold to the consumer is not merely a sport or leisure activity but a complete style of life, one which is saturated with signs and images that emphasises many of the aspirations of postmodern consumer culture.

In the twenty-first century lifestyle sports are attracting an ever-increasing body of followers and participants, from increasingly diverse global geographical settings. Take the urban sport of skateboarding; it has been claimed that the growth in skateboarding over the past ten years in the USA (based on sales), now outpaces participation in traditional sports like baseball.[11] Rinehart claims the 'alternative sport phenomenon' is 'world wide,' citing the popularity of ESPN's X-Games. In 1997 the event attracted competitors from over 20 different countries, over 240,000 spectators (in 1998), and was beamed via ESPN's different sport channels to 198 countries in 21 languages.[12] Participants of lifestyle sport range from the 'poseurs' buying into a desirable lifestyle to 'weekend warriors', the occasional participants who often participate in a range of different alternative and traditional sports, through to 'hard core' committed practitioners who are fully familiarised in the lifestyle, argot, fashion and technical skill of their activity, and spend considerable time, energy and often money doing it. While some lifestyle sports such as snowboarding and windsurfing attract significant numbers of active female participants, the majority are youthful[13] white males, from affluent Western industrialised nations.

Selling out?

Yet the landscape of alternative sport is increasingly characterised by the presence of a range of global commercial images and interests. As Kusz reminds us, extreme sport was initially 'decried' by both sports fans and pundits, seeing them as 'made-for-TV pseudo-sports created solely to peddle products to the much coveted teen male demographic'.[14] The media and consumer industries seem to have appropriated alternative sport to sell everything from deodorant to Pepsi:

> In the world of extreme sport sponsorship, pierced and tattooed skaters and skysurfers mix quite amicably with buttoned-down corporations such as AT&T and Toyota.[..] For all of the counter-culture cachet associated with ESPN's X Games and NBC's Gravity Games, the truth is that the events were co-opted from the start.[15]

Lifestyle sport stars like Tony Hawk (skater) and Kelly Slater (surfer) are individuals who, like other global sport celebrities transcend their subcultures, and 'occupy and inform national and transnational space'.[16] Commentators have therefore seen alternative and especially mediated forms of extreme sport as a 'co-opted' sporting movement increasingly associated with the global expansion and reproduction of consumer capitalism,[17] and controlled by multinational and transnational corporations and media organisations.[18]

Yet while commercialisation has been a central thread in research, the influence and impact of global commercial culture on 'local' (or 'translocal') cultures, has received little attention. Despite a number of empirical studies of lifestyle sports in different national and regional settings, none of these studies have *systematically* explored how these 'local' sporting practices are informed by, and respond to, the diverse processes of globalization.[19] In this chapter I will therefore sketch out some of the main influences that need to be considered in examining the global-local nexus in lifestyle sports. In outlining this agenda, my discussion will highlight the influences of the media, tourism and migration, the impact of global commodities in the production and consumption of equipment and sub-cultural style, and how lifestyle sports inform debates about the enduring connection between sport and national identity in the context of the proclaimed 'Brave new world of transnational culture'.[20] My discussion then turns to examining the commercialisation process, exploring some of the ways commodities are given meanings and re-worked in 'local' subcultural settings, illustrating how global consumer capitalism penetrates these lifestyle sports in increasingly complex and contradictory ways.

Lifestyles sports, however, encompass a range of different and by no means homogeneous activities, with their own histories and global development patterns. Despite evident commonalities, there is not universality in the experiences, or politics of identity in these sports. Therefore, the illustrations I draw on are either from my own empirical research on the cultures of windsurfing and surfing, conducted across different locales including around the UK coast, Hawaii, and Australia, or other lifestyle sports such as skateboarding, where there is empirical research and popular literature referring to a range of 'local' settings allowing me to draw out commonalities, as well as pointing to significant differences.[21]

In the first part of this discussion I consider what these globalisation processes are, examining their influence in the context of the diffusion of surfing culture.

The globalisation of lifestyle sport

Globalisation according to Robertson refers to an increased compression of the world, and particularly our intensification of consciousness of it made possible by escalating global connections.[22] Globalisation processes, however, are not just economic in character, but are concerned with issues of cultural meaning; 'While the values and meaning attached to place remain significant, we are increasingly involved in networks which extend far beyond our immediate physical location.'[23] Increasingly prominent in these global cultural flows are the increased meeting and mixing of cultures and identities, and the central part played by the media and communications technologies in the acceleration of this process. Robertson's term *glocalization* helps to articulate this global production of the local and the localisation of the global, the co-existence of cultural homogenisation and hetrogenisation tendencies.[24] These processes have received an abundance of critical attention, so my intention here is not to attempt any review or overview, not least because as Allison points out, 'globalisation' is a term that is 'fraught with ambiguities',[25] but to highlight issues pertinent to examining the articulation and impact of global cultural forces within alternative sport cultures in their 'local' and trans-local contexts.

Global flows, as Maguire, and other commentators have illustrated, are a profound feature of late twentieth-century sport, including the migration of elite talent, the movement of technology and the manufacturing of clothing and equipment.[26] In discussing the impact of these flows and processes on modern sport Maguire concludes that, 'Sports development has been and continues to be contoured by the interlocking process of diminishing contrasts and increasing varieties'.[27] He suggests that the emergence, diffusion and increasing popularity of alternative sports (he cites snowboarding, hang-gliding and windsurfing) is evidence of this increased heterogeneity in the range and diversity of sport cultures in world sports, a 'creolization of sport cultures' characteristic of the latest phase of 'global sportization'.[28]

Appadurai provides an insightful analysis of these dynamics, suggesting that globalisation encompasses multidirectional processes, which provide both sameness and difference; 'The new global economy has to be seen as a complex, overlapping, disjunctive order'.[29] He offers a framework for exploring this complexity, the 'disjunctures between economy, culture and politics', by examining the relationship among the 'five different dimensions of global cultural flows', dimensions he terms 'ethnoscapes, mediascapes, technoscapes, financescapes and ideoscapes'.[30] Ethnoscapes involves the 'shifting landscapes of people'[31] around the world including tourists, immigrants, refugees, guest workers and other moving groups; technoscapes refers to the flow of technology, and financescapes to the transfer patterns of global capital. Appadurai argues that the global relationship between these three scapes is:

deeply disjunctive and profoundly unpredictable because each of these landscapes is subject to its own constrains and incentives, [...] at the same time as each acts as a constraint and a parameter for movement in the others.[32]

Supplementing these three scapes are mediascapes and ideoscapes. Ideoscapes refers to images that are invested with political and ideological meaning, and mediascapes encompasses both mass media images, and the process of image production and dissemination. These scapes are the 'building blocks' of what he calls – extending Anderson's idea of imagined communities – *imagined worlds*.[33] As Carrington and Wilson suggest, 'the crux of Appadurai's framework is the assumption that the various *disjunctures*, or interactions that occur between global cultural flows – as they relate to the various scapes – provide the analyst with crucial information about the complex ways that local cultures relate to global forces'.[34]

A brief examination of the diffusion of modern surfing will illustrate the impact of these different global flows, particularly ethnoscapes and mediascapes, in extending 'surfing around the world'.[35] I examine surfing because both its form, and cultural values, have had an impact on the development and ethos of many other lifestyle sports. Snowboarding, skateboarding, windsurfing and kite-surfing, for example, all have roots in, and are all still strongly influenced by, the surfing activity and culture.

A 'travelling culture': the global diffusion of surfing

In popular consciousness the USA, and specifically California, is attributed with the birth of surfing culture;[36] however it is worth noting that surfing has a much longer, and fascinating history as a pre-Colonial body culture playing a pivotal role in Polynesian (mens' and interestingly also womens') cultural life.[37] Eighteenth- and nineteenth-century colonisation by Europeans and Americans was to constrain the activity; puritanical American missionaries thought that surfing was immoral and evil, so it was banned.[38] In the early twentieth century it was revived, predominantly by non-indigenous 'Haole' (white) Hawaiian settlers.[39]

In California in the 1940 and 50s, the political and socio-economic circumstances allowed 'modern' surfing, and surf culture, to flourish.[40] At that time, travel, particularly in the form of tourism, played a key part in its diffusion. Following Appadurai's discussion of ethnoscapes, I use the term 'travel' in an expansive way to include experiences such as tourism, immigration and migracy.[41] Nevertheless, as Urry points out, in global culture 'corporeal travel has taken on an immense dimension comprising the largest ever movement of people across national borders'.[42] Booth observes that cheaper airfares from the 1940s allowed Californians to travel to the surfing Mecca, Hawaii.[43] However, surfers in Australia – the other main location at that time – remained quite isolated, largely because the heavy Malibu surfboard made travel difficult, but also because the anti-hedonistic values of the Australian Lifesaving Club environment served to constrain regular surfing.[44] Competition also played a part in the migration process; the first international surfboard riding competition was held in 1954 in Makaha, Hawaii,[45] and despite playing an ambiguous role in surf culture, has continued to play a significant role in its global spread. (Later in the chapter I discuss the ambiguous and changing role of competitive surfing.)

As Appadurai's discussion of mediascapes and ideoscapes embraces, the growth and changing roles of the media industries, particular the emergence of global electronic culture, is seen as one of the main forms of cultural exchange in the context of globalisation. Booth outlines the various influences of the media on surfing in the 1950s and 60s. Initially the Hollywood genre of beach movies such as *Gidget* reproduced the idyllic fantasy lifestyles of California surfers' on the back of which Californian surf culture rapidly diffused around other parts of the Pacific Rim.[46] Yet whilst these mainstream films were shunned by the surfing community, specialist surf films also emerged, and quickly became important products, often consumed in communal settings, 'explaining surfing and surfers to themselves'.[47] The first subcultural magazines also emerged in the early 1960s; for example *Surfing World* was launched in Australia, initially as a vehicle to promote surf films.[48] Travel soon became synonymous with the surfing lifestyle, epitomised by Bruce Brown's classic film *The Endless Summer* (1964), often referred to as '*the* surfing film'[49] which followed the adventures (or 'surfari') of two Californian surfers around the world dedicating their life to the hedonistic voyage in search of the perfect wave.

Because of the surfer's aspiration to travel, tourism, in conjunction with specialist films and magazines,[50] was the primary way in which surfing cultural values were diffused and assimilated, particularly across national boundaries. By the early 1960s California surf *culture* had spread to Australasia, and locales in Europe including the UK.[51] Due to the unregulated nature of surfboard riding, and the subsequent dearth of organisations or clubs compared to 'achievement sport' culture, these informal interactions have continued to play an important role in the diffusion of surfing, and in producing homogeneity in information and cultural characteristics in the surf culture, and related beach cultures such as windsurfing. 'Surf safaris', competitions, car-boot sales, and trade shows all fostered links between different groups and communities I studied. Yet simultaneously the local cultures have become increasingly influenced and defined by their diverse and transient membership; for example through Australian and South African lifeguards working in Cornwall, and Cornish surfers running surfing centres in the Caribbean. Surfers are what Urry calls 'diasporic travellers'; unlike conventional tourism based upon clear distinctions between 'home' and 'away', s/he has 'no clear temporal boundaries as one activity tends to flow into the next'.[52]

Furthermore, as Appadurai suggests, the media and migration work together; [The] 'mobile and unforeseen relationship between mass mediated events and migrationary audiences defines the core of the link between globalization and the modern'.[53] The subcultural media, particularly magazines and videos, has become central to the meaning and experience of lifestyle sport, and has facilitated the creation of trans-local subcultural networks and communities that extend beyond geographically defined places. Such mediascapes present new possibilities offering scripts for 'imagined lives',[54] depicting travel as an integral part of the surf and windsurfing lifestyles, fuelling participants' fantasies of surfari and 'escape'. As one of the windsurfers I interviewed explained:

> I used to look at these pictures of Mike Waltz and Mark Angulo, sailing in these waves in Hawaii, and it just looked gorgeous, and I just used to dream about going to Maui [Jason].

Another interviewee claimed he often bumped into the same people on his windsurfing holidays, regardless of how far afield he travelled.

Maguire suggests that the practitioners of alternative sport activities more widely are the type of migrants he classifies as 'nomadic cosmopolitans', those who use their sport career to journey.[55] Cosmopolitanism, according to Urry is the intellectual and aesthetic cultural disposition toward openness to peoples, places and experiences from different cultures.[56] More broadly, it considers how globalisation processes have lead to new 'global-others' that are beyond national boundaries.[57] Cosmopolitanism suggests a post-national imaginary, that transcends these traditional social identities. Surfers and windsurfers seem to display this cosmopolitan 'disposition', expressed through their aspiration to travel, willingness to connect to other cultures (however superficially – see on), and perhaps most conspicuously through their sense of 'ethical globalism' as expressed around environmentalism practices and discourses. For example, an editorial in *Surfer* magazine calls on surfers, proclaiming [they] 'have it in their power to make a change – environmentally and socially'.[58] I revisit environmentalism and its relationship to cosmopolitanism later in this chapter.

Yet the impact of Californian surf culture's values on different locales was mediated by the local culture's different historical and socio-political conditions. For example, Booth's historical analysis points to the ways that existing differences in surfing style between the main settings of Australia, California and Hawaii affected the different ways in which surf culture was embraced, given 'local' meanings, and subsequently institutionalised.[59] Australian surfing culture developed differently to that in the USA, largely due to the pre-existence of the surf lifesaving clubs with their own anti-hedonistic ideologies, and moralistic attitudes towards 'public displays of the body'.[60] In contrast, in Hawaii surfing had developed without such 'moral constraints'.[61] These cultural differences are pertinent to understanding continuing differing attitudes to surfing 'style' and formal competition. In Australia, surfing today has become a highly institutionalised activity that has the status of a 'mainstream' sport. The Australian derived aggressive surfing ethos of 'dominating the wave' (which has achieved a hegemonic position in professional competitive surfing), is based on an aggressive masculinist ethos inherited from the surf life saving movement.[62] Whereas in Hawaii, many Hawaiians still treat surfing as part of their cultural heritage – more of a lifestyle than a sport – emphasising 'being at one' with waves and nature, not aggressive competition.[63] These local differences remind us that globalisation is not a linear or uniform process of cultural homogenisation, but involves more 'disjunctive flows' that are overlapping, complex and uncertain, their impact more disjoined and contradictory.[64]

The global village of surfing: but global for whom?

Today, surfing, like most lifestyle sport subcultures, extends beyond nation-states and is popular among participants in many industrialised nations. Yet it is important to recognise that while globalization processes have intensified the spread of these sporting cultures from the economic centre to periphery areas, this has not necessarily led to these activities being made available to, or adopted by local indigenous communities. Although surfing is practised in many less-developed countries, such as South America, Africa, and the Pacific Islands, the *main* participants are travellers, rather than indigenous communities.[65] Likewise, surfing and windsurfing is increasingly popular in South Africa and parts of the Caribbean, however, local 'black' surfers remain a minority. In areas like Indonesia, 'locals' who do participate tend to service the 'tourists' working in bars, retail and the wider tourism industries. Contrary to surf video narratives that claim surfers and indigenous island communities have a 'bond', a 'shared understanding' of the importance of the ocean, it is clear that the surfers do not share the indigenous community's material conditions, nor styles of life.[66] Contrary to these romanticised and essentialised images of the 'global village of surfing', the practitioners of these activities remain in the main part, the privileged and specifically Western white males. Moreover, as I explore later in the chapter, it is not just material conditions that function to exclude many non-Western white men. The values of meritocracy in skill and commitment underpinning surfing, windsurfing, and many other lifestyle sporting activities serves to exclude individuals – and particularly women – who tend to be less committed (in time, energy and money), less confident, and less able to reach the male defined values of physical sporting prowess and risk.

In the next section I return to exploring the relationship between local and global cultures, discussing the relationship between local and national cultures and identities.

The meaning of the 'local': the (in)significance of national identity

One central issue that has concerned globalisation theorists is the effect globalisation processes have on nation-states, particularly the extent to which 'the nation' remains an important source of identity and demarcation. While announcements of the 'obsolescence of nation states'[67] are clearly premature, commentators have highlighted the increased tensions around national identity, identifying forces that simultaneously undermine, de-stabilise and re-establish the significance of national units.[68] In the sporting context, a plethora of research has demonstrated sport's continued importance as a central site where issues of nation, and the politics of national identity, are established and con-tested.[69] Most recently, research has turned to examining the role that transna-tional corporate forces have come to play in reconstituting the relationship between sport and nation in 're-imagining' national cultures,[70] particularly the position of sport within these 'reconstructed national cultures of global industry.'[71] As Maguire, outlines, 'the role sport plays in identity politics has grown more complex'.[72]

Of course minority sports, by their very nature, are less likely to be important contexts for the expression of national identity. Nevertheless, unlike more traditional, institutional sports, (the conspicuous exception being Formula One), lifestyle sport communities and identities are not bound to particular nation-states, nor have they become important signifiers of national or regional identities.[73] For instance, in the professional World Cup competitions in surfing and windsurfing – the pinnacle of *their* sporting competition – on the winner's rostrum, instead of being draped in symbols of nationalism like flags, anthems, and nationalistic team emblems, participants' bodies (and boards) are adorned with signifiers of corporations, particularly the companies that sponsor them. Although competitors do represent their countries of origin, in windsurfing signified by the particular letter used in their sail number (like yachting each letter denotes their country of 'origin'), their allegiances and 'training teams' tend to be based around equipment manufacturers, or friendship groups, not nations. In windsurfing such nationalistic identifications become increasingly meaningless when one considers that a large percentage of the world elite windsurfers live, or strive to live, in the Mecca of the Hawaiian island Maui, or a few other centres such as the Canary Islands.[74] In Maui I met young men from Europe (France, Germany, Spain, Scandinavia, UK), Australasia, Brazil, Argentina and the Caribbean either residing on Maui's north shore, or spending large periods of time on the island. A similar picture emerges trawling the pages of windsurfing magazines. Travel articles, which are a central theme in these magazines, often narrate the adventures of the young male professional wind-surfers on global adventures to find un-crowded windsurfing and surfing venues. As illustrated above, participants are often depicted as 'nomadic cosmopoli-tans',[75] global citizens without national ties or roots, displaying the postnational imaginary', Appadurai describes in transnational groups.[76] Their status and identity in this 'imagined' subcultural community are based on their windsurfing prowess, risk taking and being the most committed hedonists.[77] As Clifford suggest, perhaps models of culture based around place and locale need to be replaced by metaphors evoking travel.[78]

These examples illustrate that national identity is not a central factor in determining or performing the self or cultural identity of these elite windsurfers. While individual participants have multiple and shifting subjectivities based on gender, ethnicity age, as well as local, regional and national identifications, often the most important 'I/ we-identities'[79] of the windsurfer is their subcul-tural affiliation; that they are 'a windsurfer'. As I have argued in depth else-where, for the *committed* windsurfer for whom windsurfing is an all-absorbing style of life, rather than the 'weekend warrior' or occasional participants (who tend to consume such lifestyle sports as postmodern 'flaneurs'), the adoption of a subcultural identity is a way of asserting a distinctive and exclusive cultural identity and a sense of community.[80] In a society where traditional forms of identity have become increasingly fractured and unstable, it is argued that collective identity – such as national identification – can become decentred, resulting in the prominence of *different* types of identities, such as around these sporting *lifestyles*.[81] As analyses of cosmopolitanism have suggested, globalisation processes may offer some groups of consumers new post-national forms of global citizenship and identity.[82]

To summarise, this discussion highlights that in windsurfing, surfing, and probably other lifestyle sports, although national identity is demarked at the highest levels, for most performers, it is a less important cultural identity than those based around the increasingly trans-national subcultural communities. Nevertheless, this is not to suggest that lifestyle sport participants do not a have a sense of place or attachment to the local,[83] but that the 'other' is not identities based other nation-states. I'll briefly exemplify this point; that issues around the meaning of space and locality are central to understanding the relationships between- and within- alternative sport and (self-other) identities.

Contesting the 'local': 'them' and 'us'

Discussing the significance of 'the local' in theories of globalisation, Bennett observes that commentators often use 'local' to denote the national rather than international context, and/or to mean specific urban or rural settings.[84] These approaches tend to conceptualise the local as an unchallenged fixed space, ignoring that the local is a 'highly contested category'.[85] Underlying the social use of space are 'competing sensibilities', such as how 'different social groups appropriate and mark out social spaces within a particular place'.[86] Borden writes about insider/outsider statuses – or the division between 'them' and 'us' – in skateboarding, demonstrating the 'territorialization of skate parks' in which 'locals' claim a skate park as their own.[87] Another case in point is the way 'the waves' are given meanings as subcultural spaces and policed by their users. In Hawaii, my research showed how this 'local' subcultural space was claimed and policed by groups of surfers and windsurfers, both overtly such as cases of surfers territorialism or 'localism', and more subtlety, for example in the exclusion of female and physically less able windsurfers and surfers via a culture of meritocracy. Underlying these exclusion processes are power relations. Examining this hierarchy of subcultural space reveals a complex micro politics of gender (both between and within each gender), ethnicity, national identities, and other insider/outsider statuses.

Another example of the significance and meaning given to 'local' space – and of trans-local communities – is evident in participants and subcultural media attitudes to ocean pollution. Despite being a global discourse, environmentalism tends to be played out in local contexts, in this case around particular beaches and beach communities. Furthermore, as Urry suggest many claims about 'saving the environment' appear to depend on some notion of the cos-mopolitan.[88] The subcultural media, and environmental groups like Surfers Against Sewage (SAS) use self – other identifications which pit 'them', in this case the politicians, governments, corporate interests – against 'us', a trans-local 'imagined community' of surfers and other water sport users based around a particular space, 'our' beaches. SAS literature in the subcultural media claims; 'together *we* can make *our* ocean safe', 'stop polluting *our* beaches'. This environmental concern of surfers is also directed at the surfing industry itself in a critique of contemporary global capitalism more broadly. In a letter in *Surfer* magazine, the author condemns *Quicksilver*, for putting commercial incentives above environmental and humanitarian ones. The incident highlighted by the reader, is of *Quicksilver's* alliance with the Indonesian government, in sponsor-ing one of the professional surfing competition held in Indonesia, causing 'socially irresponsible' 'environmental degradation' at the coral reefs.[89] As Mort argues, 'shopping as the quintessential expression of consumer choice now carriers social anxieties over eco-politics'.[90]

In the remainder of the chapter I turn to discussing the influence of global capitalism, exploring its complex and contradictory influence on lifestyle sports cultures, particularly in the ways identities are constructed, and commodities are consumed in these local, lived contexts. I examine the commodities, media and consumer industries that surround these sports, and their lifestyles, drawing on some specific case-studies to illustrate these processes, such as 'anti style' attitudes in beach cultures, and attitudes to increased institutionalisation in a range of lifestyle sports.

Commodity production and consumption

Stratton calls surfing a 'commodity-orientated subculture' arguing it supports 'two fundamentals of American capitalism, consumerism and individualism'.[91] The expansion of global consumer capitalism is particularly evident in the com-modities linked to these activities, such as equipment and clothing. In response to this growing market of lifestyle sports is an ever-burgeoning industry around the manufacture and distribution of specialised equipment and related acces-sories. Wetsuits, sunglasses, T-shirts, sandals, boards, jewellery, watches and surf wax entice the consumer, and have increasingly become part of mainstream fashion. Importers or distributors of the multinationals like *Quicksilver* and *Oakley* exist in many countries, helping to produce standardised products and promotional materials. An example of this market's ability to diversify and grow is reflected in the speed in which 'surf style' for women expanded during the mid-1990s, the catalyst being the success of the ladies' board shorts (surfing shorts for women). Then there is the sizable media industry also centrally involved in promoting the sporting equipment and lifestyle. The travel industries also play an increasingly influential role, selling 'extreme' and high-thrill sporting action to committed practitioners and adventure seeking neophyte travellers alike.[92]

There are synergies between different lifestyle sports industries and medias. Many of these companies make equipment for several lifestyle sports, albeit under different brand names. Clothing companies like *Quicksilver* and *O'Neil* sell to a range of lifestyle sport markets including surfing, windsurfing, snow-boarding and emergent activities like kite-surfing. The production of kite and windsurf sails take place in the same factories, wetsuits are produced for a whole range of water sports; some snowboards and windsurf boards are manufactured by the same corporation. This pattern is mirrored in the magazine industry, with several magazines often being produced in the same design house. For example, *Arcwind* in the UK has editorial teams working on windsurfing, kite-surfing and in-line skating magazines.

However, as I have suggested, the global flows of commodities, medias and images, do not have a simple homogenising influence on the subculture. As Appadurai argues, 'often the homogenization argument subspeciates into either an argument about Americanization or an argument about commoditization, and very often the two arguments are closely linked'.[93] Many popular and some academic discourses see sports like surfing in this way, that is, as individualistic, narcissistic, materialistic co-opted consumption practices. Yet researchers focus-ing on the lived experience of these activities, often adopting ethnographic approaches, have illustrated that lifestyle sporting cultures are also spaces in which different and potentially more transformatory relationships and identities have developed between the individual and the objects of consumption, between other (gendered) individuals, and the geographical environment.

The following discussion will use some examples to exemplify that alongside the process of commodification, lifestyle sports are at the same time a potential source of cultural transformation. In the first instance, I discuss the influence of the media, highlighting the importance of local, micro medias.

The subcultural media

Maguire suggests that the global 'media-sport complex can be explained with reference to the homogenization/Westernisation/Americanization strand of glo-balization debate'.[94] He highlights that ownership and control of global sport media rests with a few transnational corporations and media organisations such as NBC and Eurosport.[95] Recent ownership trends towards synergy in the tele-communications industries, such as the growth of the Murdoch empire in the early 1990s, have further fuelled fears about the Americanisation of popular culture, including sport. Yet, as I'll illustrate, despite the influence of American media models in lifestyle sport, they are not all-pervasive; their control is not complete, nor is it uncontested.[96]

ESPN's X-Games (formerly called the eXtreme games) is the spiritual home of the 'extreme sport' concept.[97] Rinehart claims that ESPN (owned by the Disney Corporation) maintains a dominant market share, and plays a major role in shaping what the extreme sports will 'consist of, constitute, and become' for the '[virtual] world':[98]

the omnipresence of ESPN, and the very dominance of the electronic media, provides a cultural dominance over the mere presentations of extreme, alternative sports in the electronic sportscape.'[99]

Yet despite ESPN's dominance in the televisualization of alternative sport,[100] and its increasingly global reach, its *influence* outside the USA seems to be more limited. In Britain for example, the X-Games have tended to be broadcast on subscription satellite sport channels, usually at off-peaks times. Furthermore, these trans-global media networks have yet to have a sustained impact on the subcultural medias consumed by the *participants*, rather than audiences, of these sporting activities. Even in the USA, skaters (in California) interviewed by Beal and Wilson were often indifferent to media mega-events such as the X-Games and the Olympics, a theme I return to later in the chapter.[101]

It is the specialist subcultural media, including magazines, videos, fanzines, and increasingly internet resources, that are of central importance to those *within* lifestyle sport cultures.[102] As Wheaton and Beal explore drawing on the youth subcultural work of Sarah Thornton, there is an important differentiation between *mass media* (television, newspapers, etc) and *specialist* media.[103] For the subulturalists the mass media are seen as a 'colonizing co-opting' force, whereas the specialist niche media plays a central role in the creation and evolution of these cultures, in disseminating information about their activities to their members, and the creation and circulation of the symbols and meanings of subcultural capital and notions of 'authenticity'. Booth suggests these subcultural media 'communicated cultural and technical trends and styles to devotees around the world'.[104] Stranger also confirms the importance of subcultural print and electronic image of surfing in the surfing lifestyle and aesthetic in Australia.[105] The surfers in his survey bought an average of 9.27 magazines/year and watched over 10 different videos an 'indeterminate' number of times.[106] Lifestyle sport practitioners from many different activities consume their respective subcultural videos in a similar way. They watch them repeatedly, often in 'social' group settings, and replay fragments to deconstruct the manoeuvres and techniques performed by the elite performers.

Furthermore, contrary to trans-national media ownership trends, the ownership and production patterns of the specialist magazines tend to be local and more piecemeal. Magazines are predominantly produced nationally, in the main by small publishers. Booth likewise notes that technological developments such as the camcorder have made surf videos very easy and cheap to produce. So despite the background influence of the multinational, (for example Surfboard, and clothing companies have adopted videos as a cheap and easy way to advertise their products via their featured sponsored riders[107]), he suggests they remain in the domain of the small producers; their production is 'distinctively post-Fordist'.[108] Nevertheless, as noted earlier, these magazines and videos have much wider circulation and audiences which serve in the exchange of ideas such as the latest techniques, insider information and gossip. *Windsurf* magazine, for example, a British produced publication is sold as far afield as Australia.

Windsurfing, surfing and skating videos produced by equipment manufacturers, tend to use the English language, and are distributed worldwide. As already noted, the main players in the windsurfing equipment industry have importers and distributors in many countries, producing standardised products and promotional materials. Nevertheless, despite fears about the rampant commodification and Americanisation of lifestyle sports, as the next section will illustrate, the commodities that flow from this sport-media complex are not always uncritically accepted by 'local' cultures; moreover that, 'local' consumer industries challenge the control held by international and transnational corporations.

The commodification of style and 'attitude'

Lifestyle sport cultures are based around newly created commodities such as boards and decks. However as I'll examine, the relationship between these commodities and the active participants is not one based simply on their exchange value or functionality. As Hebdige explains:

> As the consumption economy has developed, the value of commodities is seen to derive less from the laws of economic exchange governing the market or from the ability of products to satisfy primary needs as from the way they function culturally as signs within coded systems of exchange.[109]

Participants use these commodities to express particular subcultural values including an anti-materialistic attitude,[110] and to establish social position or status in relation to other consumers.

Wheaton and Beal illustrate that knowledge about the equipment brands was an important component of subcultural capital for skaters in California and windsurfers in the UK, and a way to demonstrate identity and 'insider' status.[111] In their 'readings' of magazine's advertising, windsurfers showed how they used the adverts to construct narratives of 'self' that demonstrated their own 'subcultural history' based around the *use* of equipment. Yet windsurfers were hostile to conspicuous consumption of the 'kit'. Visibly displaying skill, risk and commitment to the sport was much more important than conspicuously displaying 'appropriate' brand names.[112] They described equipment as a 'necessary evil' focusing on the aesthetic *feeling* of the product, an experience that was hard(er) to commodify.[113]

Skaters' and windsurfers' evaluation of brands, and the corporations that underlie them, was also based on the companies' commitment and understanding of their sport and lifestyle.[114] Wheaton and Beal discuss skaters and windsurfers, '"doing it" Fetishism', demonstrating how they rejected commodities not considered to be 'authentic'. For skaters, brands had authentic status, primarily through demonstrating their long-standing commitment to skateboarding and especially to the culture's 'core' attitudes; *displaying* those values marks a company as insiders and, so 'legitimate'. Similarly, windsurfers were sceptical of brands that could not demonstrate long-term ('real') commitment to windsurfing or surfing, or were targeting newcomers/beginners. Although many surf brands have become international or transnational corporations, participants favoured surfing brands that had a 'hard core' image, which came principally from 'involvement and understanding of the sport and its lifestyle'. Companies of course are aware of this process, and explicitly try to portray this attitude, using sponsorship as a way to get 'core' participants' insights on their products.[115] This knowledge is then feedback to develop themes for their products and videos that generate brand loyalty,[116] just one of the ways the 'attitude' or value system in these sports has been commodified.

A brief examination of participant's attitudes to surf style illustrates these dynamics in the commoditisation of surf style.

'Anti-style' in the windsurfing and surfing culture

When conducting ethnographic research on windsurfing my field notes often noted the homogeneity in visual appearance of the young male windsurfer. At beaches from the Caribbean to the Canary Islands, the participants wore the same style of board shorts, T-shirts, thongs, and sunglasses of the same shape and brand.[117] As one of my interviewees put it: 'there's like a uniform'. Windsurfing and surfing shops I visited around the world sold many of the same brands.[118] This uniformity in experience points to the ways these global flows in commodities (and images), Appadurai's mediascapes, have had a homogenising influence on subcultural style.

Yet although clothing and fashion is an essential part of surf culture, windsurfers didn't want to be seen to be 'buying into' an image and coined term such as 'fashion surfers' 'to describe those individuals who tried to *display* their subcultural identification solely via surf style (or by conspicuously displaying – rather than using – their equipment).[119] As one windsurfer put it, 'I object to wearing heavily branded clothing.[..] You don't like to think you are being influenced by the trade, or advertising, or the image'.[120] Furthermore, well-travelled interviewees suggested that that 'brand' display was much more prevalent in the UK and Europe, than other places around the world, referencing particularly Australia and Hawaii. Alex claimed the non-Europeans were 'less into labels ... Even in Hawaii, they wear 3 year old bits of clothing; no one is walking around wearing flashy new gear'. My own observations suggested that underlying this claim was a degree of romanticisation of the 'anti-fashion' ethos, nevertheless, it also points to a complex picture in which subcultural style has different expressions and meanings in various 'local' subcultural settings.

Moreover, there is another aspect to windsurfers' 'style denial'. During the late 1980s and early 1990s in the UK 'beach wear' and particularly surf style, exploded into mainstream men's fashion.[121] As surf style became incorporated into 'main stream' fashion, the distinctiveness and exclusivity of the windsurfers' and surfers' subcultural style decreased, which seemingly contributed to style becoming a less important aspect of subcultural identification. As a British male surfer in his 40s put it:

> In the olden days you could wear surf clothes just to show you're a surfer. Nowadays everyone wears them ... I'd avoid the big brands now. It no longer means anything to me to have surf clothing on, because everyone wears them.[122]

Denying the existence of style was a form of (verbal) 'symbolic' resistance to the commercialisation process resulting in surf style's incorporation into mainstream fashion. Stedman likewise asks on what basis do 'real surfers' express their collective identity when anyone can buy a surf T-shirt?[123] She suggests that rather than commercialism threatening to undermine the surfing culture in Australia, subcultural identity is displayed in *different* ways. So, similarly to my claims about windsurfers' display of commitment, she suggests that surfers' 'attitude' is their way of demonstrating their collective identity.[124] The meaning and uniqueness of the subcultural identification of the committed windsurfer (in the UK) and surfer (in both Australia and the UK) was not based on the consumption of these commodities, but around their 'attitude', and their sporting prowess – or ability *to do* the activities. An interesting dimension of this process that I will come on to consider is the gender politics, specifically how an aggressive sexism became part of this re-created 'alternative' attitude.[125]

This case study of surf style is also informing in illustrating that the influence of global commodity culture is neither fixed nor unchallenged; furthermore, that at the economic level, regional and national industries challenge the stronghold of the international and transnational corporations. As noted in my discussion of subcultural style, transnational and international companies like *Quicksilver* are important players in the industry, their sphere of influence via sponsorship, the production of sports videos and other subcultural resources is key. In many countries lifestyle sport magazines rely on such advertisers from *within* their sports to sustain the magazines; (for example, windsurfing magazines in the UK are largely dependent on the manufacturers of windsurfing equipment). Yet alongside these corporations are regionally based cottage industries that co-exist, and in some cases dominate, the production of material goods and services. Booth likewise recognises the enduring prevalence of small, flexible 'artisans' in the production of equipment, accessories, films and magazines in Australia.[126] The picture is clearly complex, and an area that requires detailed research; however, I will offer some insights based on differences between the British windsurfing and British surfing cultures.

In the British surf culture there is a strong history of local small scale production, particularly in the West Country, manufacturing merchandise from surfboards to wetsuits. Some of these, like *Gul* wetsuits have expanded sufficiently to impact the global market, but they exist alongside other local brands, selling largely to the UK market. Custom-made surfboards remain the preferred 'authentic' product, each one is individually crafted (the craftsman is termed the 'shaper'), often with personalised characteristics and artwork. Surfers who were members of the Cornish-based organisation Surfers Against Sewage (SAS) admitted that one reason they joined the organisation was to be able to buy SAS clothing range, its 'anti capitalist' stance gave it a 'cool' factor. However in the British windsurfing culture, although a similar local industry grew up in the 1980s, (including in the West County) in the late 1990s 'production' boards made by the international companies (often using cheap labour in the Far East) have dominated the market. In my research on the consumption of brands,[127] contrary to in the surf culture there was little evidence of windsurfers unanimously favouring 'home grown' clothing or equipment brands.

The central substantive point in this analysis of the commoditisation of style and equipment, and worth emphasising, is these lifestyle sport cultures' complex, at times contradictory and shifting, relationship to the seemingly colonising co-opting force of global consumer culture. Despite the 'resilient belief' that 'grassroots' or 'authentic' culture resists and struggles with a 'colonising mass-mediated corporate world',[128] the media and consumer industries' roles are more complex, contradictory and fluid than simply incorporation and co-option; these subculturalists are not simply 'victims' of commercialism, but shape and 're-shape' the images and meanings circulated in and by global consumer culture.[129] Whereas the commodity production process has received considerable attention, the institutionalisation process, especially as expressed through attitudes to competition provides another interesting aspect in understanding the commercialisation of these activities.

Institutionalisation and professionalisation

The historical development patterns of lifestyle sports in many ways mirror the 'sportization phases' suggested by Maguire in his discussion of the globalisation of more traditional 'achievement sports'.[130] Lifestyle sports are increasingly global in influence, international sporting rules and organisations have been established, and – in some cases – competition between 'national teams' has evolved and grown. Yet in the majority of these lifestyle sports, clubs and organisations tend to exist only where needed for access to facilities or spaces; for most, participation strives to be *unregulated* and *individualistic*. Attitudes to participating in organised competition tend to stress 'intrinsic' factors such as challenging the self or the environment, and even among elite participants' attitudes to formal man-on-man' (sic) competitions remain ambivalent. As noted earlier, whereas in achievement sport global sporting competitions such as the Olympics Games is considered the pinnacle of sporting achievement, in most lifestyle sports, practitioners have been wary of their incorporation in such institutionalised competitions, seeing it as a form of 'selling out' their alternative values and ideologies. As one snowboarder put it at the time of snowboarding's inclusion in the Olympics: 'Success is measured in exhilaration not medals or money ... How can you have a competition to measure who has had the most fun?'[131] When Olympic champion snowboarder Ross Rebagliati was temporarily stripped of his medal for allegedly smoking marijuana, he was embraced by sections of the snowboarding subculture as a champion for publicly re-establishing snowboarding's 'alternative' image.[132] Nonetheless, professional snowboarding competition has thrived – both in the Olympics and in media-made forms such as Border-X.[133]

Similar contradictions exist in the increased professionalisation and concomitant attitudes to competition in surfing, windsurfing and skating. Beal outlined how in the mid-1990s, skaters who embraced competition and sponsorship were called 'rats'.[134] Since that time competition has become much more widespread, particularly via the popularity of skating as part of ESPN's X-Games. As Rinehart argues, 'ESPN, while not defining what skating is, has come to represent for a majority of world-viewers how skating can become a 'competition,' and how skaters themselves can be encapsulated'.[135] Beal's recent research with skaters in North America also reveals changing attitudes to commercialisation, demonstrating that skaters are less critical of sponsorship and professionalism, seeing the benefits they bring to the skating community. Nevertheless, they continue to resist changes that will lead to increased regulation or a change in the ethos of skating, such as a creative/artistic sensibility, self-expression and an individualistic attitude.[136] Skaters continue to stress the importance of an 'intrinsic motivation' – that is motivations should be oriented to the act of skating, a commitment to 'the actual process' and not solely for money, or 'looking cool'. Skating – like other lifestyle sports – has diversified into different cultural forms such as the more aggressive, macho unregulated street-skating. Beal concludes that skaters are not uniformly *against* the commercial process, but show concerns about how their activity is portrayed and the resultant impact that may have; 'the skaters' assessment of commercialization is represented by some ambiguity and contradiction'.[137]

Booth has written at length about tensions and conflicts in the history of professionalisation and codification of modern surfing.[138] Initially, in the 1960s the 'Soul surfing' movement ('riding the waves for the good of one's soul')[139] explicitly rejected materialism and competition, extolling 'creativity and self-expression within a co-operative environment'.[140] Soul surfers interpreted their activity as an escape from bourgeois society, co-joining surfing with the counterculture. Surfing star Nat Young claimed he was 'supporting the revolution'.[141] Both Farmer and Pearson have argued that 'there is a competitive taboo in the surfing culture – competition against other individuals is not valued'.[142] However, surfing has increasingly embraced capitalist culture via professionalisation, and today, international professional surfing competitions are a central part of surf culture, run under the auspices of the ASP. An interesting dimension of this process is the ways in which the attempts – initially in the 1960s – to impose 'universal' international rules caused conflict between the then main 'regional' settings of California, Australia and Hawaii. Each wanted to preserve the authenticity of its different surfing 'style', underpinning which were divergent philosophies about 'mankind's (sic) relationship with nature'.[143] As noted earlier these styles reflected differing cultural values and masculine identities.

The Hawaiians tended to 'dance with the waves' whereas the Australians had developed a more aggressive and materialistic attitude and sporting masculinity. In this example then the global flow leading toward increased materialism and instutionalisation initially came from Australia not America, but nevertheless Westernisation has dominated.

Windsurfing has appropriated the ethos of soul surfing to describe the type of windsurfing (usually wave sailing) that pitted an individual against the environment, not other people. Windsurfer's idealised and constructed image of the 'soul' windsurfer as at one with 'nature', unfettered by materialism, was a reaction against both competition and commercialism. As the editorial for a British windsurfing magazine issue in the late 1990s entitled *Soul Issue* and devoted almost entirely to travel, claimed, 'Our mission was to rediscover the spirit of windsurfing, rebuild the foundations [. . .] man,[sic] board and rig at one with the wind and the waves'.[144] Nevertheless, despite this ambivalence to traditional regulated competitions, windsurfing has simultaneously embraced competition in any, and every, form it can to bring money to the struggling lifestyle of the professional windsurfer. It is hard to imagine a less 'authentic' event than the made-for-TV spectacular of indoor windsurfing. These 'competitions', run under the auspices of the PWA (World Professional Windsurfing Association), involve giant fans propelling windsurfers in slalom races and spectacular aerial antics off a ramp, accompanied by loud music and a laser show. The prize money matched that of the 'real' windsurfing competitions held in dangerous surf.

Commodification of bodies: the politics of gender

One conspicuous trend in contemporary consumer culture is the way bodies have been increasingly and unashamedly displayed, commodified and sexualised, particularly through their association with sport and exercise.[145] Lifestyle sports have not been immune from these processes. In films, advertising and television representations of beach cultures from Baywatch to Pepsi Max, female bodies are displayed in sexualised and commodified ways.

Kusz's detailed analysis of mainstream press discourses of Extreme sports, points to the ways mainstream magazine articles at the end of the 1990s have celebrated Extreme sports as the 'symbol of a new American zeitgeist' understood as the revival of traditional and specifically American values such as 'individualism, self-reliance, risk taking, and progress'.[146] Kusz examines how these discourses give a masculinised and patriotic representation of Extreme sports that re-articulates and naturalises the link between whiteness and America that he suggests 'can be read as a symptom and imagined solution to America's perceived crisis of white masculinity'.[147]

Likewise, lifestyle sport's subcultural media tend to commoditise women's bodies and experiences. The body is the site in which differences of gender, sexuality, race, ethnicity and class are constituted and made visible. Rinehart illustrates the misogynist imagery in skating magazines,[148] asserting that almost all of the images of women were sexualised, only very rarely depicting women skating.[149] Stedman's analysis of the surfing media in Australia demonstrates how the othering of female bodies and identities has shifted over the past 30 years. She charts how male surfers' broad acceptance of women before the 1980s changed to an aggressively toxic hyper-masculinity as surfers attempted to re-establish a deviant attitude.[150] In the late 1990s women's surfing participation saw considerable growth, which is only starting to be reflected by a broader acceptance in the subcultural media.

However, it tends to be the magazines and videos that target the younger, particularly 'teen' male, consumers that so explicitly sexualise, objectify and commodify women. Windsurfing magazines, for example, have a more varied male readership in terms of both class and age than skating magazines, and although they predominantly depict young male performers, representations of women include both 'beach babe' imagery that commodify the female body and photos representing women as active, competent, advanced embodied performers. Furthermore, researchers that have explored how these images are consumed, suggest that readers simultaneously constructed, and contested women, and non-white participants, as the 'inauthentic' subject or 'Other'.[151] For example, while acknowledging that images of women in bikinis will always be open to sexualised readings, windsurfers' read images that pretended the subject was 'doing it' as 'inauthentic'. As Booth outlines, the 'contradictions, ambiguities and paradoxes' associated with the growth of women's surfing are most conspicuous in the pages of the new magazines for female surfers,[152] magazines like *Wahine* and *Surfer Girl* where adverts featuring skinny models promoting makeup sit alongside 'real' muscular wet- suited women surfing monster waves.

Similarly, the expression of masculine and feminine identities in lifestyle sporting cultures is often more diverse and ambivalent than the mediated products might suggest. Gendered power relations have been examined in a range of different lifestyle sporting contexts (e.g. skateboarding, windsurfing, snowboarding, ultimate Frisbee and climbing),[153] examining how gender (and in some studies class and 'racial') identities are related to processes of inclusion and exclusion. It is argued that such sporting cultures represent both a re-inscription of traditional identities – especially in relation to compulsory heterosexuality – as well as the *potential* for more progressive sporting identities. For example, my own ethnographic research in the windsurfing culture identified that the prevalent lived masculine subjectivity – 'ambivalent masculinity' – was less exclusive of women and 'other men' than many institutionalised sport cultures, or (middle-class) work cultures.[154] 'Laddishness', particularly as played out through competitiveness over status, and masculine identification based on the subordination and commodification of women as passive, sexual objects, was largely confined to younger, elite men. Participants of both genders emphasised the supportiveness and camaraderie among men and women in the culture.[155] Nevertheless, in many lifestyle sports attitudes to gender are reflective of *dominant* attitudes to gender and sexuality. As Rinehart suggests, while oppositional options are available, groups such as skaters have opted for much more conventional, traditional gender relations.[156]

Conclusion

In this chapter I have highlighted the impact of global commodity culture on lifestyle sport cultures, and their practices and identities, highlighting the global flows in images and medias, technologies, commodities, and people. I have suggested that the articulation of identity in some lifestyle sports, particularly in the expression of self and community based around trans-local subcultural affiliations and spaces, reiterate claims that the relationship between sport and national identity is increasingly complex and needs further investigation, particularly the position different types of sports, such as alternative sport, play 'within the reconstructed national cultures of global industry'.[157] Furthermore, analysis of these post-national identities and imaginary might fruitfully draw on notions of cosmopolitism to examine participant's cosmopolitan disposition, their ability to live simultaneously in both the global and the local, and whether their acceptance of cultural diversity embraces difference and transcends national identities.

The 'alternative sportscape'[158] as Rinehart terms it, is becoming increasingly diverse and globally widespread. This diversity is particularly evident in the ever-expanding media-made events that range from sports with new twists, amalgams of previously known sports, to completely new activities. Furthermore, it isn't just the marketing departments of media corporations who are taking the initiative; ex-performers such as skateboarder Tony Hawk, have shown they too can be successful entrepreneurs in this making of the media sportscape. Tony Hawk's latest venture is the 'Boom Boom HuckJam' a live festival of extreme sport and music, in which he is director, sponsor and performer.[159] The latest financial twist to the media metamorphism of alternative sport is in its appropriation by the lucrative video game market which has propelled sportsmen like Tony Hawk into wealthy 'global mega-stars'.[160] Yet I have contended that it is those activities that transcend the mediascape and become popular *among* participants that endure beyond being short-lived fads. Lifestyle sports are fundamentally about participation and performance – the *doing* of the activity. As Borden suggests, skateboarding is a sport which produces space, time and self, which for its practitioners 'involves nothing less than a complete and alternative way of life'.[161]

Undeniably, in a global culture increasingly dominated by the exchange of commodity signs, which include mediated objects, practices and personalities, a central consequence is profitability for a variety of national, international and transnational organisations.[162] As Maguire points out 'there is a political economy at work in the production and consumption of global sport/leisure products that can lead to a relative ascendancy of a narrow selection of capitalist and Western sport cultures'.[163] Yet the case studies have also demonstrated a variety of complex and competing cultural flows, not just Americanisation. As I have exemplified, alongside the evident commodification and co-option of lifestyle sport, is its ability – like many youth cultures – to adapt and change, to remain a potential source of cultural transformation. Recent sociological research that has moved towards a more sophisticated understanding of the complex dynamics between subculture, the mass media, and global commercial culture, is better able to explore these dynamics. In outlining an agenda for empirically exploring the impact of these global cultural forces on alternative sports, I have signalled that analysis needs to move beyond cross-cultural comparisons, to exploring the impact of global flows (such as mapped out by Appadurai's scapes) on, between and within local subcultures, and their medias and industries.[164] Furthermore, the gendered, ethnic and class-based nature of these processes needs continued attention. Yet as Appadurai suggests, 'A framework for relating the global, the national and the local, in this as in other sporting contexts, has yet to emerge'.[165]

10 Afterword: more questions than answers

Lincoln Allison

We often claim, in academic social studies, that our aspiration is more to put the right questions and to clarify those questions than it is to provide definitive answers. Rarely, since the more rigorous forms of positivism have lost their appeal, do we claim to be able to predict the future. If we synthesise these two observations we are left with the task of suggesting what the key questions about the future are and on what the answers might depend. This task can coexist with a great deal of enthusiasm for future debate and investigation. In short, there are a lot of interesting questions which arise from the previous chapters when taken together.

Have International Non-Governmental Organisations (INGOs) really preempted the power and influence of states and of a range of inter-governmental organisations? Are sporting INGOs (SINGOs) and business INGOs (BINGOs) really particularly strong? Is it right to talk of the development of 'post-Westphalian' and even 'neo-Mediaeval' systems of international power which are far more autonomous of the state system than was anything in the twentieth century. Is sport a particularly advanced form of this development? In which case Juan Samaranch, Rupert Murdoch *et al.* in the Olympic Stadium in Sydney in 2000 might be a visual symbol for international power in the twentieth century as Churchill, Roosevelt and Stalin sitting on a bench in Yalta in 1945 was for the twentieth.

If so, how worried should we be about the nature of power in international organisations? In the nineteenth century liberals like John Stuart Mill and Lord Acton were also to different degrees nationalists because they perceived international organisations like the Roman Catholic Church and the Austro-Hungarian Empire as necessarily lacking many of the political virtues which might be developed in the nation-state. They were less accountable than states and less legitimate because the nature of national identity was such that a Ruritanian would always find it easier to obey a fellow Ruritanian than he would a foreigner. They tended towards a 'lowest common denominator', absorbing, for example, the normative approach to corruption of the most corrupt. This is echoed in twenty-first century debates about business ethics in the global context where 'rotten apple' theory necessarily applies insofar as it very difficult to compete uncorruptly in the matter of tendering if your competitors and the other party to a possible contract are both corrupt.

Acton's fears as a liberal catholic culminated in the declaration of papal infallibility in the Vatican Council rigged by Pius IX in July 1870. The means and the outcome were equally disturbing. Why that is particularly relevant is because the accounts given here of the politics of FIFA and the IOC seem broadly similar to the Catholic politics which disturbed Acton. The messianic figures of Brundage, Samaranch, Havelange and Blatter even seem to have papal qualities of haughtiness, self-righteousness and pretension which are knocked out of everyday, elected, state politicians. Unlike Pius IX they do not seek to have themselves declared infallible on matters of doctrine, but the impression given by both Jaou Havelange and Juan Samaranch is that they thought their judgements on what was best for football and for sport were essentially irrefutable. Like Pius XI they defended themselves by saying that what they stood for was something higher, grander and more universal than mere national politicians.

The world's press have made life easy for the SINGO emperors, subjecting them to much less of the 'critical spirit' and to much less direct scrutiny than they do national politicians. This probably goes much deeper than mere media practice: the failure of accountability is at least partly because most people still think in national terms and have much less interest in scrutinising or pillorying international figures, even allowing them their positions as ciphers for higher ideals. The question remains: will this continue? Or will there be the sort of challenge from the state which so far has been wholly absent from the agenda? The answers may depend on the development of nationalism. Sport offers an arena for an intense, shallow nationalist competition over the kind of prestige which can come from success or from the acquisition of major events. But this kind of nationalism is symbiotic with SINGO power. Could there be the development of deeper nationalist voices which see SINGO power and homogenisation as the enemies of local sporting culture. A Nordic revolt against the IOC's impact on cross-country skiing? Or an English revolt against FIFA's effects on the FA Cup or the 92-club football league? And could these voices be heard at the state level, leading governments to try to recapture control of sport in the name of democracy?

In any case, the forces of 'globalisation' do not offer a single coherent challenge, but a fragmented contest between different visions of sport. The BINGOs offer sport as the commercial opportunity of the future, an entertainment industry of almost unlimited potential. But the SINGOs talk of it as a mission, a 'social', 'cultural', even quasi-religious entity which must be governed as such. In many ways they are dependent on each other's logic, but the difference is mirrored by a completely different set of assumptions about the regulation of sport in Europe and the United States. And a final question that emerges about global regulation simply concerns whether it will be effective, given the money to be made, in dealing with the problems of doping and gambling and the force of the 'lowest common denominator' argument.

There is a great deal to play for, so to speak, for the sports' scholar and a great deal to argue about. Much of it goes to the heart of the meaning and value of sport and much of it will be of concern too to the sports' fan.

Notes

Series editor's foreword

1 Richard Vinen, *A History in Fragments: Europe in the Twentieth Century* (London: Little, Brown and Company, 2000, p.7).
2 Robert W. Stern, *Changing India: Bourgeois Revolution on the Subcontinent* (Cambridge: CUP, 2003), Second Edition, p.1.
3 Ibid., quoted in the Acknowledgement.
4 Ian Phillip, letter to *The Daily Telegraph*, Wednesday, 28 April 2004, Sport, p.54.
5 See Chapter 10, 'Afterword: More questions than Answers', in Lincoln Allison (ed.), *The Global Politics of Sport* (London: Routledge, 2004).
6 See Lincoln Allison, *Amateurism in Sport: An Analysis and a Defence* (London: Frank Cass, 2000).

1 Sport and globalisation: the issues

1 Lincoln Allison (ed.), *The Politics of Sport* (Manchester: Manchester University Press, 1986); Lincoln Allison (ed.), *The Changing Politics of Sport* (Manchester: Manchester University Press, 1993).

2 Sport, prestige and international relations

1 Trevor Taylor, 'Sport and International Relations' in Lincoln Allison (ed.), *The Politics of Sport* (Manchester: Manchester University Press, 1986, p.45).
2 John A. Vasquez (ed.), *Classics of International Relations* (Englewood Cliffs, NJ: Prentice-Hall, 1990).
3 Michael Nicholson, *International Relations*, A Concise Introduction (Basingstoke: Macmillan, 1998).
4 William Nester, *International Relations, Geopolitical and Geoeconomic Conflict and Co-operation* (New York: HarperCollins, 1995).
5 Joshua S. Goldstein, *International Relations* (New York: HarperCollins, 1996).
6 Koton and Yadowich quoted in Trevor Taylor, 'Sport and International Relations', op. cit. p.40.
7 See, for example, Hugh Carnegy, 'Hugely Important Symbol of Acceptance', China Supplement, *Financial Times*, 13th November 2000, p.VII.
8 See, for example, Nayan Chanda and Kari Huus, 'The New Nationalism', *Far Eastern Economic Review*, 9th November 1995, pp.21–28 and Yinhong Shi 'Why Against China?', *Beijing Review*, 21 October 1996, p.11. We are grateful to Shaun Breslin for information on the background to the Chinese Olympic Bid.

9   See Adrian Guelke, 'Sport and the End of Apartheid', in Lincoln Allison (ed.), *The Changing Politics of Sport* (Manchester: Manchester University Press, 1993, pp.151–70).

10   See House of Commons Foreign Affairs Select Committee Session 1999–2000 Tenth Report, 'UK Relations with the People's Republic of China'. The Chinese response was available on www.chinese-embassy.org.uk I am very grateful to my colleague Shaun Breslin for information on this issue.

11   Hans J. Morgenthau, *Politics Among Nations: the Struggle for Power and Peace* (New York: Knopf, 1960, p.27).

12   Peter Fitzsimmons, 'Warm Glow After Flame Dies', *Daily Telegraph*, 3rd October 2000, p.42.

13   Hans J. Morgenthau, *Politics Among Nations*, op. cit., p.27.

14   Ibid., p.31.

15   Peter I. Beck, *Scoring for Britain, International Football and International Politics* (London: Frank Cass, 1999).

16   See Philip Noel-Baker, *Man of Sport, Man of Peace, Collected Speeches and Essays of Philip Noel-Baker, Olympic Statesman 1889–1992*, compiled by Don Anthony (London: Sports Editions, 1991).

17   Ibid., p.37.

18   George Orwell, 'The Sporting Spirit', in *The Penguin Essays of George Orwell*, Harmondsworth, Penguin 1994, p.321. Originally in Tribune, 14th December 1945.

19   Ibid., p.322.

20   For the context see Richard Holt, *Sport and Society in Modern France* (Basingstoke: Macmillan, 1981).

21   For a straightforward account of the escalation of government support to sport see Richard Holt and Tony Mason, *Sport in Britain 1945–2000* (Oxford: Blackwell, 2000, pp.146–67).

22   Quoted in John Sugden and Alan Tomlinson, *FIFA and the Contest for World Football* (Cambridge: Polity, 1999, p.7).

23   In interviews with Lincoln Allison in 1999 as part of his research for *Amateurism in Sport, an Analysis and Defence* (London: Frank Cass, 2001).

24   Members of the Staff of the Physical Education Department of the University of Birmingham, *Britain in the World of Sport* (London: The Physical Education Association of GB and NI, 1956, p.9).

25   Ibid., p.10

26   Ibid., p.12.

27   The report of the Wolfenden Committee, *Sport and the Community* (London: The Central Council of Physical Recreation, 1960).

28   Ibid., p.72.

29   Ibid., p.78.

30   Philip Goodhart and Christopher Chataway, *War Without Weapons* (London: W.H. Allen, 1968, p.89).

31   Ibid., p.90.

32   Ibid., p.100.

33   Ibid., p.157.

34   Department of the Environment, *Sport and Recreation* (London: HMSO, 1975, p.18, para. 62).

35   See Terry Monnington, 'Politicians and Sport: Uses and Abuses', in Lincoln Allison (ed.) *The Changing Politics of Sport* (Manchester: Manchester University Press, 1993, pp.125–50).

36   As suggested in an open letter from the then Minister for Sport, Colin Moynihan, to the Director of the Sports Council, John Smith, Department for the Environment, 19th November 1997.

37   *Sport: Raising the Game* (London: Department of National Heritage, 1995, p.2).

38 John Major, 'Three Weeks That Lifted a Nation', *Electronic Telegraph*, 417, 1st July 1996, p.1.
39 For a more detailed description of the role and function of these bodies see the official website of Sport England, www.sportengland.org.uk
40 See Terry Monnington, 'The Politics of Black African Sport', in Lincoln Allison (ed.) *The Politics of Sport* (Manchester: Manchester University Press, 1986, pp.149–73).
41 See UN Development Programme, *UN Human Development Report 2000* (Oxford: Oxford University Press, 2000) and World Bank, World Development Report 1999/2000 (Oxford: Oxford University Press, 1999).
42 See D. Prokop (ed.), *The African Running Revolution, Mountain View*, Calif., World Publications, 1975.
43 See Terry Monnington, 'Crisis Management in Black African Sport', in Clyde Binfield and John Stevenson (eds.), *Sport, Culture and Politics* (Sheffield: Sheffield Academic Press, 1993, pp.113–28).
44 See Joseph Maguire, *Global Sport*, Cambridge, Polity Press, 1999.
45 We are grateful to John Roberts, West Midlands Director of Sport England, for clarifying this point. The crucial decision for releasing money on the current scale for potential medallists was the relaxation in 1997 of the ruling that lottery monies must be devoted to capital projects.

3 Not for the good of the game

1 The outgoing president of FIFA, João Havelange, boasts of his financial achievements while still at the helm in 1998. Quoted in J. Sugden and A. Tomlinson, *FIFA and the Contest For World Football. Who Rules the Peoples' Game?* (Cambridge: Polity Press, 1998).
2 For a detailed discussion of the rise of IGOs and INGOs see D. Held *et al.*, *Global Transformations – Politics, Economics and Culture* (Cambridge: Polity Press, 1999), section 1, from which these figures on the growth of such organisations have been drawn.
3 C. Archer, *International Organisations*, second edition (London: Routledge, 1992).
4 G. Morozov (1997) 'The Socialist Conception', *International Social Science Journal* 29 no.1: 28–45.
5 T. Miller, G. Lawrence, J. McKay and D. Rowe, *Globalization and Sport – Playing the World* (London: Sage, 2000), p. 10.
6 A. Tomlinson, 'Going Global: The FIFA Story', in *Off the Ball: The Football World Cup*, eds. A. Tomlinson and G. Whannel (London: Pluto Press, 1986); A. Tomlinson, 'FIFA and the World Cup – The Expanding FIFA Family', in *Hosts and Champions – Soccer Cultures, National Identities and the USA World Cup* (Aldershot: Ashgate Publishing, 1994); J. Sugden and A. Tomlinson, *FIFA and the Contest*; J. Sugden and A. Tomlinson, *Great Balls of Fire – How Big Money is Hijacking World Football* (Edinburgh: Mainstream Publishing, 1999); J. Sugden and A. Tomlinson, *Badfellas – FIFA Family at War* (Edinburgh: Mainstream Publishing, 2003); J. Sugden, 'Network Football', in *Power Games – A Critical Sociology of Sport*, eds. J. Sugden and A. Tomlinson (London: Routledge, 2002).
7 A more extensive account of this can be found in Sugden and Tomlinson, *Badfellas: FIFA Family at War*. Much of the empirical material in this chapter is drawn from chapters 1 and 14 of that book.
8 For a detailed discussion of this in a British setting see T. Bower, *Broken Dreams. Vanity, Greed and the Souring of British Football* (London: Simon and Schuster, 2003).

9   FIFA congress, Buenos Aires, 2001, Agenda Item A.1+2
10 See Sugden and Tomlinson, *Great Balls of Fire*, Chapter 10.
11 The full text of this letter, pp.4, is in the possession of the authors.
12 Petition to the Swiss court available from the authors.
13 Sugden and Tomlinson, op. cit. 1999.
14 V. Cable, *Globalisation and Global Governance* (Chatham House Papers: London, The Royal Institute of International Affairs, 1999). The quotations are from pp.102 and 103–4.
15 Obviously, these are ideal solutions with huge practical problems. For instance, when it comes to corruption, the UN and the EU have their own problems.
16 Susan Strange, *Casino Capitalism* (Manchester: Manchester University Press, 1997). The quotations are from pp.121 and 189. See too her *Mad Money* (Manchester: Manchester University Press, 199?).

4   Olympic survivals: the Olympic Games as a global phenomenon

1   This account of the 2010 bids is based upon my notes on the presentations, relayed live from Prague to the Auditorium of the Olympic Museum, Lausanne, Switzerland, throughout July 2nd 2003.
2   T. Miller, G. Lawrence, G. McKay and D. Rowe, *Globalization and Sport: Playing the World* (London: Sage, 2001, p.2).
3   Ibid.
4   M. Roche, *Mega-events and Modernity: Olympics and expos in the growth of global culture* (Routledge, 2000, p.26).
5   Ibid p. 233.
6   J. Maguire, *Global Sport: Identities, societies, civilizations* (Cambridge: Polity, 1999, p.88).
7   Ibid., p. 92.
8   Miller *et al.*, op. cit., p.12.
9   A. Bairner, *Sport, Nationalism and Globalization – European and North American perspectives* (Albany: State University of New York Press, 2001).
10 Miller *et al.*, op. cit., p.40.
11 L. Sklair, *The Transnational Capitalist Class* (Oxford: Blackwell, 2001, p.6).
12 Ibid., p.251.
13 Ibid., p.110.
14 Ibid., p.296.
15 J. Tomlinson, *Globalization and Culture* (Cambridge: Polity, 1999, p.9).
16 See Roche, op. cit.
17 These quotations are taken from the John Johnson Collection of Ephemera at the Bodleian Library in Oxford.
18 The following quotations are taken from G.Van Rossem (Ed.), *The Ninth Olympiad, Being the Official Report of the Olympic Games of 1928 Celebrated at Amsterdam, issued by the Netherlands Olympic Committee*. Translated by Sydney W.Fleming, J.H. De Bussy (Amsterdam).
19 Roche, op. cit., p.105.
20 Printed by ENIT, 1933, not paginated. Also available in the John Johnson collection.
21 A. Tomlinson, *The Game's Up: Essays in the Cultural Analysis of Sport, Leisure and Popular Culture* (Aldershot: Ashgate, 1999).
22 See A. Tomlinson, "The Making of the Global Sports Economy: ISL, Adidas and the rise of the corporate player in world sport" in D. Andrews and M. Silk (eds.) *Corporate Nationalisms* (Oxford: Berg, 2004).
23 The following details draw on the *Official Report* of the Games which I consulted at the Olympic Museum in Lausanne.

24 Thanks to Lincoln Allison for drawing out the distinction between these dimensions in response to an earlier draft.

25 This is in a copy of the programme which I consulted in the Olympic Museum in Lausanne.

26 This exhibition was entitled, 'Ella Maillart 1903–1997: Sportswoman; on the Roads of the East'.

27 A. Tomlinson, 'The Disneyfication of the Olympics? Freak-Shows of the Body', in J. Bale and M.K. Christensen (eds), *Post-Olympism? Questioning Sport in the Twenty-First Century* (Oxford: Berg, 2004, pp.147–63).

5 Alternative models for the regulation of global sport

1 Scholte, J.A., *Globalisation: a critical introduction* (Basingstoke: Palgrave, 2000).

2 Union Royale Belge des Sociétés de Football Association v Bosman (case C415/93) [1996] All ER (EC) 97.

3 Giulianotti, R., *Football: a Sociology of the Global Game* (Cambridge: Polity Press, 1999, p.95).

4 Ibid. p.35.

5 especially Houlihan, B., Sport and Globalisation in Houlihan, B (ed.) *Sport and Society: a student introduction* (London: Sage, 2003).

6 Ibid. p.351.

7 Ibid. p.355.

8 This can also apply to boxing where the harmonisation of safety standards has been advanced so that a boxer declared unfit to box in one jurisdiction cannot shop around until he can find somewhere that will allow him to fight.

9 R v Disciplinary Committee of the Jockey Club ex p Aga Khan [1993] 2 All E R 853 (CA). Most commentators consider this case to be wrongly decided. See Beloff, M. & Kerr, T., Why Aga Khan is Wrong [1996] JR 30 and Pannick, D., Judicial Review of Sports Bodies [1997] JR 150 but it remains the legal position.

10 The Supreme Court held in 1987 that the United States Olympic Committee was not a state actor so that legal action to protect its name did not constitute government action and thus the provisions of the Constitution did not apply. San Francisco Arts & Athletics Inc. v USOC, 483 U.S.522 (1987).

11 Korda v ITF (unreported, *Times*, 4 February 1999). However, in Modahl v British Athletic Federation [No.2] (Court of Appeal, 12 October 2001) it was questioned whether an athlete automatically has a legal relationship with their national association.

12 Wilander & Novacek v. Tobin & Jude [1997] 2 Lloyd's Rep 293.

13 The entry form for the Sydney Olympics contained this clause; 'In the interest of a speedy and expert resolution of all dispute arising in connection with Olympic Games, I hereby surrender any right I may have to commence proceedings in a court in relation to any such dispute or file any appeal, review or recourse to any state court or other judicial authority from any arbital award, decision or ruling issued by the CAS in particular'. (From *Sportzaken Journal*, 2000/3, p.14).

14 For descriptions of the work of Court of Arbitration for Sport, see Morris, P. & Spink, P., Court of Arbitration for Sport in Stewart, W.J. (ed.) Sport and the Law – The Scots Perspective (Edinburgh: T & T Clark, 2000, pp.61–76). Beloff, M. Kerr, T. & Demetriou, M, Sports Law, (Hart: Oxford, 1999, especially pp.217–20, & 256–63).

15 Judgment 15 March 1993. [Recueil Officiel des Arrets du Tribunal federal 119 II 271]. Extracted in Reeb, M., Digest of CAS Awards 1986–1998 *Staempfli Editions*, Bern, 1998, pp.561–75.

16 Code of Sports-Related Arbitration, Article R58.

17 This is the position under english law by virtue of the Aribtration Acts.

18 Reeb, M., Digest of CAS. Awards 1986–1998, *Stampfli Editions*, Bern, 1998, p.xxxi.
19 On this issue, see Foster, K., Is there a Global Sports Law?, 2003, Entertainment Law, Vol. 2, No.1, pp.1–18.
20 See H-J.Mertens, Lex Mercatoria: A Self-Applying System in G.Teubner, Legal Pluralism in the World Society in G.Teubner, (ed.) *Global Law Without a State*, 1997, Andover, Dartmouth.
21 Defrantz v USOC, 492 F.Supp 1181 (1980).
22 Martin v IOC, 740 F.2d 670 (9th Cir. 1984).
23 Lewis v World Boxing Council & Bruno, unreported, 3 November 1995.
24 See note 2.
25 The European Model of Sport (DG X, Brussels, 1998); for comments on it, see Hoehn, T. & Szymanski, S., *The Americanization of European Football : Economic Policy*, April 1999, p.205–40. and Weatherill, S., Resisting the pressures of Americanization: the influence of the European Community on the 'European Sport Model' in Greenfield, S. & Osborn, G. (eds.) *Sport and the law* (London: Cass, 2000).
26 One of the reasons why the US basketball team surprising failed to win the world championships despite being selected from NBA players is that the IABA plays to different rules from the NBA.
27 This changed for the 2002–3 season when two clubs were promoted from the Conference.
28 Federal Baseball Club of Baltimore v National League of Professional Baseball Clubs 259 U.S. 200 (1922).
29 Radovich v National Football League 352 U.S. 445 (1957).
30 Ice hockey in Denver Rockets v All-Pro Management 325 F.Supp 1049 (C.D.Cal. 1971) and basketball in Robertson v NBA 389 F.Supp 867 (S.D.N.Y. 1975).
31 Piazza v Major League Baseball 831 F. Supp. 420 (E.D.Pa. 1993).
32 Starting with Flood v Kuhn 407 U.S. 258 (1972).
33 On this early history see Seymour, H., *Baseball – The Early Years* (New York: Oxford University Press, 1960).
34 A useful website on defunct American sports leagues is www.geocities.com/Colosseum/Arena/6922.
35 Football Merger Act of 1996 (USC s.1293).
36 The two most interesing cases are Philadelpia World Hockey Club v Philadelpia Hockey Club, 351 F.Supp 462 (1972) and USFL v NFL, 842 F.2d 1335 (1988).
37 The litigation was a ten round judicial contest but the clearest discussion of the legal issues is the Ninth circuit appeal, Los Angeles Memorial Coliseum v NFL (Raiders I) 726 F.2d 1381 (1984).
38 Fraser v Major League Soccer, 7 F.Supp. 2d 73 (D. Mass. 1998). On appeal 97 F.Supp 2d 130 (2000). There is an extensive American literature on this case. The best articles are Maco, M., *Rules Restricting Player Movement under FIFA: Do They Violate US Antitrust Law?*, 1999, 18, New York Law School *Journal of International and Comparative Law* 407 and Mathias, E., *Big League Perestroika? The Implications of Fraser v Major League Soccer*, 1999, 148, University of Pennsylvania *Law Review* 203.
39 See note 2.
40 On the different models of regulating sport, see Foster, K. 'How Can Sport be Regulated?', in Steve Greenfield & Guy Osborn (eds.), *Law and Sport in Contemporary Society* (London: Frank Cass, 2000, pp.267–82).
41 Annex 29.
42 For a summary of the Helsinki Report, see Weatherall, S. in (2000) 25 European Law Review 270.
43 Available at www.europa.eu.int.

44 Ibid.
45 Case COMP/C.2/37.328: selling of media rights to the UEFA Champions' League on an exclusive basis. (2002/C196/03). Official Journal 17/08/02. See also IP/02/806.
46 IP/02/1951.
47 Cases COMP/35.163: COMP/36.638; COMP/36.776. GTR/FIA & others. Official Journal 13/06/01.
48 Speech by Mario Monti, European Commissioner for Competition: 'Competition and Sport – the Rules of the Game. Given at Europe's first conference on the Governance of Sport. Brussels, 26 & 27 February 2001. Available at www.supporters-direct.com.
49 Lehtonen & Castors Canada Dry Namur-Braine v FRBSB (Belgian Basketball Federation); case C-176/96. (2000) ECR I-2549; [2001] All ER (EC) 97.
50 Deliege v Liege Francophone de Judo; cases C-51/96 & C-191/97. (2000) ECR I-2681; [2000] All ER (D) 519.
51 For a more detailed discussion of these two cases, see Foster, K. 'Can Sport be Regulated by Europe?: An Analysis of the Alternative Methods', in Andrew Caiger & Simon Gardner (eds.), *Professional Sport in the EU: Regulation and Re-Regulation* (The Hague: TMC Asser Press, 2000, pp.43–64).

6 Sport and the nation in the global era

1 Tom Nairn, *Pariah. Misfortunes of the British Kingdom* (London: Verso, 2002, p.147).
2 John Urry, *Global Complexity* (Cambridge: Polity Press, 2003, p.43).
3 Toby Miller, Geoffrey Lawrence, Jim McKay and David Rowe, *Globalization and Sport* (London: Sage, 2001, p.59).
4 Joseph Maguire, Grant Jarvie, Louise Mansfield and Joe Bradley, *Sport Worlds. A Sociological Perspective*, Human Kinetics (Illinois: Champaign, 2002, p.4).
5 Ibid.
6 Ibid., p.7.
7 Joseph Maguire, 'Sport, Identity Politics, and Globalization: Diminishing Contrasts and Increasing Varieties', *Sociology of Sport Journal*, 11 (4), December, 1994, pp.389–427. See also Joseph Maguire, *Global Sport. Identities, Societies, Civilizations* (Cambridge: Polity Press, 1999).
8 Anthony D. Smith, *Nations and Nationalism in a Global Era* (Cambridge: Polity Press, p.2).
9 Ibid., p.7.
10 Alan Bairner, *Sport, Nationalism, and Globalization: European and North American Perspectives*, (Albany, New York: State University of New York Press, 2001).
11 Jay Scherer, 'Review of Alan Bairner, Sport, Nationalism, and Globalization', in *Sport History Review*, 33 (1), May, 2002, pp.78–79.
12 Ibid., p.79.
13 Miller *et al.*, *Globalization and Sport*.
14 Stephen G. Jones, *Workers at Play. A Social and Economic History of Leisure, 1918–1939*, (London: Routledge and Kegan Paul, 1986, p.6). See also Stephen G. Jones, *Sport, Politics, and the Working Class: Organised Labour and Sport in Inter-War Britain* (Manchester: Manchester University Press, 1988).
15 See Mike Cronin, *Sport and Nationalism in Ireland. Gaelic Games, Soccer and Irish Identity since 1884* (Dublin: Four Courts Press, 1999, pp.24–27).
16 Lincoln Allison, 'Sport and Nationalism', in Jay Coakley and Eric Dunning (eds), *Handbook of Sports Studies* (London: Sage, 2000, pp.344–5, p.349).
17 David Rowe and Geoffrey Lawrence, 'Beyond National Sport: Sociology, History and Postmodernity', *Sporting Traditions*, 12 (2), 1996, 3–16, p.5.
18 Nairn, *Pariah*, p.141.

19 See Grant Jarvie and Graham Walker, 'Ninety Minute Patriots? Scottish Sport in the Making of the Nation', in Grant Jarvie and Graham Walker (eds), *Scottish Sport in the Making of the Nation. Ninety-Minute Patriots* (Leicester: Leicester University Press, 1994, pp.1–8).
20 Michael Billig, *Banal Nationalism*, (London: Sage, 1995).
21 Urry, *Global Complexity*, p.107.
22 Allison, 'Sport and Nationalism', p.345.
23 Miller *et al.*, *Sport and Globalization*, p. 31.
24 Mike Ticher, 'Notional Englishmen, Black Irishmen and Multicultural Australians: Ambiguities in National Sporting Identity', *Sporting Traditions*, 11 (1), November, 1994, pp.75–91, p.75.
25 See John Hoberman, *Sport and Political Ideology* (London: Heinemann, 1984).
26 Bairner, *Sport, Nationalism, and Globalization*, p.167.
27 Carrie B. Douglass, *Bulls, Bullfighting, and Spanish Identities* (Tucson, Arizona: University of Arizona Press, 1997, p.3).
28 Phil Ball, *Morbo. The Story of Spanish Football* (London: When Saturday Comes Books, 2001, p.14).
29 See amongst others W. F. Mandle, *The Gaelic Athletic Association and Irish Nationalist Politics, 1884–1924* (London: Gill and Macmillan, 1987); Cronin, *Sport and Nationalism in Ireland*; Alan Bairner, 'Civic and Ethnic Nationalism in the Celtic Vision of Irish Sport', in Grant Jarvie (ed.), *Sport in the Making of Celtic Cultures* (London: Leicester University Press, 1999, 12–25); de Búrca, *The GAA. A History* (second edition) (Dublin: Gill and Macmillan, 1999); Marcus de Búrca, 'The Gaelic Athletic Association and Organized Sport in Ireland', in Jarvie (ed.), *Sport in the Making of Celtic Cultures*, pp.100–111; Paul Rouse, 'The Politics and Culture of Sport in Ireland: A History of the GAA Ban on Foreign Games 1884–1971. Part One: 1884–1921', *International Journal for the History of Sport*, 10 (3), 1993, pp.333–60. On the unfolding relationship between sport and politics in Northern Ireland, see John Sugden and Alan Bairner, 'Northern Ireland. Sport in a Divided Society', in Lincoln Allison (ed.), *The Politics of Sport* (Manchester: Manchester University Press, 1986, pp.90–117); John Sugden and Alan Bairner, 'National identity, community relations and the sporting life in Northern Ireland', in Lincoln Allison (ed.), *The changing politics of sport* (Manchester: Manchester University Press, 1993, pp.171–206); John Sugden and Alan Bairner, *Sport, Sectarianism and Society in a Divided Ireland* (Leicester: Leicester University Press, 1993); Alan Bairner, 'Sport, Politics and Society in Northern Ireland. Changing Times, New Developments', *Studies*, 90 (359), Autumn, 2001, pp.283–90; Alan Bairner, 'Sport, Sectarianism and Society in a Divided Ireland Revisited', in John Sugden and Alan Tomlinson (eds), *Power Games. A Critical Sociology of Sport* (London: Routledge, pp.181–95).
30 Tom Humphries, *Green Fields. Gaelic Sport in Ireland* (London: Weidenfeld and Nicolson, 1996, p.3).
31 Ibid.
32 Paul Healey, *Gaelic Games and the Gaelic Athletic Association* (Cork: Mercier Press, 1998, p.151).
33 Liam Horan, 'The challenges facing the GAA', *The Irish Sports Almanac 1999* (Inishowen, Co. Donegal: Artcam Ireland, 1998, pp.117–18).
34 Benedict Anderson, *Imagined Communities. Reflections on the Origin and Spread of Nationalism* (London: Verso, 1983).
35 Alan Bairner and Peter Shirlow, 'Loyalism, Linfield and the Territorial Politics of Soccer fandom in Northern Ireland', *Space and Polity*, 2 (2), November, 1998, pp.163–77.
36 See de Búrca, *The GAA. A History* and Mandle, *The Gaelic Athletic Association and Irish Nationalist Politics*.
37 See Cronin, *Sport and Nationalism in Ireland*.

38 Barrie Houlihan, 'Homogenization, Americanization and Creolization of Sport: Varieties of Globalization', *Sociology of Sport Journal*, 11 (4), December, 1994, pp.356–75, p.369. The relatively successful 2002 World Cup campaign can now be added to that list.

39 Ibid. See also Cronin, *Sport and Nationalism in Ireland*.

40 See R.N. Berki, *On Political Realism* (London: Dent, 1981, pp.192–227).

41 See R.N. Berki, *Socialism* (London: Dent, 1975). Berki's description of early English socialism could be applied with almost equal force (and a few minor alterations) to the ideology of Michael Cusack and other founders of the GAA. Berki could detect 'in the long-standing preoccupation with dreams of a resurrected "rural England", the almost childlike longing after the land, as testified to in countless socialist pamphlets, literary pieces, as well as the activities of early co-operative colonies, the surviving echo of peasants who had been mercilessly chased away from the common land' (p.51).

42 Berki, *On Political Realism*, p.230.

43 Ibid., p.231.

44 See for example Maguire, *Global Sport*. See also Jonathan Magee and John Sugden,'"The world at their feet". Professional Football and International Labor Migration', *Journal of Sport and Social Issues*, 26 (4), November, 2002, pp.421–37 and Pierre Lanfranchi and Matthew Taylor, *Moving with the ball: the migration of professional footballers* (Oxford: Berg, 2001).

7 The curious role of the USA in world sport

1 Alexis De Tocqueville, *Democracy in America*, translated, edited and with an 'Introduction' by Harvey C. Mansfield and Delba Winthrop. University of Chicago Press, 2000, pp.3–15. The first volume of the original French edition was published in 1835, the second in 1840.

2 Eric Hobsbawm, *The Age of Extremes: a History of the Twentieth Century, 1914–91* (Pantheon Books, 1994, p.198).

3 Andrei S. Markovits and Steven Hellerman, *Offside: Soccer and American Exceptionalism* (Princeton University Press, 2001, p.5).

4 Ibid., pp.vii–ix.

5 Ibid., p.283.

6 Ibid., pp.287–8.

7 Principally in Lincoln Allison, *Amateurism in Sport: an Analysis and a Defence* (Frank Cass, 2001).

8 One example of a Gramscian perspective on American sport is to be found in George H. Sage, *Power and Ideology in American Sport, A Critical Perspective* (Champaign, Illinois: Human Kinetics Books, 1990).

9 This account of baseball is principally informed by John P. Rossi, *The National Game: Baseball and American Culture* (Chicago: Ivan R. Dee, 2000).

10 In November 2002, for example, when I was interviewing Irakli Medzmariashvili, the Minister of Sport in the Republic of Georgia, it became clear that he was assuming that the vast majority of funding for sport in the United Kingdom came from the state.

11 James Michener, *Michener on Sport*, Secker and Warburg, 1976, pp.3–17.

12 From a column syndicated in several newspapers. Quoted in Tom Melville, *The Tented Field: a History of Cricket in America* (Bowling Green State University Popular Press, 1998, p.39).

13 Paul Gardner, *Nice Guys Finish Last: Sport and American Life*, Allen Lane, 1974. The phrase is by no means original, even as a book title: see Robert Kyle, *Nice Guys Finish Last* (New York: Dell, 1955).

14 This quotation, in slightly different forms, has been attributed to several NFL owners. This seems to be marginally the most authoritative claimant.

15 One account of Anglo-American sporting tensions during that period is Brian Dobbs, *Edwardians at Play, Sport 1890–1914* (Pelham, 1973, pp.149–64).

16 www.ncaa.org. Some of the claims made for college sport are taken from my interviews with NCAA officials quoted in Allison, op.cit., pp.123–8.

17 Howard L. Nixon, *Sport and the American Dream* (New York: Leisure Press, 1984).

18 1999–2000 NCAA Division I Manual, Article 12.

19 The starting point of the contemporary debate is often taken to be Raul Prebisch, *The Economic Development of Latin America and its Principal Problems* (New York: United Nations, 1950). For an overview of this body of writing as it relates to sport see Grant Jarvie and Joseph Maguire, *Sport and Leisure in Social Thought* (Routledge, 1994, pp.230–63).

20 The manufacturer 'Nike' is a particular focus of debate about its global role. See, for example, the Oxfam Community Aid Abroad site at www.caa.org.

21 See Bruce Kidd, 'Sport, Dependency and the Canadian State', in M. Hart and S. Birrell (eds), *Sport in the Sociocultural Process* (Iowa: Brown, 1981, pp.707–21).

22 Markovits and Hellerman, op.cit., p.32.

23 I first quoted this phrase in Lincoln Allison, 'The Soccer Boom in America', *New Society*, Vol. 35, No. 700, March 11, 1976, p.545 attributing it to a book by Leonard Schecter, *The Jocks*, which I note is not in the Library of Congress catalogue.

24 For a good example see Colin Ward, *Steaming In: A Journal of a Football Fan*, Simon and Schuster, 1989, but also a vast range of fanzines and websites such as http://surf.to/londonclarets

25 John Inverdale, 'Gloves are off in relegation debate', *Daily Telegraph*, Thursday 12 December 2002, p.S6.

26 Ibid. There is a nice historic irony to the identity of the speaker. Most of Maurice Lindsay's career has been spent in the administration of Rugby League and of the Wigan club in particular, in the one British sport which existed outside the 'amateur hegemony'.

27 Sam Wallace, '"I don't think you can have four divisions of professional football any more"' *Daily Telegraph*, Friday December 6 2002, p.S1.

28 Michael Parkinson, 'A Month in View: November!', *Daily Telegraph*, Thursday 3 December 2002, p.S5.

29 The phrase is from R. Collins 'Wall to Wall Dallas? The US-UK trade in televison' *Screen*, no. 27 vols 3–4, 1986, p.67.

30 A major thesis of Tibor Scitivsky, *The Joyless Economy* (Oxford: Oxford University Press, 1976).

8 Local heroes and global stars

1 Based on a report by Tom Wheeler: 'Tiger Woods targeted in Nike protest' http://csf.colorado.edu/forums/pvfs/2002i/msg00069.html Accessed 27 January 2003. (Some artistic licence may have been used.)

2 This corresponds to the general notion of cosmopolitanism in Ong's thesis of 'flexible citizenship. See Ong, A. *Flexible Citizenship: The Cultural Politics of Transnationality* (Durham: Duke University Press, 1999).

3 Although this appears to be a standard academic disclaimer I remain sympathetic and supportive of the concerns of feminism and gender politics more generally. The gender dynamics of heroism are covered more extensively in my MA dissertation, from which a number of thoughts in this chapter are drawn. See Gilchrist, P. *The Idea of the Sporting Hero* (University of Warwick: unpublished MA dissertation, 2002).

4 Cited in Allison, L. *Ecology and Utility* (Leicester: Leicester University Press, 1991, p.33).

5 Thoreau, H. *Walden or Life in the Woods* (London: Chapman and Hall, 1927 [1854], p.103).

6 Appadurai, A. 'Disjuncture and difference in the global cultural economy' in *Theory, Culture and Society* (Volume 7, 1990), pp.295–310.

7 Frazer, J.G. *The Golden Bough: A Study in Magic and Religion* (London: Macmillan, 1963). Boas, F. 'The Origin of Totemism', *American Anthorpologist* (Volume 18, 1916), pp. 319–26. Durkheim, E. *The Elementary Forms of Religious Life* (London: Allen & Unwin, 1912/1971).

8 Frazer, J.G. cited in Freud, S. *Totem and Taboo* (London: Routledge & Kegan Paul, 1960, p.103).

9 Wundt cited in ibid., p.106.

10 Allison, L. *Ecology and Utility*, p.149.

11 The precise nature of the group of people or community referred to throughout is a source of contention. The sports hero has and does serve as a 'symbol or emblem, linking the style of the performance with a sense of a wider community – a class, a city, a region, an ethnic group or religious denomination, a nation and, most strikingly, perhaps even an empire'. Holt, R. and Mangan, J. Prologue: European Heroes: Myth, Identity, Sport, *International Journal of the History of Sport* (Volume 13, Number 1, 1996), p.10.

12 Appadurai, A. *Modernity at Large: Cultural Dimensions of Globalisation* (Minneapolis: University of Minnesota Press, 1996, chapter 5).

13 James, C.L.R. *Beyond a Boundary* (London: Serpents Tail, 1994).

14 Holt, R. and Mangan, J. 'Prologue', p.5.

15 Ibid., p.8.

16 This generalisation is posited by Allison, L. *Amateurism in Sport* (London: Frank Cass, 2001, pp.149–50).

17 Inglis, F. 'The State of Play: Capital, Sport and Happiness' in Allison, L (ed.) *Taking Sport Seriously* (Aacher: Meyer & Meyer, 1998, pp.155–72).

18 Boorstin, D. *The Image: A Guide to Pseudo-Events in America* (New York: Random House, 1992, p.61).

19 Voting for the contestants in the second series of 'Big Brother' in the UK in 2001, for instance, outstripped the combined votes for the Conservative Party at the General Election of that year.

20 Durkheim, E. *The Elementary Forms of Religious Life*, p.381. See also Jarvie, G. and Maguire, J. *Sport and Leisure in Social Thought* (London: Routledge, 1994, chapter 1).

21 Weber, M. *Charisma and Institution Building* (London: Unwin Hyman, 1963, p.xviii).

22 See Andrews, D.L., Carrington, B., Jackson, S.J. and Mazur, Z. 'Jordanscapes: a preliminary analysis of the global popular', *Sociology of Sport Journal*, Volume 13, Number 4, pp.428–57.

23 Jameson, F. *Postmodernism, or, the Cultural Logic of Late Capitalism* (Durham: North Carolina, Duke University Press, 1991, p.275).

24 Mauss, M. 'A category of the human mind: the notion of person; the notion of self', Carrithers, M., Collins, S., and Lukes, S. (eds) *The Category of the Person* (Cambridge: Cambridge University Press, 1985, p.19).

25 Featherstone, M. 'The Heroic Life and Everyday Life', *Theory, Culture and Society* (Volume 9, Number 1, 1992, p.177).

26 Conrad, P. 'Blend it like Beckham', *The Observer*, Review Section, Sunday 25 May, 2003, p.1.

27 See Gans, E. *Originary Thinking* (Stanford: Stanford University Press, 1993, p.151).

28 Shakespeare, W. *Coriolanus*, Lee Bliss (ed.) (Cambridge: Cambridge University Press, 2000, p.54 (4.7.49–50)).

29 Ibid, p.252 (5.3.35–6).
30 Jameson, F 'Postmodernism, or The Cultural Logic of Late Capitalism', *New Left Review* (Number 146, July–August 1984), p.58, p.60.
31 Rojek, C. *Celebrity* (London: Reaktion Books, 2001).
32 Whannell, G. *Media Sport Stars: Masculinities and Moralities* (London: Routledge, 2002, chapter 15).
33 *The Economist*, 'The World of Sport Survey', June 6 1998, p.7.
34 Adorno, T.W. and Horkheimer, M. *Dialectic of Enlightenment* (New York: Herder and Herder, 1972, p.158).
35 *European TV Sports Databook* (London: Kagan World Media, 1995, p.4).
36 LaFeber, W. *Michael Jordan and the New Global Capitalism* (New York: W.W Norton and Company, 2002, p.67).
37 See Wilton, Iain. *CB Fry: King of Sport* (London: Metro, 2002, pp.208–9).
38 Appadurai, A. *Modernity At Large*, Chapter 2.
39 Fukuyama, F. *The End of History and the Last Man* (London: Hamish Hamilton, 1992).
40 Held, D. *et al. Global Transformations: Politics, Economics and Culture* (Cambridge: Polity Press, 1999, p.3).
41 Van Hoecke, J., Van Hoecke, W., De Knop, P. and Taks, M. 'The Contribution of "Local Heroes" in the Athlete Endorsement Mix', *The Cyber Journal of Sport Marketing.* Available at http://www.cjsm.com/ vol4/hoecke43.htm Accessed on 25 November 2002.
42 Tomkins, R. 'Advertisers lose out on sporting chance', *Financial Times*, 21 June 2002, p.21.
43 'Pub name "may damage Rooney"' BBC News website: http://news.bbc.co.uk/1/hi/england/2834073.stm Accessed March 9 2003.
44 Kelso, P 'Money worries that haunt world cup', *The Guardian*, January 28 2003. Hopps, D. 'Players unite to take on ICC', *The Guardian*, September 21 2002.
45 There are fears that the Rugby World Cup in Australia 2003 could be beset by similar problems.
46 Rojek, C. *Celebrity*, p.46.
47 See Fiske, J. *Reading the Popular* (London: Unwin Hyman, 1989).
48 Law *et al.* discuss the nature of global media integration and point out that the codes and objects in which to express our differences may be severely limited as media output becomes homogenised. See Law, A., Harvey, J. and Kemp, S. 'The Global Sport Mass Media Oligopoly', *International Review for the Sociology of Sport*, Volume 37, 3–4 (2002), pp.279–302.
49 Habermas, J. 'The Public Sphere' Chapter 14 in Mukerji, C. and Schudson, M. (eds) *Rethinking Popular Culture: Contemporary Perspectives in Cultural Studies*, (Berkeley: University of Los Angeles Press, 1991, p.398).
50 Savigny, H. 'Public Opinion, Political Communication and the Internet', *Politics* (Volume 22, Number 1, 2002), pp.1–8.
51 Sklair, L. *The Transnational Capitalist Class* (Oxford: Blackwell, 2001).
52 Falk, R. 'Resisting "Globalisation-from-above" through "Globalisation-from-below"' *New Political Economy*, Volume 2, Number 1, 1997, p.20.
53 Kant, I. 'An Answer to the Question "What is Enlightenment?" Reiss, H. (ed.) *Kant: Political Writings*, Second Edition (Cambridge: Cambridge University Press, 1991, p.54). This literal translation is *'Dare to be wise'*.
54 Some scepticism, however, should be retained as to the uses of new technology to reinvigorate political participation. See Hand, M. and Sandywell, B. 'E-topia as Cosmopolis or Citadel: On the democratising and de-democratising logics of the Internet, or, toward a critique of the new technological fetishism', *Theory, Culture & Society*, Volume 19, (1–2), 2002, pp.197–225.
55 Urry, J. *Globalisation and Citizenship* (draft) http://www.comp.lancaster.ac.uk/sociology/soc009ju.html. Accessed February 13 2003.

56 Ibid.

57 Cited in La Feber, W. *Michael Jordan and the New Global Capitalism*, p.91.

58 Ibid., p.92.

59 Ibid. p.107.

60 Allison, L. 'Sport and Politics' Chapter 1 in Allison, L. (ed.) *The Politics of Sport* (Manchester: Manchester University Press, 1986, p.17).

61 Hooks, B. Cited in See Andrews, D.L *et al*, 'Jordanscapes: a preliminary analysis of the global popular', *Sociology of Sport Journal*, p.452.

62 Hargreaves, J. *Heroines of Sport: The Politics of Difference and Identity*, (London: Routledge, 2000, p.4).

63 Kellner, D 'The Sport Spectacle, Michael Jordan, and Nike: Unholy Alliance?' Chapter 3 in Andrews, D. L. (ed.) *Michael Jordan, Inc: Corporate Sport, Media Culture, and Late Modern America* (Albany: State University Press of New York, 2001).

64 Cited in ibid. p.59.

65 Law, A., Harvey, J., and Kemp, S. *The Global Sport Mass Media Oligopoly*.

66 Sklair, Leslie 'Social movements for global capitalism: the transnational capitalist class in action', *Review of International Political Economy* (Volume 4, Number 3, Autumn 1997), pp.521.

67 Friedman, M. 'The Social Self and the Partiality Debates' in Card, C. (ed.) *Feminist Ethics* (Lawrence: Kansas, University of Kansas Press, 1991, p.171), emphasis in the original.

68 Manifold, J. 'The Recruit' in Gardner, B. (ed.) *The Terrible Rain: The War Poets 1939–45* (London: Magnum Books, 1966, p.31).

69 Giardina M.D. 'Global Hingis: Flexible Citizenship and the transnational celebrity' Chapter 12 in Andrews, D.L. and Jackson., S.J (eds) *Sport Stars: The Cultural Politics of Sporting Celebrity* (London: Routledge, 2001, pp.205–6).

70 Bauman, Z. *Globalization: The Human Consequences* (New York: Columbia University Press, 1998).

71 Ohmae, K. *Borderless World: Power and Strategy in the Interlinked Economy* (London: HarperCollins, 1989).

72 See Barnard, F.M. (ed) *Herder on Social and Political Culture* (Cambridge: Cambridge University Press, 1969, p.7).

73 Maguire, J. *Global Sport: Identities, Societies, Civilizations* (Oxford: Polity Press, 1999).

74 James, C.L.R. *Beyond a Boundary*.

75 Lichfield, J 'France unites in football victory' *The Independent*, July 10th 1998, p.14. Lichfield, J. 'For once united', *The Independent*, July 12 1998, p.4. Lichfield, J. 'This is the France we want to see: valiant, stubborn and multi-racial', *The Independent*, July 14 1998, p.3.

76 Davies, P. *The National Front in France* (London: Routledge, 1999). Mayer, N. 'The French National Front', in Betz, H-G. and Immerfall, S. (eds) *The New Politics of the Right: Neo-Populist Parties and Movements in Established Democracies* (Basingstoke: Macmillan, 1998, pp.11–25). Webster, P. 'Le Pen: Populist who rose from ashes', *The Guardian*, April 22, 2002.

77 Pires, R. Cited in Tallentire, M. 'Le Pen in, France out says Pires', *The Guardian*, Friday May 3 2002, p.30.

78 Ibid.

79 As a flippant aside, the joke of the day was 'What is the difference between the French football team and Jean-Marie Le Pen?' '*Le Pen reached the second round*'.

80 Spivak, G. C. 'Can the subaltern speak?' in *Marxism and the Interpretation of Culture*, C. Nelson and L. Grossberg (eds) (Urbana, Illinois: University of Illinois Press, 1988, pp.217–313).

81 MacIntyre, A. 'Is Patriotism a Virtue?' in Beiner, R. (ed.) *Theorising Citizenship* (Albany, New York: State University of New York Press, 1995, pp.209–28).

82 Melnick, Merrill J. and Jackson, Steven J. 'Globalization American-Style and Reference Idol Selection', *International Review for the Sociology of Sport*, 37 (3–4) (2002, pp.429–48).
83 Maguire, J. *Global Sport: Identities, Societies, Civilizations*.
84 Melnick, M. J. and Jackson, S.J. Op Cit. p.443.
85 See Carrington, B., Andrews, D.L., Jackson, S.J. and Mazur, Z. 'The Global Jordanscape' in Andrews, D.L. (ed.) *Michael Jordan, Inc.* (New York: State University of New York, 2001, Chapter 7).
86 Caust, L. 'Community, Autonomy and Justice: The Gender Politics of Identity and Relationship', *History of European Ideas* (Volume 17, Number 5, 1993, pp.643–4).
87 See Barker, F. 'Nationalism, nomadism and belonging in Europe: *Coriolanus*', Chapter 9 in Joughin, J. J. (ed.) *Shakespeare and National Culture* (Manchester: Manchester University Press, 1997, pp.233–65).
88 Ibid. p.252.
89 Bob Fisher, Amelia Hill and David Fickling 'Uproar as America's Cup slips towards "traitors"' *The Observer*, 23 February 2003, p.25. 'Alinghi skipper hails cup win'. http://news.bbc.co.uk/go/pr/fr/-/sport1/hi/other_sports/sailing/2812427   Accessed March 5 2003.
90 Holt, R. 'Champions, Heroes and Celebrities: Sporting Greatness and the British Public' in Huntington-Whiteley, J. (ed.) *The British Book of Sporting Heroes* (London: National Portrait Gallery Publications, 1998, pp.12–25).
91 MacIntyre, A. *After Virtue*, Second Edition (London: Duckworth, 1985, pp.187–91).
92 Such a fight, I believe has been conceptually and theoretically prepared by MacIntyre, A. op. cit. Allison, L. *Amateurism in Sport*, Morgan, W. *Leftist Theories of Sport* (Chicago: University of Illinois Press, 1994).
93 Tonnies, F. *Community and Association* (Routledge & Kegan Paul, 1955, pp.37–9).

9 Selling out?

1 This term is from R. Rinehart, '~~Emerging~~ Arriving Sport: Alternatives to formal sport', in *Handbook of sport studies*, eds. J. Coakley and E. Dunning (London: Sage, 2000, p.507).
2 For a good over view of alternative sport and extreme sport, and the various terms, see Ibid. and R. Rinehart, 'Inside of the outside: Pecking orders within alternative sport as ESPN's 1995 "The eXtreme Games"', *Journal of sport and social issues* 22, no. 4 (1998), 398–414.
3 I am referring here to Raymond William's categorisation. R. Williams, *Marxism and Literature* (Oxford: Oxford University Press, 1977). See also Rinehart, 'Inside of the outside: Pecking orders with in alternative sport as ESPN's 1995 "The eXtreme Games"'.
4 See N. Midol and G. Broyer, 'Towards an anthropological analysis of new sport cultures: The case of whiz sports in France', *Sociology of Sport Journal* 12 (1995, 204–212; R. Rinehart, *Players All: Performances in contemporary sport* (Bloomington & Indianapolis: Indiana University Press, 1998); B. Wheaton, 'Just Do it: Consumption, commitment and identity in the windsurfing subculture', *Sociology of Sport Journal* 17, no. 3 (2000): 254–74. Rinehart, '~~Emerging~~ Arriving Sport: Alternatives to formal sport'.
5 I use the term lifestyle sport as this is a term that initially emerged during my ethnographic research, seems to be one participants identify with and that for me best encapsulated these cultures. For a fuller discussion of this term and others such as alternative, extreme, new, postmodern etc. see B. Wheaton, ed., *Understanding Lifestyle sports: consumption, identity and difference* (London: Routledge, 2004).

6 Bourdieu calls these activities new sports, and terms these entrepreneurs the 'new' and 'petite bourgeoisie'. P. Bourdieu, *Distinction: A social critique of the judgement of taste* (London & NY: Routledge & Kegan Paul Ltd, 1984, p.220).

7 Bale, for example, suggests such activities present a challenge to the 'western sport model', and Maguire notes they challenge the 'achievement sport' ideology. J. Bale, *Landscapes of modern sport* (Leicester: Leicester University Press, 1994). J. Maguire, *Global Sport: Identities, Societies, civilizations* (Cambridge: Polity Press, 1999). See also Midol and Broyer, 'Towards an anthropological analysis of new sport cultures: The case of whiz sports in France', Rinehart, 'Arriving Sport: Alternatives to formal sport'. Wheaton, 'Just Do it: Consumption, commitment and identity in the windsurfing subculture'.

8 The idea of lifestyle sport as postmodern sport is discussed in Wheaton, ed., *Understanding Lifestyle sports: consumption, identity and difference*. However, see also L. Allison, *Amateurism in sport: An analysis and a defence* (London: Frank Cass, 2001, p.43, 44), and Rinehart, 'Arriving Sport: Alternatives to formal sport'.

9 D. Kellner, 'Popular culture and the construction of postmodern identities,' in *Modernity and Identity*, ed. J. Friedman (Oxford: UK and Cambridge, USA: Blackwell, 1992, p.141).

10 D. Philips and A. Tomlinson, 'Come on Down? Popular Media Culture in Post-War Britain', in *Homeward Bound – Leisure, popular culture and consumer capitalism*, ed. S. Wagg (Routledge, 1992).

11 See B. Beal and C. Wilson, ' "Chicks dig scars": Commercialisation and the transformations of skate boarders' identities', in *Understanding Lifestyle sports: consumption, identity and difference*, ed. B. Wheaton, 2004. Likewise according to professional skateboarder Andy Mac, there are 12-million skaters in the United States, which is more than play baseball. Cited in 'Skateboarding ... seeking respectability', in *The Sports Factor* (Radio National (Australia), 2003).

12 Rinehart, 'Arriving Sport: Alternatives to formal sport', p.505.

13 While image of these sports tend to be dominated by those of teenage males, in many activities participants include men in their 30s, 40s and 50s. For a discussion of this youthfulness (and the wider context of the aging Gen-X) see I. Borden, *Skateboarding, space and the city: Architecture and the body* (Oxford: Berg, 2001).

14 K. Kusz, ' "Extreme America": The Cultural Politics of Extreme Sports in 1990s America', in *Understanding Lifestyle sports: consumption, identity and difference*, ed. B. Wheaton (forthcoming).

15 J. Ostrowski, 'Corporate America cozies up to the tattooed extreme world', *Street & Smith's SportsBuisness Journal*, Sept 18–24 2000. p.24.

16 D. Andrews and C. Cole, 'On issue: the nation reconsidered', *Journal of sport and social issues* 26, no. 2, May (2002): 123–4.

17 See Rinehart, 'Inside of the outside: Pecking orders with in alternative sport as ESPN's 1995 "The eXtreme Games" '; Rinehart, 'E̶m̶e̶r̶g̶i̶n̶g̶ Arriving Sport: Alternatives to formal sport'.

18 The term transnational corporations, and the idea of transnational practices come from L. Sklair, *The transnational capitalist class* (Oxford: Blackwell, 2001).

19 Robinson also highlights the need for an examination of globalisation processes in new sports. See V. Robinson, 'Men, masculinities and rock climbing', in *Everyday culture working paper* (The Open University, 2002, p.3–19).

20 J. Clifford, *Routes travel and translation in the late twentieth century* (London: Harvard University Press, 1997, p.9).

21 Key academic sources on surfing I've used include J. Fiske, 'Reading the Beach', in *Reading the Popular* (Unwin Hyman, 1989); R. Farmer, 'Surfing: motivations, values and culture', *Journal of Sports Behaviour* 15, no. 3 (1992): 241–257; D. Booth, 'Surfing 60s: A case study in the history of pleasure and discipline', *Australian Historical Studies* 103 (1994): 262–79; D. Booth, 'Ambiguities in Pleasure and dis-

cipline: The development of Competative surfing', *Journal of Sport History* 22, no. 3 (1995): 189–206; L. Stedman, 'From Gidget to Gonad Man: Surfers, feminists and postmodernisation', *Australian and New Zealand Journal of Sociology* 33, no. 1 (1997): 75–90; M. Stranger, 'The aesthetics of risk: A study of surfing', *International Review for the Sociology of Sport* 34, no. 3 (1999): 265–76; J. Abell, 'Values in a sporting sub-culture: An analysis of the issues of competitiveness and aggression in surfing', (MA in politics, sport and society, University of Warwick, 2001); D. Booth, *Australian beach cultures: The history of sun, sand and surf* (London: Frank Cass Publishers, 2001); M. Henderson, 'A Shifting line up: men, women and Tracks surfing magazine', *Continuum: Journal of media and Cultural Studies* 15, no. 3 (2001): 319–32.

22 R. Robertson, *Globalization: Social theory and global culture* (London: Sage, 1992).

23 C. Barker, *Cultural Studies: Theory and Practice* (London: Sage, 2000, p.113).

24 Robertson, *Globalization: Social theory and global culture*.

25 Allison, *Amateurism in sport: An analysis and a defence*. p.44.

26 Maguire, *Global Sport: Identities, Societies, civilizations*.

27 J. Maguire, 'Sport and globalization', in *Handbook of sport studies*, ed. E. Dunning (London: Sage, 2000, p.367).

28 Maguire, *Global Sport: Identities, Societies, civilizations*. p.87, p.2.11. In a similar vein, Bale suggest such adventure experiences activities are part of a green wave that – along with other alternative body cultures – present a challenge to, and critique of, the 'western sport model'. Bale, *Landscapes of modern sport*.

29 A. Appadurai, *Modernity at Large: Cultural dimensions of globalization* (Minneapolis: University of Minnesota Press, 1996, p.32).

30 Ibid. p.33.

31 Ibid. p.35.

32 Ibid. p.35.

33 Ibid. p.33.

34 B. Carrington and B. Wilson, 'Global Clubcultures: Cultural flows and late modern dance music culture', in *Young People in Risk Society: The restructuring of youth identities in late modernity*, ed. M. Cieslik and G. Pollock (Aldershot: Arena, 2002).

35 D. Booth, 'Surfing films and videos: adolescent fun, alternative lifestyle, adventure industry', *Journal of sport history* 23, no. 3 (1996): 313–27. p.319.

36 See Booth, *Australian beach cultures: The history of sun, sand and surf*. p.91.

37 There are many interesting dimensions to surfing in its 'residual' cultural form possibly dating back to 2000 BC. For a description see B. Finney and J. Houston, *Surfing: a history of the ancient Hawaiian sport* (San Francisco: Pomegranate Artbooks, 1996). See also A. Gabbard, *Girl in the curl: a century of women in surfing* (Seattle: Seal Press). For a discussion of the significance of pre-colonial, colonial and post colonial body cultures see J. Bale and M. Cronin, 'Introduction: Sport and postcolonialism', in *Sport and postcolonialism*, ed. M. Cronin (Oxford: Berg, 2003).

38 D. Booth, 'Surfing: The cultural and technological determinants of a dance', *Culture, Sport, Society* 2, no. 1 (1999): 36–55. p.44. See also Finney and Houston, *Surfing: a history of the ancient Hawaiian sport*.

39 Finney and Houston, *Surfing: a history of the ancient Hawaiian sport*.

40 See Booth, *Australian beach cultures: The history of sun, sand and surf*. p.91.

41 Appadurai, *Modernity at Large: Cultural dimensions of globalization*. See also Clifford, *Routes travel and translation in the late twentieth century*.

42 J. Urry, *Globalizing the tourists gaze*, www.comp.lancs.ac.uk/sociology/soc056ju.html (Department of Sociology, Lancaster University, 2002, accessed February 12 2003).

43 Booth, *Australian beach cultures: The history of sun, sand and surf*. p.91.

44 Ibid.

45 Booth, 'Surfing: The cultural and technological determinants of a dance', p.47.

46 Booth, *Australian beach cultures: The history of sun, sand and surf*. p.91, 93.

47 See Ibid. p.94.

48 See Ibid. p.97.
49 See Booth, 'Surfing films and videos: adolescent fun, alternative lifestyle, adventure industry', As Booth notes *Endless Summer* (and *Endless Summer 2*) is an interesting case in illustrating the commercial potential of surf films both within and outside of the surf culture.
50 See Booth, *Australian beach cultures: The history of sun, sand and surf.* p.95.
51 See Finney and Houston, *Surfing: a history of the ancient Hawaiian sport*; Abell, 'Values in a sporting sub-culture: An analysis of the issues of competitiveness and aggression in surfing'.
52 Urry, *Globalizing the tourists gaze* (accessed).
53 Appadurai, *Modernity at Large: Cultural dimensions of globalization.* p.4.
54 Ibid. p.36.
55 Maguire, *Global Sport: Identities, Societies, civilizations.* p.105.
56 J. Urry, *The Global media and cosmopolitanism*, www.comp.lancs.ac.uk/sociology/soc056ju.html(Department of Sociology, Lancaster University, 2000, accessed February 12 2003). He argues that there are dangers with suggesting that 'cosmopolitanism' is a 'specific cultural type' distinguishable from locals, tourists, migrants and so on, so sets out a 'model of cosmopolitanism' listing key predispositions and practices.
57 Ibid (accessed).
58 *Surfer*, February 1996 p.34. See for example, the environmental movements based around surfing such as the SAS, Surfers Against Sewage (UK), and Surfers Alliance (US). These discourses around environmentalism – and their effectiveness – are discussed in B. Wheaton, *Privatised consumption and Eco movements in 'Surfers against sewage'* (Paper presented at Leisure Studies Association conference, Gloucester, 1999).
59 Booth, 'Surfing films and videos: adolescent fun, alternative lifestyle, adventure industry', p.319. See also Booth, *Australian beach cultures: The history of sun, sand and surf.*
60 Booth, 'Surfing: The cultural and technological determinants of a dance', p.45.
61 Ibid.
62 See Booth, 'Ambiguities in Pleasure and discipline: The development of Competative surfing'.
63 Ibid.
64 See Appadurai, *Modernity at Large: Cultural dimensions of globalization.* Robertson, *Globalization: Social theory and global culture.*
65 Although Finney and Houston, *Surfing. a history of the ancient Hawaiian sport* explore the existence of pre colonial surfing forms in many counties. For example, Maoris in New Zealand enjoyed body surfing, as did indigenous people of coastal Africa. Finney and Houston, *Surfing: a history of the ancient Hawaiian sport.*
66 Despite these contradictions these attitudes point to the surfer as cosmopolitans.
67 Clifford, *Routes travel and translation in the late twentieth century.* p.9.
68 See for example; Ibid; J. Urry, *Global complexity* (Cambridge: Polity, 2003).
69 For a discussion of this literature see Alan Bairner this volume.
70 M. Silk and D. Andrews, 'Beyond a boundary? sport, transnational advertising and the reimagining of national culture', *Journal of sport and social issues* 25, no. 2, May (2001): 180–201.
71 D. Andrews and C. Cole, 'On issue: the nation reconsidered', Ibid. 26 (2002): 123–124. p.123.
72 Maguire, *Global Sport: Identities, Societies, civilizations.* p.176.
73 Although surfing's role in the complex identity politics of in Hawaii is a striking exception that requires further investigation – see on.
74 In surfing, competitors from the USA are differentiated into USA or Haw – the latter indicating that they are Hawaiians.

75 Maguire, *Global Sport: Identities, Societies, civilizations* p.105.
76 Appadurai, *Modernity at Large: Cultural dimensions of globalization* p.177.
77 For a discussion of these values in the windsurfing culture see Wheaton, 'Just Do it: Consumption, commitment and identity in the windsurfing subculture'.
78 Clifford, *Routes travel and translation in the late twentieth century*.
79 Maguire, *Global Sport: Identities, Societies, civilizations* p.186, citing Elias, 1996 p.153.
80 Wheaton, 'Just Do it: Consumption, commitment and identity in the windsurfing subculture'.
81 S. Lash, *Sociology of Postmodernism*, 1st ed. (London & NY: Routledge, 1990, p.37).
82 Urry, *The Global media and cosmopolitanism* (accessed).
83 Maguire calls these types of sport migrants with no attachment to place 'mercenaries' Maguire, *Global Sport: Identities, Societies, civilizations*. p.105.
84 A. Bennett, *Popular music and youth culture: Music, identity and place* (Basingstoke: Macmillan press itd., 2000, p.53).
85 Ibid. p.53
86 Ibid. p.53.
87 Borden, *Skateboarding, space and the city: Architecture and the body*.
88 Urry, *The Global media and cosmopolitanism*.
89 *Surfer*, Feb., 1996; p.20.
90 F. Mort, 'The politics of consumption', in *New Times: The changing Face of politics in the 1990's*, ed. M. Jacques (London: Lawrence & Wishart, 1989, p.170).
91 J. Stratton, 'On the Impossibility of Subcultural Origins', in *The Subcultures reader*, ed. K. Gelder (London & NY: Routledge, 1997, pp.183–4).
92 C. Palmer, 'Death, danger and the selling of risk in alternative sports', in *Understanding Lifestyle sports: consumption, identity and difference*, ed. B. Wheaton, 2004.
93 Appadurai, *Modernity at Large: Cultural dimensions of globalization*. p.32.
94 Maguire, *Global Sport: Identities, Societies, civilizations*. p.145.
95 Ibid. p.150.
96 Ibid. p.148, 210.
97 See K. Kusz, 'Extreme sports, white masculinity and the white male backlash politics in late 1990s America', in *North Amercian Sociology of Sport Association* (Cleveland: 1999); Kusz, 'Extreme America: The Cultural Politics of Extreme Sports in 1990s America'.
98 Rinehart, '~~Emerging~~ Arriving Sport: Alternatives to formal sport'. p.507.
99 Ibid. p.507.
100 T. Miller and others, *Globalization and sport: playing the world* (London: Sage, 2001, p.65).
101 Beal and Wilson, ' "Chicks dig scars": Commercialisation and the transformations of skate boarders' identities'.
102 See B. Wheaton and B. Beal, ' "Keeping it real": Subcultural media and the discourses of authenticity in alternative sport', *International Review for the Sociology of Sport*, vol.38, No.2, pp.155–76: S. Thornton, *Club cultures: Music, media and subcultural capital* (Cambridge: Polity Press, 1995).
103 Wheaton and Beal, ' "Keeping it real": Subcultural media and the discourses of authenticity in alternative sport'.
104 Booth, 'Surfing films and videos: adolescent fun, alternative lifestyle, adventure industry', p.322.
105 Stranger, 'The aesthetics of risk: A study of surfing'. See also Margaret Henderson, 'A Shifting Line-Up: men, women and *Tracks* surfing magazine', *Continuum: Journal of Media and Cultural Studies*, Vol.15, No. 3, 2001, pp.319–32.
106 Ibid., p.273.

107 Booth, 'Surfing films and videos: adolescent fun, alternative lifestyle, adventure industry', p.321.
108 Ibid., p.324.
109 D. Hebdige, 'After the Masses', in *New Times: The changing Face of politics in the 1990's*, ed. M. Jacques (London: Lawrence & Wishart, 1989, p.81).
110 Wheaton and Beal, '"Keeping it real": Subcultural media and the discourses of authenticity in alternative sport'.
111 Ibid.
112 Wheaton, 'Just Do it: Consumption, commitment and identity in the windsurfing subculture'.
113 Wheaton and Beal, '"Keeping it real": Subcultural media and the discourses of authenticity in alternative sport'.
114 Ibid.
115 Ibid.
116 Ibid.
117 I claim that this apparent lack of heterogeneity or 'individuality' was not because I could not 'read' or appreciate the subtleties in subcultural style; my interviewees concurred that there was a recognisable subcultural style, which newcomers soon became quite competent at 'reading.'
118 Although European, Australian and North American collections of the same brand are often different.
119 Wheaton, 'Just Do it: Consumption, commitment and identity in the windsurfing subculture'.
120 Interviewee quoted in B. Wheaton, 'Consumption, lifestyle and gendered identities in post-modern sports: the case of windsurfing' (PhD, University of Brighton, 1997).
121 As part of a wider differentiation and fragmentation of the male fashion market. See S. Nixon, *Hard Looks: Masculinities, Spectatorship and Contemporary Consumption* (London: UCL Press, 1996).
122 Interviewee quoted in Abell, 'Values in a sporting sub-culture: An analysis of the issues of competitiveness and aggression in surfing'. Mike Doyle's description of the evolution and development of surf wear industry from a California-based cottage industry in the early 1960s, illustrates a similar process of commercialisation, incorporation and resistance M Doyle, *Morning glass: The adventures of a legendary waterman* (Three Rivers, CA: Manzantia Press, 1993). Yet where the historical and cultural context of the UK in the 1990s differs is that it was not just particular brands, but the whole 'image' that was becoming incorporated into the mainstream. With this prevalence of advertisements in men's magazines and the clothing available in the high street – even in male order catalogues – surf style rather than individual brands became a 'style', available to anyone with the financial resources to 'buy into' it. Doyle, *Morning glass: The adventures of a legendary waterman.*
123 Stedman, 'From Gidget to Gonad Man: Surfers, feminists and postmodernisation', p.80.
124 Ibid.
125 Ibid.
126 Booth, 'Surfing films and videos: adolescent fun, alternative lifestyle, adventure industry', p.323.
127 Wheaton and Beal, '"Keeping it real": Subcultural media and the discourses of authenticity in alternative sport'.
128 Thornton, *Club cultures: Music, media and subcultural capital.* p.116.
129 T. Skelton and G. Valentine, 'Cool places: An introduction to youth and youth cultures', in *Cool Places: Geographies of youth cultures*, ed. D. Chambers (London: Routledge, 1998).

130   What Maguire following Elias calls achievement sports. See Maguire, *Global Sport: Identities, Societies, civilizations.*

131   Snow boarder, interviewed on Ski Sunday, BBC television 5 Jan 1997.

132   His medal was later re-instated. Snowboarding's inclusion in the Olympics has caused much debate, and this incident needs to be seen in the context of a wider fracture in snowboarding culture at that time and its belief that the FIS (international ski federation) was trying to appropriate snowboarding for its own commercially driven ends.

133   See also Rinehart, 'E̶m̶e̶r̶g̶i̶n̶g̶ Arriving Sport: Alternatives to formal sport'.

134   B. Beal, 'Disqualifying the Official: An exploration of Social Resistance Through the Subculture of Skateboarding', *Sociology of Sport Journal* 12, no. 3 (1995): 252–67.

135   R. Rinehart, 'Book review of Iain Borden, Skateboarding, space and the city: Architecture and the body', *International Review for Sociology of Sport* 38, no. 2 (2003): 261–6.

136   Beal and Wilson, ' "Chicks dig scars": Commercialisation and the transformations of skate boarders' identities'. See also Borden, *Skateboarding, space and the city: Architecture and the body.* These authors outline skater's claims about resistance to corporate takeover.

137   Beal and Wilson, ' "Chicks dig scars": Commercialisation and the transformations of skate boarders' identities'.

138   Booth, 'Ambiguities in Pleasure and discipline: The development of Competative surfing', Booth, *Australian beach cultures: The history of sun, sand and surf.* p.112.

139   Booth, *Australian beach cultures: The history of sun, sand and surf.* p.113.

140   Ibid. p.113.

141   Ibid. p.113.

142   Farmer, 'Surfing: motivations, values and culture'.

143   Booth, *Australian beach cultures: The history of sun, sand and surf.* p.101.

144   Kasprowicz, M. Opening editorial, the Soul Issue, *Windsurf* Magazine, May 1997, p.6.

145   See M. Featherstone, 'The body in consumer culture', *Theory Culture and Society* 1, no. 2 (1982): 18–33.

146   Kusz, ' "Extreme America": The Cultural Politics of Extreme Sports in 1990s America.'

147   K. Kusz, ' "I want to be a minority": The politics of youthful masculinities in sport and popular culture in 1990's America', *Journal of Sport and Social Issues* 25 (2001): 390–416; Kusz, ' "Extreme America": The Cultural Politics of Extreme Sports in 1990s America.'

148   R. Rinehart, 'Babes on boards: Women as co-opted sports models', in *North Amercian Sociology of Sport Association* (Cleveland: 1999).

149   Ibid.

150   L. Stedman, 'From Gidget to Gonad Man: Surfers, feminists and postmodernisation, *Australian and New Zealand Journal of Sociology*, vol.33, No.1, pp.75–90.

151   Wheaton and Beal, ' "Keeping it real": Subcultural media and the discourses of authenticity in alternative sport'.

152   Booth, *Australian beach cultures: The history of sun, sand and surf.*

153   Wheaton, 'Just Do it: Consumption, commitment and identity in the windsurfing subculture', Beal, 'Disqualifying the Official: An exploration of Social Resistance Through the Subculture of Skateboarding', A. Thornton, 'Ultimate Masculinities: An ethnography of power and social difference in sport', (PhD, Ontario Institute for Studies in Education of the University of Ontario, 1998); K. Anderson, 'Snowboarding: the construction of gender in an emerging sport', *Journal of Sport and Social Issues* 23, no. 1 (1999): 55–79; Borden, *Skateboarding, space and the city: Architecture and the body.*

154 B. Wheaton, ' "New Lads?" Masculinities and the New Sport participant', *Men and Masculinities* 2, no. 4 (2000): 436–58.

155 Ibid.

156 Rinehart, 'Book review of Iain Borden, Skateboarding, space and the city: Architecture and the body'.

157 Andrews and Cole, 'On issue: the nation reconsidered', p.123.

158 Rinehart, 'Emerging Arriving Sport: Alternatives to formal sport'. p.507.

159 T. Layden, 'What Is This 34-Year-Old Man Doing On A Skateboard? Making Millions', *Sports Illustrated*, 10 June 2002.

160 See M. Borden, *X-Treme Profits: The economy stinks. Tech's a mess. Not exactly fun and games out there – unless, like Activision, you're making videogames.* [InfoTrac Web: Expanded Academic ASAP] (Fortune, 4 March 2002, accessed 2002).

161 Borden, *Skateboarding, space and the city: Architecture and the body.* p.1.

162 M. McDonald and D. Andrews, 'Michael Jordan: corporate sport and postmodern celebrityhood', in *Sport stars: the cultural politics of sporting celebrity*, ed. S. Jackson (London: Routledge, 2001, p.20–21).

163 Maguire, *Global Sport: Identities, Societies, civilizations.* p.93.

164 See Carrington and Wilson, 'Global Clubcultures: Cultural flows and late modern dance music culture'.

165 Appadurai, *Modernity at Large: Cultural dimensions of globalization.* p.188.

Index